Apocalypses

APOCALYPSES

Prophecies, Cults and Millennial
Beliefs through the Ages

EUGEN WEBER

Random House of Canada

Canadian Cataloguing in Publication Data

Weber, Eugen, 1925 –
    Apocalypses: prophecies, cults and millennial beliefs through the ages

(The Barbara Frum lectureship)

Includes index.
ISBN 0-679-30984-5

1. Apocalyptic literature – History and criticism.
2. Millennialism – History.   3. Prophecies – History.
4. Cults – History.   I. Title.   II. Series.

BT876.w422 1999   291.2'3   c98-932554-7

Jacket image: *Commentaire sur l'apocalypse: les locustes*,
from a mid-eleventh century Latin manuscript (number 8878, folio 145 v.).
Courtesy of Bibliothèque nationale de France.

Printed and bound in the United States of America

10 9 8 7 6 5 4 3 2 1

For Jacqueline
My first, last, everlasting day

CONTENTS

INTRODUCTION

That day, when sent in glory by the Father,
The Prince of Life his best elect shall gather;
Millions of angels round about him flying,
While all the kindreds of the earth are crying,
And he, enthroned above the clouds, shall give
His last just sentence, who must die, who live.

– HENRY VAUGHN

W HEN the University of Toronto invited me to deliver the 1999 Barbara Frum Lecture, I was asked, appropriately enough, to talk about *fins de siècle*. The more I worried that particular bone, however, the less meat I found on it. Centuries, in our calendric sense, appear to be an esoteric sixteenth-century invention, a hesitant usage of the seventeenth century. The special attention focused on a century's end, with the halo of references that we associate with the turn of the nineteenth century into the twentieth, was a one-shot affair. Like our own century's tail end, that of the eighteenth century, and of every other, attracted no endist label; anyone tackling *fins de siècle* in the plural would have gathered a very sparse harvest.

Yet ends and beginnings played a large part in humanity's experience of itself, not least in that Judeo-Christian tradition that forms the backbone of Western history from Asia Minor to the Pacific's shores. Hebrew history plunges its roots in the Pentateuch; the history of Christendom is irrigated by the New Testament, which culminates in the book of Revelation. Apocalypse—the revelation or unveiling of the world's destiny and of mankind's—has fascinated Jews and their Christian offspring at least for the last 2200 years.

Christians and Jews knew, or thought they knew, how the world began, and had a fair idea how it was supposed to end, though precise circumstances remained debatable. Knowledge of the end affects the terms and manner of progression to it. For a long time, Christian history developed in the concurrence of prophecy and interpretation within a destiny that had been foretold. Apocalypse and the thousand-year millennium that would precede Christ's Second Coming (or in some versions follow it) were major parts of this process, and loomed incommensurably larger than calendric dates. Indeed, the measuring of worldly time was mainly relevant insofar as it served divine timing.

The Christian year began with Advent: the weeks that lead up to the Incarnation, Passion, and Resurrection of Christ. Liturgically, it does so still. Now, as ever, the first familiar act celebrated at Christmas and at Easter is only an introduction to the climactic conclusion, when the long struggle between satanic darkness and divine light is at last resolved in the triumph of good over evil. Advent may lead up to the birth of Christ, but it culminates in his Second Coming. And that is what the rite, the lessons, and the sermons of the rite are about: the judgment to come, and before it the Son of Man coming in a cloud with great power and glory, and the terrors that precede his coming, and the magic interlude between his preliminary and his final victory over Satan.

That is what people were exposed to, one generation after another during hundreds of years; that is what they grew up and grew old regarding as history, and as premonitory history, as real as the seasons were real and as sure. This whole scenario entered the language, the mindset, the store of common references, and aroused great passion and controversy. When, gradually, after the seventeenth century, it began to seep out of educated consciousness, it did so only partially and incompletely. That being so, one may well wonder why a motif and motivating agency so strong and so pervasive was for so long ignored in modern times, especially by historians.

Just thirty years ago, Christopher Hill began his Riddell Lectures of 1969 with a similar remark that sheds light on my question. Historians—Hill calls them intellectual snobs—"have ignored the lunatic fringe that believed in the imminence of the end and the necessary preliminary of Antichrist,"[1] paying no heed to Milton, Cromwell, Newton, and so many others who shared a belief in the imminent end of the world. Great historian of seventeenth-century England that he is, Hill saw the need to look with attention on beliefs of that time because beliefs influence and inflect action— as they encouraged Cromwell, for instance, to readmit Jews to England in hope of advancing the time of the Lord's return. Yet Hill's scholarship characterized, and hence intellectually marginalized, the believers he studied as a lunatic fringe. That was not so until the seventeenth or even the eighteenth century, and many eighteenth- and nineteenth-century reformers would have to be counted among the lunatic fringe: Lord Shaftesbury and his friends, the supporters of Jewish emancipation and of Zionism, and abolitionists who, in England and North America, eventually brought the slave trade to an end.

Prophecies make little sense to rational modern scholars and they embarrass advocates of a Christianity that, in the past two hundred years, has learnt to present itself as rational too. Before the eighteenth century ended, *The Holy Bible Adapted to the Use of Schools and Private Families* (Birmingham, 1783) had omitted most of Paul's epistles and the whole book of Revelation as too incendiary. In the following century, textual criticism cleared most of the supernatural out of Christian beliefs, or explained it away. In 1925, Wilhelm Bousset, a great student of Antichrist, authoritatively declared that Antichrist's legend "is now to be found only among the lower classes of the Christian community, among sects, eccentric individualists, and fanatics."[2] In 1957, another serious scholar, Norman Cohn, memorably assigned the apocalyptic tradition to the "obscure underworld of popular religion."[3] Christianity was being recast. It has been through the ages, but now its supernatural foundations were being meddled with. Reconstruction can shore up or help to weaken structures. Subtract one aspect of the supernatural, and the edifice may crumble. Within a few years, a distinguished theologian like Karl Tillich dismissed belief even in the afterlife as "a corrupt form of theological expression, disseminated among the relatively poor and uneducated."[4] If some people don't think as we, the educated, think, it must be because they are uneducated, poor, or crackpots.

They may, on the other hand, be sociologically all right and simply mistaken. Or they may not be mistaken at all. Condescension is not the right approach. *The Oxford Dictionary of the Christian Church* arrived at that conclusion. Conceived before the Second World War, its first edition consigned millenarianism to the dustbin of history. Published in 1997, on the millennium's eve, the third edition reveals the luxuriant growth of millenarianism in Asia, Africa, and South America. History, Hill reminds us, is not an exclusively rational process and, in any case, one man's reason is another man's nonsense. I have always been interested in the reasons of unreason, or of what others denounce as unreason. So, when the University of Toronto suggested *fins de siècle*, I turned to apocalypses.

I had little apprehension of the topic before I looked into it, and no scholarly acquaintance with it. But if curiosity kills cats, it nourishes historians. I went back to the Bible, I read hundreds of the thousands of books bearing on the subject, and the more I read the more fascinating the topic looked. I hope that the following pages convey some of the excitement of the chase and of discovery.

They do not reflect, as my other books do, research in original sources; only curiosity and empathy, not uncritical, but aware of the limits both of my scholarship and of human understanding. The treatment is not exhaustive, the approach is subjective, and the coverage reflects not models or reductive theories but what caught my attention and answered some of my questions. My adventure, like most adventures, was generated by chance and curiosity. This book—an account of my journey through apocalypses, millenarianisms, their prophets and their believers—is like a travel book. It offers more narrative than interpretation, more description than explanation, and it is addressed not to specialists but to those curious to learn about beliefs and attitudes that have metastasized both throughout our culture and far beyond the Western world.

Apocalypse long furnished the key to human history. Even if today it provides only a plain folks' gloss on history, it deserves serious attention.

It might be useful at this point to provide a précis of that contentious account of what the last times will be like.

Steeped in Old Testament imagery and terminology, John's revelations come in a series of eschatological visions. The first is of Jesus Christ, his head and hair white like wool, as white as snow, his eyes as a flame of fire, in his right hand seven stars, and out of his mouth a sharp two-edged sword. The Risen Lord commands John to write what he sees and send it to seven Asian churches: "I stand at the door and knock . . . He that hath an ear, let him hear what the spirit saith unto the churches."

Handel explained that he wrote the *Messiah* after he "saw the heavens opened and God upon his great white throne." For John, too, a door opened in heaven before his second vision—of God seated on his throne in dazzling majesty amid a heavenly entourage, in his right hand a scroll (in our versions, a book) sealed with seven seals containing his secret plans for the universe. John weeps because no one, it seems, is fit to unseal the book, but he soon dries his tears. "The Lion of the tribe of Judah, the root of David . . . prevails to open the book and loose its seven seals." The Lion of Judah turns out to be a Lamb with seven horns (representing omnipotence), and seven eyes (representing omniscience), all perfect because the number seven is a symbol of perfection.

As the Lamb begins to open seals, he brings forth four horses and their riders, all agents of destruction; reveals the souls of those who had been slain for bearing witness to the word of God; and, with the sixth seal, shatters the universe as a token of the great day of God's wrath. Chapter 7 provide a respite, while 144,000 servants of God are sealed—their seal in this case the token of a divine pledge: for them there shall be neither hunger nor thirst, "and God shall wipe away all tears from their eyes."

The opening of the seventh seal ushers in angels and trumpet blasts that amplify terror, torment and great woes presented in unnerving detail. The seventh and last trumpet calls forth great voices that proclaim the kingdom of God and of his Christ. One would think the matter settled, but there is much still to come. Two garish interludes evoke the perils of a woman clothed with the sun pursued by a great red dragon, the machinations of dreadful beasts, prototypes of Antichrist, penultimately a scenario of downfall and liquidation involving further beasts, doomed unbelievers, Babylon and its great whore, and war between diabolic swarms and the hosts of heavens. Satan, bound only to rise again after a thousand years, will be finally disposed of in a lake of fire, along with death and hell.

The closing chapters promise and describe a new heaven, a new earth, and the holy city of Jerusalem coming down from God out of heaven, while God (once again) wipes tears from survivors' eyes, and John is enjoined to tell all of the things he has seen, and that must shortly take place.

CHRONOLOGIES

AND *FINS DE SIÈCLE*

If a young man mislays his hat, he says he has mislaid his hat.
The old man says: "I have lost my hat. I must be getting old."

— DR. JOHNSON

TIME AND ITS DIVISIONS are social constructs. Chronology, like other "ologies"—astrology, archaeology, sociology, eschatology—serves ulterior ends and reflects realities quite different from abstract measures.

Herodotus measured time by generations, as the Etruscans did, and by reigns, as the Egyptians and the Mesopotamians did. Polybius measured time by quadrennial Olympiads; and hard-bitten anticlericals, reluctant to refer to Christ, still did so at mid-nineteenth century.[1] At the end of the sixth century, Gregory of Tours began his *History of the Franks* in the Jewish manner, with the creation of the world—a world he expected to last 6000 years, still, he calculated, 208 years away. But most history, like most people until quite recently, ignored abstract chronology. Time was not linear, but multiple, subjective, and specific to particular situations.

Consider the way Thucydides describes the beginning of the Peloponnesian War, midway through a thirty-year truce. "In the

15th year [of the truce], in the 48th year of the priesthood of Chry-
sis in Argos, when Enesias was ephor at Sparta and Pythodorus
still had two months to serve as Archon at Athens, 6 months after
the battle of Potidea, just at the beginning of Spring, a Theban
force . . . about the first watch of the night, made an armed entry
into Platea [which was an ally of Athens]."[2]

So Thucydides knows about months and years, but he
locates events in time according to tenured priests and rulers,
seasons, and memorable events like battles, plagues, and earthquakes. Sixteen hundred years after Thucydides, things have
not changed. In the thirteenth century, Robert de Clary begins
his history of the Fourth Crusade, the one that took Constantinople: "It happened in that time when Pope Innocent [III] was
apostolic of Rome and Philip [II] was king of France and there
was another Philip [Philip I of Swabia] who was emperor of
Germany, and the year of the Incarnation was 1200 and 3 or 4"[3]
So what we're dealing with is not time, but times that overlie
each other.

We think of our chronology in terms of BC (Before Christ)
and AD (Anno Domini), which is as good a way of placing events
in time as any other. But the Christian perspective was never the
only one. The Chinese, who marked the years by the harvest,
recorded events by referring to monthly cycles within given
dynasties. The Hindus based years on astronomical cycles, and
reckoned dates from the consecration of their kings. The Egyptians first named years by their main event, then by the name of
kings, as did Mesopotamians. The first Olympic games were
held in 776 BC, and the use of the Olympiad as a quadrennial
measure continued from the fourth century BC through the
fourth century AD. Roman chronology began with the foundation of Rome in 753 BC. Jews improved on Romans by counting
years since the creation of the world, calculated back through
Biblical generations. Since the Jewish year begins in autumn,
it does not easily reconcile with those of Christian chronology,

but 1999 is 5759. As for the Islamic calendar, it begins with the Hegira, Muhammad's emigration from Mecca to Medina, traditionally dated in July 622.

Though cognizant of years, calendars are actually structured to count days and relate them to phases of the sun and moon. The Egyptians counted by decades, as French Revolutionaries sought to do. The Hebrews seem to have invented the seven-day week, though they may have cribbed it from the Mesopotamians. The seven-day week of Creation, with its day of rest, was then translated into Mosaic legislation requiring every seventh year to be observed as a sabbath, when debtors and Israelite slaves were freed and land lay fallow. A belief gradually grew that the first six days of Creation week represented thousand-year periods in which the world toils in labor and pain, after which the world would end and creation would enjoy rest and happiness for a seventh millennium: the true sabbath.

Romans, and Etruscans before them, subdivided first the lunar months and then the solar year into specifically named days, and counted forward or back from those. They also used *nundinae*: nine-day intervals from market- to market-day. Devised by Julius Caesar in 46 BC, the Julian calendar moved the beginning of the year from March to January, to replace the lunar by a solar year that kept better pace with the seasons; but the seven-day week was established in the Roman calendar only in AD 321, when Emperor Constantine also designated Sunday as the first day of the week, dedicated to rest and worship, hence *dies dominica*—the day of the Lord.

The New Testament is largely indifferent to chronology. Paul blamed the astrological superstition of those who observed "days and months and times and years" (Galatians 4:10) and discouraged the Colossians from heeding new moons, sabbaths, and allegedly holy days, "which are a shadow of things to come" (Colossians 2:16–17). In the perspective of an imminent Second Coming and of the passing of the temporal order, worldly time was of little moment. That may be why Paul neither dated letters nor provided the date of historical events. He shared this attitude with other Jewish apocalyptists of his age such as Ezra, whose Apocalypse etches terrible trials followed by a glorious, incorruptible age when all years and other time divisions would be no more, "and thereafter will exist neither month nor day, nor hours."[4]

Mundane chronology signified little, unless as part of a greater sacred scheme. How this worked may be seen from the story of jubilees—another Hebrew concept connected to that of sabbatical years—which were celebrated every fifty years. The fifty-year intervals had nothing to do with decimal thinking, but with the completion of seven weeks of years (7 x 7 = 49). The fiftieth year that followed was the year of jubilee. Land was left fallow, estates were returned to their original owners or to their heirs, debts were remitted, and slaves recovered their freedom. In imitation of this plan, Pope Boniface VIII proclaimed a Church Jubilee for the year 1300, offering remission of guilt and punishment to pilgrims who visited Rome. The Holy Year was to be repeated at hundred-year intervals. The profits it brought to Rome were so great, however (at the church of S. Paolo fuori le Mura, for example, two priests were on constant duty with rakes to gather up the coins the faithful tossed on the altar)[5] that intervals were reduced to fifty years, and even to thirty-three (in memory of Christ's lifespan). Then, in 1475, arguments based on the brevity of human life and each generation's access to holy pardon introduced jubilees every twenty-five years.

Quarter-century Holy Years have been celebrated since that time with fair regularity, but interspersed with extraordinary jubilees designed to invoke divine assistance against Turks, plagues, Protestants, or schismatics, to celebrate success, or to mark the accession of popes. Benedict XIV, for example, proclaimed an extraordinary jubilee on his accession in 1740, and also presided over a regular jubilee in Holy Year 1750. In this long story, calendric and decimal timing seem to have played subordinate roles; the interests of the church and its memorials have remained paramount.

In the Christian West, the times that counted most were those of the church. The liturgical year, which was recorded in breviaries and missals, began with Advent: the Sunday following the feast of St. Andrew on November 30. Into the sixteenth century and sometimes beyond, the public year might begin on January 1, but more often at Christmas, Annunciation, or Easter—especially Easter. But even Easter, crucial to Christian rites, could in early days be observed according to local calculations: in the fifth century, Rome might celebrate it in March, and Alexandria in April; in 590, most parts of Gaul picked March 26, while Gregory of Tours chose April 2.

Gregory of Tours followed a monk known as Dennis the Short (Dionysius Exiguus), who tried to work out a reliable method to set the date of Easter. Calculating (and probably miscalculating) from Alexandrian tables, he placed the birth of Christ at an improbable date.[6] Yet that is where our chronology comes from. Calendar dating appears in the tenth century, but for a long time it was not much used; and those who used it hesitated between dates and religious feasts. Letters of change referred to either or both until the fourteenth century. For a couple of centuries after that, loans might be dated by the calendar, but the payment could fall due on a religious feast. Papal briefs of the late fifteenth century were dated from Christmas, while papal bulls followed the Florentine style and used Easter. At Milan, after the fifteenth century, the official year began on January 1, Feast of the Circumcision, but notaries referred to the Nativity until the eighteenth century; in Piacenza, they preferred March 25, the Annunciation, which coincided with the vernal equinox.

The sixteenth century is crucial because, after 1560, the French year began on January 1, and after 1582, most Catholic countries adopted the Gregorian calendar, which Protestants accepted only two centuries later. As Voltaire would put it, Protestant mobs preferred their calendars to disagree with the sun than to agree with the pope. In England, where legal documents and statutes were dated by reign, not year, the calendar year began at the spring equinox, until England adopted the Gregorian calendar in 1752 and the beginning of the year shifted from March 25 to January 1.

The chronology used most commonly today, based on years before and after Christ, came into general use only in the seventeenth century. Now, three hundred years later, it is going out of use again because politically correct publishers and media prefer the Common Era to Anno Domini. So, now, we get CE and BCE (Before the Common Era), even when it is not quite clear who has got what in common.

But the new calendars of early modern times were more about heavenly events that could affect health and horoscopes than about everyday life. Life could do without dates. Imprecision, inexactness ruled the roost. Months were hardly noticed, and even years were ignored. People did not know their age exactly. Born into a Florentine family of good standing, Dante tells us only that he was born "under the sign of Gemini," meaning some time between mid-May and mid-June, in the year of the battle of Benevento, which was fought in 1265. Erasmus knew that he had been born on the eve of the feast of St. Simon and St. Jude (which falls on October 28), but the year of his birth is still given as "around" 1467. Rabelais, whose father was a lawyer, "may" have been born in 1493, or possibly 1494. And though most sources confidently tell us that Luther was born on November 10 (St. Martin's Eve) in 1483, Lucien Febvre more cautiously adds "probably."[7]

This situation continued for some time. Felix Platter, a distinguished and much-traveled physician who died in 1614, had little use for the calendar and, whether in letters or in his journal, rarely gave precise dates of important events in his life.[8] So, for a while longer, chronology continued to escape even the educated. Calculations were for initiates; precision was irrelevant. "Time," remarks a seventeenth-century work, "did not appear of any importance to them."9 Parish registers noted baptism, but not birth date. And until the mid-eighteenth century, most French had only an approximate sense of their age, which they envisioned in round numbers, "rounded off by dozens or by tens."

Generally speaking, time past was not historical and subject to exact computation, but legendary and jumbled, with little or no difference between the time of Alexander, Charlemagne, or King Arthur, and small sense of just how far real time can stretch. At the mid-nineteenth century still, a London coster girl could tell the journalist Henry Mayhew: "We often talks about religion. My father told me that God made the world . . . it must be more than a hundred years ago."10

Heedlessness of dates reflected a broader unfamiliarity with numbers, which remained mysterious to the great majority, and largely irrelevant too. It was hard to compute using Roman numerals, which offered expressions of quantity, but no simple way to multiply or divide. Addition and subtraction were not easy either: when St. Augustine wanted to discourage those trying to count the years to the end of the world, he admonished them to "relax your fingers and give them a little rest."11

No wonder that, into the seventeenth century, even educated people lacked elementary calculating skills. Arabic numerals were hardly known in Europe before the thirteenth century, and took a long time to supplant Roman numerals. Mathematics gained ground by the sixteenth century, but those who could handle complicated calculations remained rare. Numerical operations called for special wisdom, and numbers mattered more for what they could reveal than for the quantity or chronology they might represent. Still, by the mid-eighteenth century, numbers had become familiar and people got used to dates. As this happened, they also started to interfere with dates—not because they did not know what they were doing, but because they had specific ends in mind.

In 1788, Sylvain Maréchal's *Almanach des honnêtes gens* is dated from the First Year of Reason (l'An premier de la Raison) and his year reasonably begins in March. On July 14, 1790, the *Moniteur universel* dates itself "first day of the second year of Liberty" (du premier jour de la Second Année de la Liberté). Then, on September 22, 1792, the Convention, having abolished the monarchy the day before, went on to abolish the Christian Era. All official documents would henceforth be dated from year I of the French Republic; and in 1793 the Republic adopted a decimal calendar appropriate to the rational era, which lasted until an imperial decree reestablished the Gregorian calendar in 1805.

Many readers know this story. What they may not know is that, in accordance with the decree of 7 Messidor, year III, the *Annuaire du Bureau des Longitudes* continues to publish every year a concordance between the Republican calendar and the Gregorian.

A French historian, Daniel Milo, has argued that *siècles* came into their own with the Revolutionary system that structured time decimally, as it did other measures, and thereby confirmed the century as the standard historical unit—and also opened the way to thoughts of a *fin de siècle*.[12] Milo makes an important point, though it is probable that the new era did not devote much thought to conclusions. The 1790s was a dawn when it was bliss to be alive, or else it was a nervous time. Either way, the turning point it focused on was millennial rather than secular. Pietists from Russia to New England focused on the end of the *world*, not of the century; and so did Julie de Krüdener, the lady who prayed with Alexander I, and who persuaded the tsar to influence his fellow monarchs to sign the Holy Alliance.

So, no *fin de siècle*, yet, but more references to the century, to *enfants du siècle*, to *l'esprit du siècle*, and so on. The French dictionary of quotations that I keep on my desk lists four citations of *siècle* before 1800, and nineteen for the nineteenth century. It is hardly a scientific survey, but the proportions are about right for a century that savored exactness and positive knowledge, and also realized that centuries do not necessarily coincide with calendar dates.

Centuries had not done so for a long time, signifying more usually a generation, a period, an epoch of variable length. Roman emperors described their reign as a *saeculum*. When Heinrich Bullinger, the Zwinglian theologian, preached on the *fin du siècle* in Zurich in 1557, he meant *the coming judgment and the end of times*.[13] But this indeterminate usage became more focused, again in the sixteenth century, when Michel Nostradamus published his prophecies as *centuries* of 100 stanzas each, and the Protestant "centuriators" of Magdeburg organized their historical chronology by centuries. By the late seventeenth century, *siècle* has come into its own, and in December 1699 we learn from the most popular French periodical of the day, the *Mercure galant*, that the century to come raises hotly debated questions: "Some claim that it's about to begin, others contend that it will only begin in 1701."[14]

Once the eighteenth and early nineteenth centuries began to use *siècle* in the modern historical and chronological sense, the usage became first natural, then unavoidable, reflecting also the attraction of round numbers. In 1772, a year after it was published, William Hooper, MD, translated an early science-fiction book, Sébastien Mercier's *Mémoires de l'an 2440*, and changed 2440 to 2500. Most English and American editions have kept the easy secular date.

But what about *fin de siècle*? Sooner or later, beginnings suggest ends, and ends suggest decline. The *saeculum* of a Roman emperor quite often ended in tragedy and failure. Hebrew and Christian apocalyptic works that have survived from the centuries before and after the birth of Christ imply as much. The Hebrew Apocalypse of Baruch was far from the only declaration that "the youth of the world is past, the vigor of creation is at its end; the coming of [last] times is near."[15] Christian chronology, which was essentially end directed, also intimated a sense of decline and senescence. For St. Cyprian, martyred at Carthage in AD 258, the world was at its dusk. It lingered there a long time. In illustrated calendars, months often age from a baby in January to a decrepit old man in December. There was no reason why centuries should not follow suit: end of a century, of a "generation," of a "world"—perhaps of *the* world. More often and more likely, end of an age, not *ages*; end of one time, not of all times.

That was precisely what a Lorrainer, Wendelin Baar, indicated in the wake of the French Revolution while he discussed the Apocalypse and the ways of God with man. A millennialist, Baar expected the coming of Christ to rule over a terrestrial kingdom; but he warned his readers not to confuse the end of their time with the end of times. The earth would be renewed, not annihilated: *fin de siècle* did not mean *fin du monde*—end of the world.[16] Yet, even though millenarianism has never been specially interested in centuries, the fascination of round numbers and of regularly recurring anniversaries, especially of significant dates related to the Incarnation, survives. Numerical regularities seem to answer a need for order in a confusing world, not least for order affecting time and times.

The Christian Church was also great at anniversaries. Commemorations were repeated each year or at other intervals, as in the case of the Holy Year Jubilees instituted in 1300, which inspired Dante to set his *Divine Comedy* in that year. But if we leave the very great aside, secular anniversaries are an invention of the nineteenth century, the first to be related to a number and identified as such in its own time. The year 1876 marked the centennial of American independence, 1889 that of the French Revolution, 1900 that of the century itself. It seems appropriate that this should have happened in the age *par excellence* of clocks and watches, timetables and calendars.

Anniversaries are marked by significance, appraisals, apprehensions, and trepidations. So are ends and beginnings, which stimulate excitement and, sometimes, anxiety. Suicides peak on Mondays and in springtime; heart attacks occur at higher rates at the end of years and at their beginnings. Norman Cohn tells us that in ancient Egypt end times were particularly favorable to demons: ends of a day, a month, a year, or a decade were moments when order was disturbed and evil spirits could be expected to be especially active.[17] It need not surprise us, therefore, on the eve of a newly relevant time period, to find Stéphane Mallarmé expressing the anxiety of attending *la finale d'un siècle*; and across the Channel, Thomas Hardy echoes him. Dated December 31, 1900, Hardy's "Darkling Thrush" was originally entitled "By the Century's Deathbed."

But the end of an epoch does not necessarily coincide with the end of a hundred-year span. The feeling that the world and time are coming to an end does not need a century's closure. *La fin des temps*, the end of days, has been part of Christian and pre-Christian experience far longer than thinking in centuries has been. As Wendelin Baar warned, *la fin des siècles* does not necessarily coincide with *a* fin de siècle, or *the* fin d'*un* siècle. But the two notions can quicken and spur each other. A number of calculators placed Doomsday in 1900, as others would in the year 2000. Vastly more, however, have chosen other dates—notably, anniversaries of Christ's Passion;[18] and a lot have simply equated the end of *their* world with the end of *the* world.

It is, for example, tempting to connect late nineteenth-century Wagnerism, and especially Wagner's *Götterdämmerung*, with *fin de siècle* catastrophism. It is true that the first performance of *The Ring* took place in 1874, and that the poem on which *The Ring* is based was completed in 1853, when Wagner was thirty-five. That's my point, or one of my points. The poem, and the operas, are about love and about unwittingness, but, above all, they are about endings. Wagner said so from the beginning in revealing terms: "All that mankind did, ordered and established," he writes to a friend in 1854, "was conceived only in fear of the end. My poem sets this forth."[19]

If, as George Bernard Shaw declared, both Wagner and Marx prophesied the end of our epoch, that may explain why Wagnerism in France and Britain, and in France *before* Britain, came into its own at the *fin de siècle*, just as visions, prophecies, and mysticism revived. *Fin de siècle* France was full of bleeding hosts, cyboriums crying tears, apparitions, prodigies, comets, meteorites, and even flying serpents, earthquakes at home, and news of exploding volcanoes abroad. Readers of Nostradamus knew that he expected the end of the world in 1886, but he could have been out by a decade or two. At any rate, in December 1899, we find George Gissing in Paris, writing a book to be called *Among the Prophets*, which, he explained, "deals with new religions and crazes of various kinds."[20]

We haven't paid enough attention to new nineteenth-century religions, most of which were old religions. But if they revived, as Catholic enthusiasm revived and Wagnerite enthusiasm flourished on the midden of decadence, that was because (or *also* because) *fin de siècle* could be made to coincide with *fin des siècles*, the end of time.

How easily discomforting experiences are linked to expectations of catastrophe comes out in a sermon and pamphlet of 1829, entitled *The Last Days*, where the rise in "juvenile depredations and felonies," "the dislocation and corruption of family ties," the decline of authority, and the wreck of a dissolving society are signs that threaten the end of the world. Chronological indices can only reinforce such premonitions, and the 1880s and 1890s brought grist aplenty to their mills. The world was deteriorating: statistics demonstrated its degeneration. Crime soared on all sides; so did venereal diseases, alcoholism, tuberculosis, and mental maladies, while birth rates fell in more advanced societies. Society was sick, rotten, rotting; the Western world weakened with age. And the more troubles its peoples thought they faced, the more hopes they heeded about some miraculous or catastrophic resolution.

Pierre Chaunu, who regards the notion of decadence as a correlate of the notion of progress, sees in it an aspect of modernity.[21] But about the year 100, the scribe who goes under the name of Ezra, reporting on his conversations with the archangel Uriel concerning the end of the age, applied it to the modernity of his day. Ezra's generation, says Uriel, was inferior to its predecessors, and the world of Ezra's day less vigorous than that of yore, "even as creation is already grown old and is already past the strength of youth." That is not unlike the spirit in which a work of 1687, printed at the height of the Sun King's radiance, set out to tell the story of French decadence. Thereafter, as Chaunu suggests, progress and decadence proceeded side by side, with decadence the inferior partner until the Romantic age. François Guizot found that the Romantic poets and chroniclers of his time "all believed themselves at the end of the world." Cardinal Newman, a roaring Romantic himself, confirmed that judgment in his Advent sermons: "The world grows old—the earth is crumbling away—the night is far spent—the day is at hand."[22]

Once again, progress advanced side by side with the notion of decadence. In retrospect, most things were changing for the better; in practice, many folk were irked by the discomforts that change implied, both psychic and material. Nostalgia for a largely imaginary past outran the benefits of the present. Things were not what they used to be, the world was not as it used to be; too rapid change made consciousness and self-consciousness more acute, and provoked and dramatized self-criticism, self-doubt, anxiety, and guilt. Public inquiries, inspections, examinations, surveys, and statistics, all characteristic of the age, confirmed the degeneration of the race. Print, which was more available than ever, as well as politics, publicized decadence and made it fashionable. The century's approaching end made it inescapable.

Millennialism, which often identifies the end of chronological cycles as moments of crisis, now identified crisis with the end of a particular chronological circle. A lot of critics and journalists in the 1890s complained that they didn't know, that no one really knew, what *fin de siècle* meant. But *we* know what it was taken to mean, and so did Mallarmé: The flesh was sad, alas! and all the books were read.

It's in this context, in this mood, that Émile Zola, in the aftermath of exile, transferred his depression to the *fin de siècle*: "I wonder if we're not moving towards some final cataclysm," he wrote to a friend at home. "I expect a catastrophe, I know not what, in which we shall all be swallowed up.... I really believe in the end of everything."[23] That was in 1899, and it reflected dejection over the persistent injustice perpetuated on both Zola and Captain Dreyfus. But the mood had been there before. In the urban trilogy that Zola started to write in 1894, the *fin de siècle* coincides with an epoch's end—*fin de race, de génération, du monde*, society rotting away, inevitable catastrophe predicted by the calendar.[24] So even before he got involved in the Dreyfus Affair, Zola's eschatology was less economic or social than millenarian.

Contemporary science could suggest similarly apocalyptic visions. In 1893, the astronomer Camille Flammarion had published *La fin du monde*, full of quotations from the Apocalypse; and his friend, Anatole France, was more explicitly pessimistic: "L'espèce humaine n'est pas capable de progrès indéfinis . . . Quand le soleil s'éteindra . . . les hommes auront disparu depuis longtemps. Les derniers seront aussi dénués et stupides que les premiers."[25] [The human species is not capable of indefinite progress . . . When the sun goes out . . . humankind will have long disappeared. The last humans will be as naked and stupid as the first]. This was France, the stoic, playing the role of Seneca. But Henry Adams expressed similar feelings in slightly different terms: chaos was the law of nature, order was the dream of man, and science revealed that man could not go on trying to impose his dream on nature. Humanity would succumb under the avalanche of unknown forces that the *fin de siècle* was beginning to reveal. Meanwhile, "drifting in the dead waters of the *fin de siècle* . . . one lived alone."[26]

It was this stubborn *absence* that Adams identified. Its loneliness colored the pessimism of a lot of intellectuals, corroborated what people took to be the verdict of the second law of thermodynamics (world energy ebbing, the world running down), and justified mopey *littérateurs* like Octave Mirbeau, whose dreary *Vingt-et-un jours d'un néurasthenique* (a *fin de siècle* complaint for a *fin de siècle* title published in 1901) ends on the image of men who are already dead moving about a dying world, facing a future without a future.

This desperate nihilism also fueled the *Crise de la conscience catholique* (*souffrance, désarroi, désespoir,* and so on), and consumed Léon Bloy, the bizarre Christian writer who expected a Second Coming any day after the 1870s. Bloy was convinced, as he wrote in 1884 in *Le désespéré,* that the Lord God would soon come down and burn up all human rottenness and corruption. He was disgusted when the *fin de siècle* did not deliver: "Je suis fort mécontent de cette dernière année du siècle. Elle pouvait et devait être l'année du Chambardement." But he went on waiting. In 1915, two years before he died, he was still *au seuil de l'apocalypse* [on the doorstep of the apocalypse].[27] And Bloy was not alone. The end of the nineteenth century and the beginning of the twentieth saw a spate of futuristic fiction full of astronomical, ecological and political catastrophes, and at least one novel about the final twenty-first-century struggle of Christ and Antichrist, culminating in Armageddon and the End of the World.[28]

We'll find out about that if we live a bit longer. Meanwhile, let's go back to Anatole France's declaration that humankind is incapable of indefinite progress. Progress in the accepted sense means advance toward an end; and linear progress suggests endings, just as calendric progress suggests an end and, by implication, decline. Like other organisms, years grow weary; centuries grow old and degenerate. Nietzsche in 1888 assimilated humanity's forward march to decadence: "Step by step further into decadence, that is my definition of modern progress."[29] To call decadence, as Chaunu does, a gift of modernity is anachronistic, but not unfair. Modernity, which is about the here and now, is necessarily about the passing of the present, of ourselves, of current fantasies that we assume as norms, of trends and fashions that have decay built in.

But these were implications, not givens, until inference turned to affirmation, demonstration, and ostentation. These attributes found strong support in 1893 when a Hungarian physician, Zionist, and social critic who lived in Paris under the name of Max Nordau published a long pamphlet on *Degeneration*, which offered allegedly scientific proof that the world was going to the dogs. Characteristically modern works, Nordau argued, reflect diseased creators; and the diseased creators reflect the nervous exhaustion of the race. Society is sick, and its products prove it.

A couple of years after *Degeneration*, when George Bernard Shaw was invited to discuss the book in an American review, he wrote a fighting essay entitled "An Exposure of the Current Nonsense about Artists Being Degenerate."[30] The essay is far more cheerful than Nordau's about society, humanity, and the present, which may be due to the fact that Shaw was trying to learn to ride one of the technological triumphs of the *fin de siècle*, a bicycle, and obviously enjoying the experience.

But the bicycle, with its recently invented brakes and pneumatic tires, was seen by doomsayers as just another nail in the coffin of civilization. Women were riding bicycles, contributing to the decline of morals and accelerating the collapse of social harmony. New-fangled sports, rambling, and cycling threatened rank, order, and culture. Léon Bloy perceived this link when he told an editor in 1900 that "la bicyclette tuera le livre" (Ceci tuera cela).

Newly obtrusive and newly mobile criminals, robbers, bag-snatchers, muggers, gangsters, and *hooligans* (a word that enters English shortly before 1900, while *apache* enters French in 1902) use bikes to rob and stab and make their getaway. Juvenile delinquency is rife. Indeed, a lot of activities are publicized and a lot of notions are bandied about that come to us with a familiar sound: aggression, perversion, homosexuality, incest, drugs, immigrants, nerves, neurasthenia, depravity, unemployment, loneliness, isolation, transgression, anomie, and urbanization. Urban predators run wild in the streets, children brandish knives and pistols, parents are indifferent to the moral and physical well-being of their offspring, and the uncouth masses gain access to the precincts of their betters.

All these trends had been invoked with horror throughout the century. They had inspired arguments for schools to civilize the dangerous offspring of the dangerous classes, and they went on to inspire the founding of Boy Scouts and other civilizing agencies for young males, first in Britain, then in France. Delinquency was also quickly identified with socialists, syndicalists, and anarchists, whom the popular press compared with criminals, and who were often portrayed as hooligans or apaches. But intrusive insecurity and disgust also, as they had done before, inspired efforts at social redemption: regenerate society; emancipate women, the young, and the oppressed; and abolish social evils—poverty, overwork, ugliness, rapacity, blighted health and lives. Kicking over the traces also meant kicking off fetters and leading strings.

The *fin de siècle* was also less decadent and morose, more exhilarating and more fun than sensitive contemporaries let on. Before he died in 1892, Ernest Renan declared that the nineteenth century may not have been the greatest of centuries, but was certainly the most amusing. A look at the recent compilation on the *Fin de siècle*, edited by Mikulas Teich and Roy Porter, makes clear what a busy, vibrant, generally forward-looking time it was. Holbrook Jackson's book about the 1890s gives the same impression; and while Jackson writes about England, André Billy also presented *L'époque 1900* (1885–1905) as lively, attractive, and fruitful.[31]

Billy talks about a certain *dévergondage*, which suggests profligacy, extravagance, abandon, but hardly decay. His view goes well with the impression of Jackson, who lived those years on both sides of the Channel, and who sees what was described as decadence as self-indulgent, but also vital and curious, and finds its petulances and flippancies and febrilities arising *not* out of senility, "but out of surfeit, out of the ease with which life was maintained and desire satisfied."[32]

In other words, posturing and parading were forms of self-indulgence made possible by a society that was, or was growing, newly richer and newly freer; and the great password of the *fin de siècle* was never *old*, but *new*. *Art nouveau*, of course; but also new woman, new hedonism, new criticism, new journalism, new sports (and renewed Olympic Games), new discoveries, new kinds of science, and even new history.

The painter Jean-François Raffaelli was worried by the moral perversion engendered by Anglo-Saxon art nouveau, and about the pederasty engendered by Liberty fabrics. Joris-Karl Huysmans grumped about lousy *fin de siècle* housemaids. But there was more to excite than to depress: "All new eyes, new minds, new modes, new fools, new wise" (Thomas Hardy).[33]

When we hear about the flesh that's weary and the books all read, we might look at the complaint in perspective. Verlaine did in 1889:

A bas Baju! [The editor of *Le Décadent*]
Qu'il meure bien vite.

A bas le symbolisme, mythe
Et termite, et encore en bas
Ce décadisme parasite!

Down with Baju!
Let him die fast.
And down with symbolism at last
That silly symbol of the past.
Down too with decadence—a parasite
That should slink off into the night.[34]

And if Verlaine was not impressed by decadence, neither in another vein was Gustav Mahler. His Second Symphony in 1894, "The Resurrection," would be an anti-*Götterdämmerung* whose last movement features the trumpets of the Apocalypse ushering in the Last Judgment, but whose choral finale proclaims not annihilation, but redemption.

Now let me quickly move on to our own *fin de siècle* and place it in the perspective I have tried to sketch. First, let's recapitulate: A mentality that takes calendars and centuries for granted develops in the seventeenth century and asserts itself in the eighteenth century, when it begins to associate temporal progress with senescence, decay, and decline. From this position, there's but a step to assimilating material and social progress with obsolescence, calendrical conclusions suggesting crises even when they do *not* coincide with a crisis that they could serve to emphasize.

So *fin de siècle* is an invention of the last *fin de siècle*, which is what it called itself. Its negative connotations are related to natural evocations, but also to a long millennial tradition that contributes images, language, stereotypes, and attitudes which suggest that the end of an age, a generational experience, or a class assumption can be linked to the end of a world, and perhaps of *the* world.

My generation has lived through similarly nervous times and, if the end of the world hasn't come about, yet, that of *a* world probably has. Unfortunately, our *fin de siècle*, however popular with copycats, looks less impressive than the coterminous end of the billennium. Official bodies, learned institutions, business enterprises, and the media focus less on the end of a mere century than on the end of one millennium and the beginning of another. So, *fin de siècle* will have to wait another hundred years for a proper revival—if any.

APOCALYPSES
AND MILLENARIANISMS

Come up hither and I will shew thee things which must be hereafter.

– REVELATION 4:1

S HORTLY after the Second World War had ended, the British Army posted me to our occupation forces in Germany, where I spent several months in Münster, in Westphalia. Much of the center of town had been turned to rubble. But the great Gothic tower of St. Lambert's Church rose above the ruined gables and arcades of the market; and from the tower three great iron cages hung, where the last remains of radical Anabaptist leaders had been left to rot four centuries before.

For a few years in the 1530s, the little town of about ten thousand people, comparable with Calvin's Geneva, had been the New Jerusalem of a Thousand-Year Reich, ruled by a prophet in his twenties: John of Leiden. Like other true believers of his time, John was a chiliast: he was convinced that the world order was about to end in terrible torments, to be followed by the millennium, a thousand years of blessedness, during which the saints would reign. Having proclaimed himself King of Zion and Messiah, he instituted a theocratic reign of terror and polygamy, abolished private ownership of money and commodities, banned all books save the Bible, and sustained a long siege before being captured, tortured, put to death, and hung up with two companions as an object lesson to millenarians to come.

John's revelation—his apocalypse, for that is what the Greek word means—had turned out wrong, but that never discouraged prophets. In Münster itself, shortly after my passage there, a gentleman called Michael Schmaus published a forecast of last things, *Von Den Letzten Dingen* (1948), affirming that the millennium was imminent. A history of exploded predictions would fill an anthology. The index of Mgr. Ronald Knox's study of religious *Enthusiasm* (1950) lists ten dates between 1260 and 1834 when a Second Coming was expected; and any diligent researcher could easily add ten hundred more.

To mention only a few that might concern our immediate future, William Butler Yeats, the poet who predicted a Celtic Armageddon in 1899, seems to have expected the end of the Christian era in 2000, when the rough beast, "its hour come at last," would slouch to replace Jesus. So does the Reverend Tim La Haye, and so did several other ecclesiastics: Protestant ministers like Robert Fleming in the eighteenth century, Robert Scott in the nineteenth century, or the Catholic canon Rodriguez Cristino Morondo in the twentieth century. Nostradamus appears to have expected the end, or the beginning of the end, in 1999 (the seventh month of 1999 to be precise), while numerological readings vary between 1999 and 2001. So, apparently, does the Mayan calendar. Tynetta Muhammad, a numerologist belonging to the Nation of Islam, has recalculated the code of the Koran to conclude that we may expect the end in 2001.[1]

The "rapture," which in some views is to remove the minority of saints from earth during the horrors of tribulation, has become part of doomsday chic. Rapture wristwatches proclaim "One hour nearer to the Lord's return." Bumper stickers re-quest "Beam me up, Lord." Dashboard signs warn, "If you hear a trumpet, grab the wheel." The *Rapture Alert Newsletter* published by Salem Kirban, whose *Guide to Survival* (1968) sold half a million copies, offers predictions of the end seasoned by recipes for Mrs. Kirban's chicken soup.[2]

Unfortunately, visions of the end are less about soup and solace than about horror and destruction. In common usage, "doomsday," the day of judgment, becomes annihilation; "apocalypse" means disaster, cosmic catastrophe, the end of the world. The revelation of God's plan for the world and for his church narrows into predictions about how times (history) and time will end; "eschatology," the doctrine of end times, becomes the chief aspect of apocalypse.

Jewish prophets, of whom we are the heirs, had produced a rich harvest of sightings of God intervening to destroy the wicked, both Israelites and their enemies, and to set up his kingdom on earth in spectacularly horrid circumstances. Zachariah 14:12 describes the plague wherewith the Lord would smite Jerusalem's enemies: "Their flesh shall consume away while they stand upon their feet, and their eyes shall consume away in their holes, and their tongue shall consume away in their mouth." Joel, for his part, describes the day of the Lord which is nigh at hand (2:10): darkness, gloom, clouds, and thick darkness, devouring fire, devastation, and much running to and fro. "The earth shall quake . . . the heavens tremble, the sun and the moon shall be dark, the stars shall withdraw their shining."

Christ and his apostles were heirs of this tradition. Peter, the senior apostle, made it clear that "the day of the Lord shall come as a thief in the night; in which the heavens shall pass away with a great noise, and the elements shall melt with fervent heat, the earth also and the works that are therein shall be burned up" (2 Peter 3:10). Not a very unobtrusive intruder in the night, but vivid enough to make the point.

The true heir of fire-and-brimstone prophets was another John, writing from exile on the barren isle of Patmos toward the end of the first century. His revelations echo the imagery of other angry exiles: Daniel, Zachariah, Ezekiel, and the rest. Our Bible, which opens with the Beginning, closes on John's grand and gruesome visions of "things which must shortly come to pass" before a new heaven and a new earth were vouchsafed. The swarming imagery of trumpets, thrones, seals, vials of wrath, lamps of fire, angels, plagues, lightnings, thunderings, earthquakes, falling stars, fire, blood, hail, black sun and bloody moon, a menagerie of fantastic beasts including dragons, demon frogs, scorpion locusts, and dire-hued horses, water turned to wormwood, Gog, Magog, and a cast of thousands was mostly drawn from the lumber of the past. It would, however, inspire the future, even to our own day. Its bizarre but powerful evocations were to provide generations to come with metaphors, allegories, and figures of speech, with warnings, guideposts, and inspiration.

Not the least influential of John's prophecies was his vision of Christ's Second Coming as a warrior on a white horse, his eyes as a flame of fire and a sword in his mouth to smite Antichrist, the Devil's catspaw, and cast him in a lake of fire burning with brimstone. Then, while the fowl of heaven feast on the flesh of God's foes, an angel comes down from heaven to chain "the dragon, that old serpent, which is the Devil and Satan," bind him for a thousand years, "cast him into the bottomless pit and shut him up . . . till the thousand years shall be fulfilled" (20:1–3) True, after the thousand years are over, Satan "must be loosed a little season" to wreak more havoc before God's fire devours Satan's creatures, and the Devil, his beast, and his false prophet are finally cast into the lake of fire and brimstone to "be tormented day and night for ever and ever." Preceding that happy closure and the dire penultimate crises that foreshadow it come a thousand years of blessedness—indeed, "one thousand" represents a long indefinite duration. The millennium forms a sort of antechamber of the new heaven and new earth in which God wipes away all tears from men's eyes, "and there shall be no more death, neither sorrow, nor crying, nor pain, for the former things are passed away" and all things are made new.

If, then, apocalypticism is about judgments, accountings, and ends, millennialism (or millenarianism) is about new beginnings: restoration and regeneration. Ezra, Enoch, and others had looked to rejoicing in the marvels of the Lord for a span of 30 or 400 or 1000 years, according to the particular text selected. John, and Jesus and his angels, promised an eternity of justice, bliss, and glory in the light of God; and that time was at hand.

It is still at hand today, as it was in the day of John of Patmos or John of Leiden. But it has grown more complex over time. Whether they were uttered before Christ or since, apocalyptic prophecies are attempts to interpret their times, to console and guide, to suggest the meaning of the present and the future. Typically, they relate fear to hope: tribulation and horror will usher in public and private bliss, free of pain or evil. And, inevitably, they speak to their times. A medieval historian, Bernard McGinn, describes them as mirrors held up to the age, attempts by each era to understand itself in relation to an all-embracing scheme of history—preferably God's plans for man.[3] Sooner or later these plans included the Parousia—the arrival or return of Christ in glory, which we now call the Second Coming—to terminate the present world [dis]order and usher redeemed humanity into a better world (Matthew 24; 1 Corinthians 15).

Most social historians link apocalypticism with political crisis, social change, or material distress. But this does not tell us much. Change, pain, distress, and insecurity are part of every age; so are hope, confusion, and simple curiosity. When the apostles on the Mount of Olives asked about signs of Jesus' Second Coming and of the end of the world, their master listed wars, rumors of wars, nation rising against nation and kingdom against kingdom, famines, pestilences, earthquakes, deceivers and false prophets, betrayals, hate, iniquity abounding and love waxing cold. Paul writing to Timothy, his friend and companion, went into further detail about the last days when "men shall be lovers of their own selves, covetous, boasters, proud, blasphemers, disobedient to parents, unthankful, unholy, without natural affection, truce breakers, false accusers, incontinent, fierce, despisers of those that are good, traitors, heady, high-minded [proud], lovers of pleasures more than lovers of God" (2 Timothy 3:1–4). If that's what we're supposed to look for, no wonder that every era produces apocalyptic visions appropriate to its circumstances.

Basic themes and preoccupations endure, specifics alter, the recipes for action inspire peaceful dissent or militant chiliasm, serve private salvation (quietism, inner light, withdrawal from the world), meliorism interested in reform, or radical ideologies that bring not peace but a sword.

Given human nature, radical alternatives can be popular. The righteous deserve compensation. As St. Ireneus, a great theologian and bishop of Lyon in the second century, explained: "In that very creation in which they toiled and were afflicted and were tried in every way by suffering, they should receive the reward of their suffering . . . and . . . in the very creation in which they endured servitude, they should also reign." In the early fourth century, Lactantius, the tutor of Emperor Constantine's son, was more explicit: the reward of the righteous lay in the lurid fate of the unrighteous. "That multitude of the godless shall be annihilated, and torrents of blood shall flow, [and Christ] will hand over all heathen peoples to servitude under the righteous . . . and this kingdom of the righteous shall last for a thousand years."[4]

Liberation is sweet; bloody vengeance is sweeter; ruling the unrighteous will be sweetest of all. "Then the rain of blessing shall descend from God morning and evening, and the earth shall bear all fruits without man's labor. Honey in abundance shall drip from the rocks, fountains of milk and wine shall burst forth. The beasts of the forests shall put away their wildness and become tame . . . no longer shall any animal live by bloodshed. For God shall supply all with abundant and guiltless food."[5]

We are not told how this abundance would trickle down to the enserfed heathen. But the religio-historical forecasts were enticing and, as in sixteenth-century Münster, they could stimulate religio-hysterical crowds determined to achieve the kingdom of God by force: aggressive ascetics, parousian paroxysms, messiahs and apocalyptic beasts in conflict—or rolled into one, as in John of Leiden.

All ages are marked by perils, lawlessness, social disorders and upheavals, breakdown of morality and family, perils, turbulence and troubles that can serve as signs and stimulate expectations. They are portents; and there are always portents, always apocalyptic apprehensions, always fears and hopes to suggest millennial themes. Joining pessimism and optimism together, the millenarian message is infinitely adaptable to the circumstances of every age.

Sooner or later, also, millenarianism linked religion and politics, and precipitated pre-political attitudes into political movements with social and economic goals related to its religious goals—as suggested, for example, in the Sermon on the Mount (Matthew 5–7). Religion, which had been the handmaiden of politics, became its inspiration and, eventually, as the supernatural was slowly naturalized and secularized, its justification. One kind of salvation suggested another, one kind of revelation suggested another, one kind of revolution suggested another. But, for many centuries, the two marched hand in hand, with political, social, and economic rules, as well as their breach, justified by reference to Holy Writ and, often, to its revelations.

There were always aspirants to the complete and radical change that they expected would replace their corrupt, unjust environment with a new world order. But the despair, or the moral and physical discomfort, that spurs violent millenarian movements to destroy whatever prevents happiness and salvation varies with circumstances.

For a long time, chiliasm had been an answer to persecution. Belief in the imminence of the end brought comfort in the midst of danger and pain. When in the fourth century the Roman Empire became Christian, the actuality of eschatological questions, of speculations about the shape of the last things and the Second Coming, became less pressing, and criticism of literal expectations, which had been rising since the third century, came into its own. Beliefs that early Christians had taken for granted were disparaged as misleading or, at least, bizarre.

In the early fifth century, Augustine delivered what looked like a knockout blow to literal readings of the Apocalypse: God's timetable was inscrutable, the city of God lay in heaven, the city of man lay on earth, and never the twain would meet. The Savior "comes throughout this present age in the person of his church" (*City of God* 1.4), the Apocalypse is an allegory that shows the way to salvation, but it was silly to get excited about the millennium. By 431, the Council of Ephesus had followed suit, denouncing the more carnal, this-worldly aspects of millenarianism as errors and phantasies.

Yet the age of the world as an indicator of the proximity of the end remained a burning issue. In 410, when Alaric's Goths sacked Rome, too many Christians held that "from Adam all the years have passed . . . and now comes the day of Judgment." At the mid-fifth century, Vandal invasions recalled calculations that the world would end in the year 500, 6000 years after Creation, and spurred new calculations to show that the name of the Vandal king Genseric represented 666: the number of the Beast. Wise men like Isidore of Seville, who died in 636, and the Venerable Bede, who died one hundred years later, recalculated the reach and terminus of six thousand years; and even rustics pestered learned clerics to study the age of the world and know when it would end.[6]

So millennial dreams persisted, as did apocalyptic nightmares—both too precious to dispense with. Etymologically, the term "superstition," which we associate with irrational beliefs, means a superfluous structure irrelevant to the tectonics of a creed. Is millenarianism a superstition in this sense? Or is it integral to Christianity? My short answer to these questions would be yes, and yes. Christianity no more rests on Revelation or needs it to make its point than Judaism needs Daniel or Ezekiel. But Christianity would not be recognizable without the revelations of Revelation, and it would look very different without the contribution that its Apocalypse and a variety of millenarianisms made to its history.

Determinism, the view that all events are somehow inevitable, let alone predestined, is incompatible with the Christian doctrines of autonomy and free will. The more specific a prediction, including predictions of the end, the more offensive it was to free will. The end was near. "But of that day and hour knoweth no man, no, not the angels of heaven, but my Father only." On the other hand, believers were supposed to watch for it and be ready (Matthew 24:36, 42, 44). That was an invitation to endless speculation.

It was increasingly argued that the revelations of John, like those of Daniel before him, were not to be taken literally, but figuratively. The Revelation is a skein of mysteries, signs, images, and hints to be decyphered. Its visions are symbols to be approached analogically, one word or figure representing something else. Thus, when John describes the rider on a white horse, called Faithful and True, and tells us that "out of his mouth goeth a sharp sword, that with it he should smite the nations," the image is interpreted to represent the Word of God.

Scriptural numbers, likewise, symbolize spiritual messages: three stands for the Trinity, four for Creation, three plus four equal seven, perfection; three times four equal twelve, plenitude. Jerusalem has twelve gates. The number six, which falls short of seven, is incomplete; and 666 is a culmination of incompleteness: the Beast ever yearning for divine truth but never able to attain it. Seven, in contrast, seems omnipresent: seven seals, seven trumpets, seven visions, seven vials, seven angels with trumpets, seven angels with last plagues, and even a seven-headed dragon testify to its powers. Like the number twelve, 1000, too, is a symbol of plenitude, and Augustine explains that it is a perfect number, ideal for allegorical expressions of notions like "lots," or "totality," or "all generations," but not for anything exact.

Exactness, or the quest for it, comes into its own when exegetes begin to calculate the date of the millennium or the Judgment. The mighty angel who addresses John (11:3) refers to a waiting period to last forty-two months or—the same thing—1260 days. Christians agreed with Jews that, in prophetic language, days stand for years. "One day in the [Lord's] world of justice is like a thousand years," explained a third-century Roman priest.[7] So Joachim of Fiore, who died in 1202, was not the first Christian to calculate the end of the present age, only the first to place it in the year 1260. Joachim's calculations began in the year 1, and many were to challenge his choice of a starting date. Daniel 8:14, on the other hand, had heard a saint speak of 2300 days before the end. In 1452, Cardinal Nicholas of Cusa thought that these 2300 years should begin in 559 BC, when he presumed that Daniel's vision had occurred. That delayed the Second Coming until the early eighteenth century. Scores of exegetes reached different conclusions.

We shall encounter some of these prophecies as we go. The point now is that, as D.H. Lawrence once reminded his readers, symbols have many meanings, and no one explanation can be taken as final or exhaustive. In fact, like other prophecies, John's Apocalypse "has no one meaning. It has meanings."[8] We shall see that different readers, believers and unbelievers, raised a variety of questions, reached a variety of conclusions, and reacted in a variety of ways. Was the millennium literal or allegorical, earthly or spiritual? Did Daniel or John intend to be read figuratively or to the letter? Do they offer intimations or timetables? Why count time from the Nativity, as Joachim did, and not from the Annunciation, or the Passion of Christ? And why should all but Christian parameters be ignored when, as Cusa knew, God spoke to others before Christ was born?

Would fulfillment of Biblical prophecy be trenchant and violent or gradual: a cumulative progress to salvation? Was the end imminent, or advance to redemption immanent? The implications were momentous. If the millennium were a gradual improvement of present conditions, then Christ would appear only after it was complete (post-millennialism). If the transition to the millennium was to be violent and abrupt, then it would be associated with the Second Coming.

Nothing could be known for sure. The catastrophes revealed by John and his fellows could have happened already, or may be unfolding even at this time, unbeknownst to us. According to the Council of Ephesus, Christ's kingdom was the church, and the Christian church and the millennium were coterminous. For Protestants, who denied the divine relations of Catholic authority and doubted that their circumstances were millennial, the thousand years of Christ's reign lay over the horizon. Some eschatologists placed the end of days within history; others, in an extratemporal state under the rule of Christ. Were the events that were symbolically described historical or ahistorical? Were they, in other words, part of a linear progression, or were they due to take place on a spiritual plane outside historical time?

There was yet another possibility to envisage: Creation is a beginning, and a beginning implies an end. But in the New Testament as in the Old, the end was a beginning too: a new heaven and a new earth. When the world ends, it could be argued that all that ends is the world we know. The end of the world was really only the end of one world, not the end of time but of our times, not the annihilation of mankind but the end of a way of life and its replacement by another.

Cycles—lunar, seasonal, chronological—are part of everyday experience. Days dawn and darken, moons wax and wane, tides ebb and flow, humans and other animals are born, grow old, and pass away. But new young replace those who declined and died, and every new year is a new beginning. As autumn, winter, spring, and summer follow one another, the sun shines longer or more briefly, crops are sown and are harvested, and the order of the day—of work, rest, meals, courtship, and the generations— recur over and over.

If nature presents a compelling picture of recurrence, why should the world's fate not be part of it? Crops, humans, and kingdoms do not last indefinitely. Nor can the universe. Everything decays and ends, but decadence is preliminary to renewal and revitalization. "Just as the disappearance of the moon is never final because a new moon inevitably follows," wrote Mircea Eliade, the great sociologist of religions, "so the disappearance of man is never final either, for after flood or whatever a new humanity is born."[9]

Stoicism, the most powerful philosophy of late antiquity, identified the original element of our universe as fire and expected a cosmic conflagration, after which all would be fire again, but only temporarily: "The great march of centuries begins anew," wrote Octavian's friend, the poet Virgil, who died nineteen years before Christ's birth: "The maiden returns, Saturn is king again,/ A new race descends from on high."[10] The fiery consummation was not final, as the Last Judgment was in Christian lore, but the conclusion of one cycle was preceded and followed endlessly by other similar ones.

Seneca, the stoic philosopher who died in AD 65, expected final conflagration to obliterate the creation: "All we see and admire today will burn in the universal fire that ushers in a new, just, happy world." And, since every generation reads the world's end in contemporary calamities, the great eruption of Mount Vesuvius in AD 79, when Pompei was buried by the volcano's lava flow, was taken as the signal of the cosmic conflagration that was about to follow. Recurrence, what Eliade called the myth of eternal return, ruled over a history consisting of repetitions.

Regeneration of the world and life also lay at the core of Zoroastrianism, a religion that flourished in Iran and neighboring lands for some twelve centuries after 600 BC, and is still followed by the Indian Parsis. Originally, Zoroaster's (or Zarathustra's) world was due to be consumed very soon in a mighty conflagration, after which the good would rise again to share in the coming kingdom. When conflagration did not come, Zoroastrians formulated an alternative cosmic drama in four 3000-year acts, where Ormuzd, the god of light, struggles against Ahriman, the spirit of dark and evil. The fourth trillennium begins with the birth of Zoroaster, and the end of each of its millennia is marked by the appearance of savior figures, each a godlike prophet, each miraculously conceived by a virgin, each renovating the world and helping to perfect mankind.

The third and last such savior, a son of Zoroaster, would usher in the new creation. The World Savior comes in glory; a great ordeal by fire and molten metal ensues, followed by the final battle between good and evil. Then, after the triumph of righteousness, Ormuzd regenerates a world saved from impotence, decay, and demons: "There will be abundance everywhere; there will be no more want of food; the world will be pure, man liberated from [evil spirits] and immortal for ever."[11]

A great many apocalyptic myths involve destruction followed by reconstruction. Deucalion, son of Prometheus, and his wife, Pyrrha, survive the deluge wrought by Zeus' ire and reconstruct the human race. In the third century BC, Berosus, a Babylonian priest writing in Greek, popularized the Chaldean doctrine of the Great Year, according to which the universe is eternal, but periodically destroyed and reconstructed every Great Year, whose number of millennia varies according to the account you chose to read. When monsters slay the Nordic gods at Ragnarok and the world is destroyed by fire and flood, the world-tree Ygdrasil survives and bears a new man, Lif, and a new woman, Lifthrasir, to generate the next human race. Even the American

Indian ghost-dance religion of the late nineteenth century was about regeneration; the world would perish soon, but another earth, this one like paradise, would take its place. So cyclical catastrophe is normal, but never final.[12]

Cyclical myths are optimistic: death is followed by resurrection, cataclysm by a new creation. But even cosmic recurrence has an end. History, in the Zoroastrian scriptures, will end one day when all will render an account of what they have done in the great historical struggle between good and evil, and those who are found not guilty will know beatitude and eternity. For Hebrews, too, when the Messiah comes, the world will be saved once and for all, and history will cease to exist. The same was true for Christians.[13] But, just as apocalyptic predictions and millennial expectations became mixed up and gave rise to endless speculation and argument, so the scenario of recurrent regeneration could confuse and be confused with predictions of progression toward an appointed end.

Shelley, the atheist poet, could not help writing about the eternal return:

> The world's great age begins anew,
> The golden years return,
> The earth doth like a snake renew
> Her winter weeds outworn . . .

Cyclical experience, in seasons and in life, was the warp; apocalypse was the woof; and on their common weave the great sequential rhythms of decades, centuries, and millennia imposed their abstract patterns. Over the centuries, human minds and imaginings were going to arrange and rearrange them endlessly, in designs that we can describe as harmony or cacophony, according to taste.

IN DARK AND BLOODY TIMES

Dies irae, dies illa,
solvet saeclum in favilla,
teste David cum Sibylla.
Quantus tremor est futurus
quando judex ext venturus,
cuncta stricte discussurus;
Tuba, mirum spagens sonum
per sepulchra regionum
coget omnes ante tronum.

Day of anger, day of terror,
all shall crumble into ashes,
Witness David and the Sibyl.
What a tremor will assail them
when the Judge shall come to judgment
shattering all at once asunder!
Sounds the trump with awful note
through the tombs of [deathly] regions
summoning all before the throne.

    – THOMAS OF CELANO, 1250

A LONG TRAIL of wild and somber Jewish prophets precedes John's grimly imaginative predictions of the old consumed and the new conceived. Hard times, defeat, persecution, and insecurity often generated compensatory fantasies that brought comfort in distress and assurance of divine intervention. The book of Daniel, probably put together in the second century BC, in times of bloody persecution and resistance, was the first Jewish apocalyptic writing properly speaking; but far older prophets, like Amos and Isaiah in the eighth century BC, and Joel, had foretold the day of the Lord and his judgment, and had described its setting. They and others also promised the coming of a deliverer and restorer, the Messiah, under whose glorious rule the Jews would live in peace.

Christianity is the daughter of Jewish revelations, and Christ is a messiah within the Jewish tradition, though one most Jews failed to accept. John's Revelation, addressed to his first-century contemporaries, used notions, images, and expressions that were familiar to his readers, including millenarian visions of a time of justice and plenty to follow tribulation. It would be easy to pick these images up in later times, even if the apostles had not thought much about them. But they had.

Before John, Jesus and his followers had expected the imminent coming of God's kingdom and the beginning of a golden age. When Jesus died and rose again, hopes of a prompt return survived and grew apace. Over the centuries, foreign wars, internal conflict, and the everyday misbehavior of fallible folk triggered dire predictions. But the first century brought particularly hard times for Jews, and for the Jewish heretics who believed in Christ. Romans were fighting Romans, Jews were fighting Jews, Jews were fighting Romans and losing with terrible results, Romans as well as Jews persecuted Christians, and, as Paul wrote to the Romans (8:22), the whole of creation was groaning in travail. Ninety years or so into the Christian era, when John was exiled on Patmos and recorded what he saw and heard, hopes of deliverance surged with great urgency. Three centuries earlier, the archangel Gabriel had advised Daniel to keep quiet about his vision because it depicted things that would happen "many days hence" (Daniel 8:26). By John's time, his prophecies and those of his Christian fellows were to be broadcast openly, for, as we are told, "the time is near" and the Messiah is "coming soon" (22:10, 12).

A contemporary of John, the Jewish apocalyptist known as Esdras, was just as sure that times were swiftly closing. He painted a spectacularly terrifying picture of the end, after which the few survivors would rejoice in the Messiah's light for 30 or 400 or (as John preferred) 1000 years. An end to the world was a good way of escaping its perils, a solution for insoluble problems. It was even more desirable if it ushered in an age of material and moral perfection under the aegis of the Lord's anointed.

Christians who, like the Jews, knew plenty of worldly woes had peculiar predicaments of their own. Biggest of these was the delay of Christ's return in glory, which most of his early followers expected to take place within their lifetime, or soon thereafter. Sufferings and depravities would get worse, they knew, but the Parousia (Christ's Second Coming) would bring them to an end. It was not clear, however, as Christ delayed his promised return, just what Christians should do. In the event, they did what many Christians have done since then: some adjusted to a new timetable of long-term progress; others kept expecting the Parousia from one day to the other.

Late in the second century, the Holy Spirit became incarnate in an Anatolian prophet named Montanus, for whom the Last Judgment was at hand and the New Jerusalem would soon descend from heaven near a Phrygian town. In preparation, Christians should cut themselves off from the corrupt, corrupting world and lead ascetic lives. Montanism, which reacted against the growing institutionalization and secularization of the church by a return to original fervor, won converts from one end of the Mediterranean to another. Tertullian, a church father of Carthage, embraced the fervent eschatological expectations that inspired Montanism. Its rigor and ecstatic prophesying would resurface in centuries to come—not least in French Jansenism and its offshoots. But this appearance also spurred a reaction from those who believed that the church was here to stay and did not want its pitch queered, its mission destabilized, by heedless enthusiasts.

Early in the third century, St. Hippolytus, an important Roman theologian and foe of heresies, wrote a commentary on the book of Daniel that was meant to discourage the sort of eschatological expectations that had lately driven a bishop to lead his flock into the desert to meet the returning Lord, whence they could only be rescued by government intervention. But it was an Egyptian contemporary of Hippolytus, Origen, who provided the crucial argument against apocalyptists. The Scriptures, wrote Origen, could be interpreted literally, morally, or allegorically. Of these, he preferred the last, and his allegorical interpretations, honed on Greek myths, went a long way to exploding literal readings of problematic stories like that of Eden and its tree of knowledge, Noah and his ark, or Lot and his daughters.

Literalism, Origen suggested, was too "Jewish" to be doctrinally correct; the message of the Scriptures was symbolic, and that was how it should be read. A century after Origen, St. Jerome, who had translated the Bible into Latin, agreed that sensible folk avoided literalness. He dismissed chiliasm (the theory that Christ would return to rule on earth for a thousand years before the final consummation) as simply Jewish fables.[1]

Literalism was not the preserve of Jews alone; we live with it today. But apocalypticism was beginning to embarrass moderate, rational Christians, and it would embarrass them even more after the Christian church was accepted and coopted by the state in the fourth century. Available for limitless predictions, speculations, and imaginings, apocalypse was too destabilizing. Its origins had been lost from sight; its imagery was more acceptable when translated as allegory and symbolism. Tarring it with Jewish origins was an effective way to marginalize it; also a convincing one. As late as 1873, Ernest Renan, the great French scholar, recognized Revelation as "the most Jewish . . . of New Testament writings" and "Israel's last word" in the Christian world.[2]

But the man who effectively solved the philosophical problems of anti-apocalypticists was an Algerian-born Roman intellectual whom asthma forced to give up a professorship in Milan to become bishop of Hippo, not far from Carthage. The young Aurelius Augustinus (354–430), better known as St. Augustine, had been troubled by contradictions between the accounts of Jesus' origin given by Luke and Matthew. He had solved that problem by treating the texts as not literally but symbolically true. Why not apply the same method to John's Apocalypse, and interpret it not in a material but a spiritual sense?

A metaphor is a figure of speech that colors or enhances a term, as when we describe Wall Street as a *hive* of activity. Allegory is often the extension of metaphor, as when we describe the truth as *naked*, and dwelling at the bottom of a well. Biblical apocalypse was to be read allegorically, as a discussion of good and evil, the latter being part of time, and of the history whose end would necessarily see the end of evil. But the struggle between good and evil was even now unfolding; literalist readings of prophecy, millenarianism, Armageddon, and the rest were to be avoided, and end-of-time speculation should be avoided too. The City of God was not of this world or for this world. Christians could struggle toward it by restraining violence and injustice, but millenarian perfection could only be attained in another life. If history had failed to end on time, that was because the kingdom of God was already there. Parousia had come with Christ; and his church, which represented humanity and forgiveness, *was* the kingdom of God on earth.

The things to come had not yet come, explained Augustine; "yet already there is in the mind an expectation of things to come." Not yet, yet already here—in the mind. Christ's eschatology had been a short story oriented to an early conclusion. That of Augustine was closer to novels through which we wind, knowing they will end, but not when or how. And there could be no peeking. God was inscrutable, his message opaque; Christians knew *how* the story would end, not *when*. God determined the time and fashion of ultimate redemption. But we alone were responsible for personal redemption while the Last Judgment loomed over the horizon. "Do not be slow to turn to the Lord," advised Augustine, "nor delay from day to day, for His wrath shall come when you know not." Since Christ's coming, regeneration no longer depended on cosmic revolution or explosive resolution, but on individual effort to salvation; not on divine destruction, but on human decisions and effort. Helped by divine grace, God's creatures could speed the process by prayer, charity, and reform.

In 431, one year after Augustine's death, the Council of Ephesus made this approach official: the notion of collective salvation on earth was error and fantasy. Apocalyptic promises applied not to mankind in some earthly garden of Eden, but to individuals and their life after death. Henceforth, talk of last things would be only partly about the end to come, for the end had begun, and Christians already lived in an eschatological age. As Frank Kermode put it, "no longer imminent, the End became immanent."3

The world would end one day, but there was no knowing when. All people die, but all they can know or do about it is that they should live as if death could come at any moment. When it came, they would be judged. When the end came, all would be judged. Guessing, fussing, fretting were pointless and, worse, they went against the will of God and his church. A story is told about the sixteenth-century saint, Aloysius Gonzaga, when he was still a Jesuit novice, and he and his fellow students were playing at ball during a break. Their talk turned to salvation, and the question was raised: "If suddenly, right this moment, you learned that the Last Judgment were to take place in half an hour, what would you do?" While his friends imagined prayer, penitence, or appeals to a patron saint, Aloysius said: "I would go on playing." Charles Péguy, who retells the apocryphal story, comments: "It doesn't depend on us that the event take place; it depends on us to deal with it."[4] The church told its children how to do so.

The issue had been resolved. Or had it? Distinctions are for scholars; confusions for normal folk. And even scholars confused belief in Christ's Second Coming with speculations about the swiftness and manner of his coming; experience of all manner of tribulation around them with signs of the great tribulation to come; and the commonplace operations of Satan in a fallen world with the manifestation of apocalyptic beasts and Antichrist. When the moderate, rationalistic Christianity of a Pauline church marginalized the Apocalypse, it forgot or sought to forget the immoderate, enthusiastic nature of primitive Christianity: materialistic conceptions, visions, impossibilities, paradoxes, incoherencies, contradictions, and self-contradictions. Apostles and church fathers changed their minds, mixed their metaphors, and borrowed from their opponents many notions or implications they had once decried.

A religion that regarded the natural and supernatural realms as divinely interlaced could only confirm mentalities that made no distinction between the natural and the supernatural. Fairies, sprites, imps, and ogres were part of everyday experience; noble families claimed descent from fairy ancestors, as Lusignans and Luxemburgs (sometimes Plantagenets as well) did from Melusine; springs and "good fountains" consecrated to fairies were everywhere. No wonder that Joan of Arc had her first vision near a fairy spring, the *bonne fontaine aux fées*.[5] No wonder, either, that meteorites recalled the falling stars of Scriptures, or that the Norman historian Ordericus Vitalis, recording a meteor shower "falling like the hail" in April 1095, linked the ominous sighting with Biblical predictions. "The heavens themselves," as Shakespeare knew, "blaze forth the death of princes." Comets portended dire events, and divine or satanic powers intervened constantly to affect both people's lives and natural phenomena:

to bring rain or fend it off, to change the color of the sky or douse the light of heavenly bodies. Prayers, if well received, could affect fate or, at least, weather. Like fairies around a royal cradle, supernatural powers could inflect destiny or give warning of it.

Not yet, but here, in the mind, the Judgment was near; the world stood close to the end of time. Church services, which everyone attended, but also church architecture, sculptures, and frescoes, bore witness to the original Fall, far in the past, and to the Last Judgment, in the near future, with man's brief compass in between. Only God's goodness postponed it and kept mankind from being swallowed in a worse hell than they saw around.

How long would He stay his hand? The calculations of Bishop Gregory of Tours, who died in 594, suggested some time between 799 and 806, which allowed mankind a spell to breathe and pray.[6] But in September 589 a terrible earthquake ravaged Antioch, killing tens of thousands; and in November 589 fearsome floods devastated Gaul and Italy, after which plague killed thousands, including Pope Pelagius II. No wonder his successor, Gregory I (590–604), judged that the end was a good deal closer than the calculations of his Gaulish namesake indicated. Pelagius, the late pope's epitaph pronounced, had been caught "in a falling world" that was rapidly decomposing. Gregory saw this clearly: "The world grows old and hoary and hastens to its approaching end." Inundations, famine, pestilence, and invasions may account for Gregory's lifelong obsession with the world's ending: he was a practical man who combined piety and character, and probably drew the conclusions of what he saw and heard around. All we know, or think we know, is that the missionaries whom he sent to England in 596, led by the prior of his own monastery, a future St. Augustine (one more!), first Archbishop of Canterbury, were part of his preparations for the coming end.[7] So the conversion of England, like the later voyages of Columbus, were heavily influenced by anticipation of end times.

It was hardly extraordinary that clerics versed in the Scriptures should relate contemporary travails to events and signs that
Scriptures had predicted, or that the apocalyptic terrors they
evoked should amplify the terrors of mundane existence. Clearly,
as Adalbert of Laon (just north of Paris) wrote in the tenth
century, the world had gone mad: "Laws are dissolving, peace
evaporating, customs changing, and order reels as well."[8] The
dissolution of law and social order was one more forewarning
of the approaching end. Belial, the lawless one, had migrated
from Jewish apocalyptic literature to become Antichrist; and
Antichrist was also *Ante*christ—a necessary forerunner of the millennium. We shall encounter them again with their chaotic escort
whenever everyday mayhem rises to paroxysm; but they fitted
the turmoil and havoc of a thousand lawless years after the fifth
century and, not least, the anarchic decades before the year 1000.

The millennium of the year 1000 has inspired much debate.
We have seen that to count centuries and millennia from the uncertain date of the birth of Christ is as anachronistic as it is to
speak of a tenth and eleventh century as if those who lived in
them knew about them. Neither system, as a system, existed in
the minds or experiences of those days. Yet the Apocalypse, as
Joachim of Fiore was to put it, carried "the key of things past, the
knowledge of things to come"; its appeal was as irresistible as the
catastrophic resolution that it promised. Chronology remained
an uncertain art, but the obsession of anniversaries and commemorations made scholars, preachers, and those whom they
taught or preached to be aware of dates, even when these events
were not precisely dated.

Expectation of the end had not waited on the year 1000.
Seventh-century documents turned out by princely and ecclesiastical chancelleries refer to "evident signs announcing the early
end of the world."[9] Around the year 700, that venerable Briton,
Bede, grumbled that rustics importuned him about the time left
in the millennium. In 793, Elipand, bishop of Toledo, accused

Beatus, abbot of Liebana, of having prophesied the end of the world. It was Easter eve. "In terror, the people fasted all night and until the ninth hour on Sunday, when [one of them] feeling hungry declared 'Let us eat and drink, for if we are to die, we might as well die full.'"[10] In the late ninth century, the fall of the last Carolingians and of the Roman Empire that Charles the Great restored brought more confirmation of a looming end, predicted not by Apocalypse alone but by diffuse feelings of the world's twilight and senescence. It was not by coincidence that the coronation robe of Otto III, crowned emperor in 996, would be embroidered with scenes from the Apocalypse.

Dreadful apprehensions of the approaching end were an integral part of medieval minds, which seized on what came to hand for their confirmation. They seem to have found plenty of kindling in the second half of the tenth century in chancelleries, sermons, and debates about whether to expect the ending, and to fear it, refute it, or prepare for it. That response was not necessarily because 1000 years had been properly counted since Christ had come and the devil had been bound (though evidently not tightly). And, even accounted for, were the 1000 years to be read literally or symbolically, as standing for "totality" or "all generations"? Few cared for accuracy of reckoning or language. They cared that the Bible said that Christ *would* return, and, according to John's Revelation, after 1000 years, Satan would be unchained and become Antichrist.

Augustine had insisted that signs and wonders of the day should not be related to the apocalyptic prophecies of Daniel and Revelation. Prodigies, he had warned, are deceptive. But the times teemed with prodigies, prophets, monsters, earthquakes, storms, and eclipses, all of which induced apocalyptic panics in armies and congregations. In 989, Halley's comet swept through the skies, proof that not much time was left. Likewise, a rumor that the end would come when the feast of the Annunciation coincided with Good Friday. This happened in 992, when Easter fell on March 22, and eager calculators established that the world would end before three years had passed.

The three years passed and nothing much happened in 995; nor in "the millennium of the birth of the all-vivifying Word." Then, the hopes or fears of those who cared about such things, such as the monk Raoul Glaber, shifted to the thousandth anniversary of the Passion, when Augustine's millennial countdown had begun. For 1033, premonitory signs appeared more satisfying: a great famine was followed as usual by pestilence, even cannibalism, so that "folk believed that the order of seasons and the laws of the elements that had governed the world until then had crashed back into eternal chaos, and feared the end of humankind."[11] Yet once again, the end did not come on time.

The eleventh century furnished still more momentous events. In 1009, Jerusalem's Church of the Holy Sepulchre, and Christ's tomb within it, were destroyed by order of Calif Hakim. In 1028, a great rain of blood off the coast of Aquitaine struck fear along Mediterranean coastlines. In 1066, the Normans conquered England, and one historian has suggested that William the Conqueror's great survey of his lands, ordered in 1085, came to be known as the *Domesday Boke* because it evoked the Day of Judgment but, even more, the great register of the day of doom, the *Liber vitae*, or *Book of Life*.[12] In 1071, the Turks conquered Armenia and most of Asia Minor, including Syria and the Holy Land, while pope and emperor squabbled. In 1095, Pope Urban II proclaimed the First Crusade, an armed pilgrimage really, designed to help Christianity "flourish again in these last times, so that when Antichrist begins his reign there—as he shortly must— he will find enough Christians to fight."[13] Two hundred years later, when the Crusades properly speaking were over, crusading ideas that had spurred the Christian reconquest of the Muslim-occupied Iberian peninsula would help to shape Spanish and Portuguese expansion overseas.

The Apocalypse would not go away. In the mid-twelfth century, a German mystic, Elizabeth of Schonau, accused of prophesying the Last Judgment, wrote to Abbess Hildegard of Bingen to defend herself: "I should never have presumed to do it, since its arrival defies mortal knowledge." St. Hildegard (1098–1179) undoubtedly agreed about the doctrine, but she knew herself to be a divinely appointed prophetess. A voice from heaven had addressed her in 1141 and ushered in twenty-six visions of salvation history leading to the Last Judgment. Her writings contain numerous references to last times and to imagery based on the Apocalypse, including its beasts, and winds whose energies would only be unleashed at the world's end.[14]

Meanwhile, south of Hildegard's Rhineland, in the mountains of southern Italy, a Calabrian monk was about to renovate apocalyptic thinking. The catastrophes and persecutions that John of Patmos envisaged made sense to persecuted first-century Christians and could only be escaped by personal salvation or catastrophic conclusion. Joachim of Fiore (1135–1202) "saw history moving through purifying catastrophes from one stage to a better one."[15] History had not been very relevant to salvation, which could only come at the end of time. Joachim suggested that salvation could come within history, through history, as the church reformed and purified itself and the world around it.

The twelfth century had seen the beginnings of accounting and budgeting in counting houses and chancelleries. In 1202, a Pisan mathematician, Leonardo Fibonacci, would introduce arabic numerals and, most important, the number zero, which facilitated calculation. Although he died in the year when Fibonacci's *Liber abaci* was published, Joachim was a great numerologist in the traditional vein, and his history was patterned by divisions into sevens and threes. Seven ages, inspired by Jewish lore, placed his own times near the end of the sixth age, which would be followed by a sabbath of repose and peace between the coming of the Antichrist, expected around 1260, and the Last Judgment; or three states, inspired by the New Testament and the Trinity.

In the latter perspective, history, like the Godhead, was divided into three: the age of the Father, of the Old Testament and the Law; the age of the Son, of the New Testament and Grace; and the Age of the Spirit, proceeding from both, when new religious orders would convert the whole world, and a new human race would lead free, contemplative lives in a purer, better universe. Joachim and his followers expected the Third Age to begin around 1260, after a brief reign of Antichrist, who would probably be followed by a new Adam or a new Christ. The Joachite periodization of a progressive history was to influence or confirm many secular millenarians all the way to the Comte de Saint-Simon at the beginning of the nineteenth century.

Evidently, the Parousia could figure in beginnings as strikingly as it did in ends, and could become a part of history as easily as part of its precipitation. Again, though, the spectacular consummation expected in the last days attracted greater attention. Enormously popular, especially as a source book for preachers, *The Golden Legend*, completed in 1265, listed the fifteen signs of Doom—rising seas, collapsing buildings, rains of fire or blood and the rest—that were widely publicized in play cycles that touched the illiterate masses as well as the literate few. One of the signs to watch for was the appearance of Antichrist, the man of sin, whose identity provided fascinating food for discussion. When Richard I, the Lionheart, passing through Italy in the 1190s on his way to the Third Crusade, asked to meet the great prophet, Abbot Joachim of Fiore, the king's first question was about where and when Antichrist would be born.[16] As time passed, the abbot's admirers had to adjust his predictions on this score as on others. There was always more to Joachim's message than eschatological premonition.

A hundred years after Joachim's death, Dante, who believed in progressive revelation and recognized his predecessor as a prophet, placed him in Paradise. Before long, however, Joachite notions were going to influence the friar followers of Francis of Assisi (1181–1226), whose thinking sanctified poverty and humility in the service of active charity. Was St. Francis a millenarian? Pope Gregory IX, his personal friend, believed that the world was in its evening and declining. St. Bonaventure, general of the Franciscan order from 1257 to his death in 1274, saw in St. Francis the Angel of the Sixth Seal of Revelation, harbinger of the church's Seventh, or Seraphic, Age.[17] Writing in 1297, the friar Petrus Olivi opined that Antichrist would surely surface between 1300 and 1340, after which the world would enter the Age of the Holy Spirit, due to end around the year 2000 with Gog and the Last Judgment. Olivi was a leader of the Spiritual Franciscans, dedicated to poverty and strict observance, whose apocalyptic sense of mission was reinforced by reference to Joachim and by the dissemination of pseudo-Joachite prophecies exalting poverty, austerity, and expectations of the end.

One fervent Joachite and extremist dropout of the Spiritual Franciscans was Fra Dolcino of Novara. Preaching abolition of property and probably of marriage as well, Dolcino established a communist peasant commune in Piedmont and held off orthodox crusaders for several years before being crushed in 1307, more by cold and hunger that by arms. Dolcino would be burnt alive a few months after his capture, but during preliminary tortures he announced that Antichrist would come in three and a half years, and that after his defeat, he himself would return to earth to preside over a purified church. Cola di Rienzo, too, who in the 1340s set out to reestablish Rome as capital of a "sacred Italy" that would spread peace and justice through the world, was deeply influenced by Joachim's prophecies. When cast out of Rome, he found refuge among Joachite monks in the Abruzzi mountains who recognized in plagues and earthquakes of the day proof that the reign of Antichrist was nigh and the Age of the Spirit was to follow. God, these holy ascetics suggested, was trying Cola in preparation for his apocalyptic task, which was to persuade the emperor to lead the universal reform that Joachite prophecies foretold. But the emperor could not be persuaded, and Cola was massacred by a Roman crowd in 1354.

One French fellow-traveler of the Spirituals, Jean de Roquetaillade (d. 1365), published a guide to the tribulation (*Vade Mecum in Tribulatione,* 1356) that present-day aficionados might find useful. Since he insisted on evangelical poverty and the imminent coming of Antichrist, he was imprisoned for most of his adult life. Roquetaillade expected Antichrist in 1366, to be followed in 1369 or 1370 by a millennial Sabbath. Jerusalem, under a Jewish king, would become the center of the world; but the king of France, "called to be the very poor husband of the universal church," would finally inherit the imperial crown.

A special ecclesiastical tribunal concerned with the detection and prosecution of heresy came into existence in 1184, when a papal bull directed bishops to make inquisition (inquiries) for heresy in their diocese and hand over those who would not recant to secular authorities for punishment. When bishops did not prove effective, Gregory IX in 1233 decided that full-time inquisitors should be recruited among Franciscan and Dominican friars. So Spiritual Franciscan heretics, imprisoned, tortured, or handed over to secular authority for dispatch, were often dealt with by fellow Franciscans. On the other hand, a Dominican hellfire preacher like St. Vincent Ferrer (1357–1419), author of a work on *The End of Days (De Fine Mundi)*, could also set Spain, France, England, and Italy atrembling with his predictions of Antichrist and the Last Judgment.

Eloquent prophet of an apocalyptic future, Ferrer called himself the Angel of the Apocalypse. The signs of a Second Coming that Jesus indicated as he sat upon the Mount of Olives (Matthew 24) were clear for all to see: wars and rumors of wars, nation rising against nation, betrayals, hatreds, false prophets, iniquity abiding, and love waxing cold. Faith lay in ruins, and Antichrist was already born and would soon meet St. Michael in mortal combat in the skies. That would be the end of days, which only a few faithful would survive. The fateful Joachite date of 1260, when the age was to end, rendered more impressive by ambient plague and famine, had spawned the violent penitence of flagellant bands who hoped that, by whipping themselves in public for thirty-three and a half days (representing the Lord's years on earth), they might convince God to suspend the death sentence he had passed on the world.[18] Ferrer revived this movement: in thirty-three and a half years, he promised, atoning flagellant saints would usher in the Third Age. In the fifteenth century, as in the fourteenth and the thirteenth, provocatively penitent flagellants waged war not only on Antichrist but also on the established order and the social, clerical, and money powers that were part of the anarchy that masqueraded as order. That some were burnt for their brutally subversive activities testifies that chiliasm, which could be invoked by the church, could easily turn against it.

The world was foundering under its load of sin and evil; and this burden included a clerical hierarchy and a clergy that forgot their calling and their duty to God, that bought and sold offices and prayers, and that fornicated, intrigued, and amassed worldly goods. What hope of salvation was there when those who controlled access to salvation did not do their job? As war, plagues, and famines more deadly than usual scourged the fourteenth-century West, the ballads of worldly court poets like Eustache Deschamps assured their hearers that the end of the world was near, and apocalyptic interpretations mingled with chiliastic hopes in an explosive mixture.[19]

"Prophecies foretelling a blood-bath and the massacre of clergy and the powerful" were rife. In 1348, bubonic plague (the Black Death) began to scour Europe. For Matteo Villani, the chronicler of Florence who lost his brother to it, the plague came as a second flood, a divine judgment for men's sins.[20] Past centuries had been bad enough; the present one was worse; and coming centuries would bring no improvement. In the intermittent devastations of the Hundred Years' War (1337–1453), the furious Turkish threat nibbling at Central Europe, ferocious risings, and the Great Schism (1378–1414), when rival popes excommunicated each other, evil relentlessly preened itself. Harbinger of imminent apocalypse, Antichrist could not be far off. Perhaps he was already here.

John Wycliffe (1330–1384), the English scholar, was sure of that. In 1379, one of his pamphlets, *De Papa*, concluded that the pope was "Antichrist heere in earth, for he is agens crist both in lif and in lore." Much influenced by Wycliffe's writings, some of which he translated into Czech, John Huss (1372–1415) made the university of Prague, whose rector he was, a center of Wycliffite doctrines critical of clerical morals and Roman anarchy. Many in that day saw the Great Schism as preliminary to the advent of Antichrist, but Huss proved a bit too specific: one of the "egregious errors" for which he would be burnt at the stake was his equation of pope and Antichrist.[21]

Huss's execution made him a national hero, and his martyrdom set off fifteen years of Bohemian war in which Hussites fighting for ecclesiastical reform, communion in both kinds (bread *and* wine), and a vernacular liturgy prefigured many aspects of the Reformation. The more extreme among them professed radical social doctrines, rejected churches and feast days, oaths, courts of so-called justice, and worldly dignities, and sought to spread the kingdom of God by force of arms. They set up a mountain stronghold not far from Prague and called it Mount Tabor, after the Biblical site of Christ's transfiguration, symbol of his messiahship and early return in glory. Taborite priests preached that, with his Second Coming, the enemies of truth would be exterminated and the good preserved. Meanwhile, Antichrist stood at the gates. The armed communities in which God's saints took refuge, a saving remnant in a Noah's ark of faith, sought to recapture an imaginary Biblical past where saints could survive Antichrist's deluge and God's wrath.[22]

Antichrists swarmed in fifteenth-century Europe, and crusades against them were launched on all sides. Thus, English troops recruited as crusaders against Hussite Taborites were going to be diverted to France to face the threat of another false prophet— Joan of Arc (1412–1431). The farmer's daughter from Domrémy in Lorraine was soon greeted or execrated as a prophetess leading an eschatological army against the king's enemies: a *sainct voyage* not very different from dimly recalled crusades and evoking similarly wondrous images. Joan's coming, the people said, had been predicted by Merlin the sorcerer; she could fly through the air (the people of Troyes in Champagne opened their gates in fear of such feats); and, above all, Saint Michael stood beside her.

"Prince of the citizens of heaven," premier among the angels guiding John through his revelations and aiding the Woman of the Apocalypse, destined to destroy Antichrist in the last days, the archangel Michael was patron of warriors and of Joan of Arc. Leader of celestial armies against the hosts of Satan in the Apocalypse, his was the only male voice that the maiden heeded, as his flaming sword opened the way for her, and his figure inspired the vision of countryfolk who, in July 1429, saw an armed man riding through the air on a great white horse. It was the voice of Michael that Joan most missed when her saintly "voices" deserted her in the end.[23]

By 1431, when Joan was burned at the stake in Rouen, Huss's ashes had long been scattered to the winds. The man who presided over his trial and execution was dead, too, but he had given much thought to apocalyptic matters. Admirer of Joachim, whom he compared to St. Hildegard, the great scholar and churchman Cardinal Pierre d'Ailly (1350–1419 or 1420) turned to astronomical calculations and to astrology to quash prevalent expectations of Antichrist and the Apocalypse. D'Ailly was also concerned to resolve the Great Schism of Western Christendom, which he helped to settle as papal legate to the Council of Constance in 1414. But schism and apocalypse were related. In a *Concordance of Astronomy and History* that he composed in 1414, D'Ailly argued that a restored church would help avert disaster, and he demonstrated that an apocalypse was astrologically impossible because Antichrist was not due until 1789.

What might have seemed convincing in 1414 carried less weight three score and four score years later. Astrologers and prophets recognized 1484 as a great turning point for Christianity and for the world, when history and religion would undergo great disturbance. The conjunction of Jupiter and Saturn marked the completion of an astrological Great Year, while the entrance of the sun into the house of Aries opened a new Great Year and brought religion to a turn as well. In the later 1480s, a fervent and austere Dominican friar, Girolamo Savonarola, began to call on Florentines to mend their ways. The kingdom of God was at hand, and it was time to build an Ark of repentance as refuge in the coming Flood. Influenced by the storm of eschatological prophecies around him, Savonarola's prophetic preaching confirmed what the eschatologists prophesied. The king of France, Charles VIII, threatened to invade Italy. In the friar's increasingly prophetic language, Charles would be a new Cyrus, but also the scourge of God wielding the sword of divine vengeance. By the early 1490s, apocalyptic excitement had mounted enough to let Savonarola establish a kind of theocratic democracy in Florence and, when Charles's army marched down the peninsula, Florence opened its gates to him.

The French expedition represented the Flood, about which Savonarola preached, but by the end of 1495 the French tide had receded and Savonarola's radical republic was left high and dry. Arrested and condemned for schism and heresy, the Dominican was burned in 1498. His followers remembered him as a martyr.[24] Among these were a Dominican prioress and future saint, Catherine de Ricci, who was noted for sanctity and good counsel. Her correspondents and "spiritual children" included other saints of the church like Charles Borromeo and Philip Neri. Another was Sandro Botticelli. In 1500, two years after Savonarola's death, Botticelli painted a Nativity scene with a Greek inscription scrolled across the top:

> I Sandro painted this picture at the end of the year 1500 in the troubles of Italy in the half time after the time according to the eleventh chapter of St. John in the second woe of the Apocalypse in the loosing of the devil for three and a half years. Then he will be chained in the 12th chapter and we shall see him trodden down as in this picture.[25]

So chiliasm marched on. No wonder that the Fifth Lateran Council (1512–17), most of whose attention focused on internal and international politics, found little time for church reform, but enough to denounce popular apocalyptic tendencies. Two years after the council closed, Martin Luther affixed his ninety-five theses to the door of the palace church in Wittenberg. The Reformation had begun, and apocalyptic chiliasm stood on the verge of a new Flood.

REVIVALISTS
AND ANTICHRISTS

The tribulation and the destruction of Babel
approach with violence, the storm roars on
all sides, it will rage; a vain hope betrays
for the destruction of the tree draws near.

    – JAKOB BOEHME, 1623

ITALIAN RENAISSANCE humanists invented the notion of the Middle Ages (a term coined in 1469) to celebrate their own days and to highlight their difference from the thousand darkling years that had gone before. Yet, as we saw, those in the ages we now describe as "middle" thought of themselves as living in end times. Many were to do so in later ages; and none so fervently as those who suffered through the sixteenth and seventeenth centuries. The imaginary rift between medieval and modern times was linked by many bridges; and one of the processions that marched freely from one side to the other was made up of enthusiastic believers in the imminent end of the world.

The signs of Jesus' Coming were there for all to see: wars and rumors of wars, nation rising against nation, and all the usual iniquities, both public and private. The world was condemned. It wasn't only that it was evil, but that it was dark—quite literally so when windows were few and artificial light was lacking, when murky forests lapped close to villages and fields, brimming with sinister forces like spooks, spirits, witches, imps, elves, goblins, and devils. Now, having banished the memory of children lost in dark forests to the realm of fairy tales, we find it hard to envision the times when such fears were more than imaginings, when the violence and apprehension of material reality shaded quite naturally into a supernatural that was just as real. One sixteenth-century scholar, Nicolas Cardan, has recorded how, on waking one morning, he saw the sun shine through his shutters, with flecks of dust dancing in its golden rays. Imagining that he saw a monster in the dust biting off heads with its bloody fangs, he panicked, jumped out of bed, and fled the house in nothing but his shirt.

Bosch, Bruegel, Dürer, Cranach, and their contemporaries have recorded this world of anxious imaginings, teeming with shaggy devils pricking up goat-like ears, prancing on intimidating hooves, horrifying and tormenting. Yet these fantastic monsters were no worse than the brutality of a world where the best entertainment was cruel executions by boiling in oil or cudgeling to death; where unwary travelers could bump into rotting corpses hanging from roadside gallows; or where a Swiss physician riding to Lyon passed "a Christian in a shirt" with a bundle of straw tied to his back, to fuel the fire that would shortly consume him.[1]

In contrast to this decaying world of darkness, the contemporary clerks, scholars, and gentlemen who named the Renaissance presented it as a resurrection: a revival of texts, art, systems of government, and ways of thinking long dormant; a *renovatio*, or renewal, of knowledge long lost and now plumbed anew; a palingenesis, or the beginning of a new world cycle after the old had worn itself out. But the renewal that Renaissance humanists referred to was mostly reserved for a small elite with access to the redemptive knowledge of *gnosis*—those spiritual mysteries of the origin and destiny of man which offered privileged access to redemption.

A mixture of Greek, Jewish, Egyptian, and Zoroastrian speculations alternately denounced as pagan or heretic, gnosticism had survived on the margins of Christianity since the first century. Manicheanism, which "unveiled" the primeval conflict between light and darkness and which seduced Augustine before he rejected it, carried gnostic doctrines through the Middle Ages in a variety of forms. Then, just when these notions had been crushed or seemed to have petered out, humanists began to explore the Greek and Latin writings attributed to Hermes Trismegistus, translations from an Egyptian god, Thoth-the-Very-Great. Thoth was the god of knowledge, and hence of science (including alchemy), astrology, cosmology and every kind of esoteric lore. Hermes was his hetero-Christian incarnation; and the hermetic writings attributed to him were, by definition, difficult, obscure, and secret—the sense that the term retains today. As such, hermetic writings remained the prerogative of small numbers, but continued to be plumbed.

The gnosis of initiates did not carry them far from Biblical lore. The "modern" interests of Renaissance humanists were about present times (*modo* means "now"), but they also involved a return—past the dark tunnel of the Middle Ages—to the higher, purer wisdom of the ancients: of Greece and Rome, and of the Bible, too. The Platonist Giovanni Pico della Mirandola believed both in the *Dignity of Man* (1486) and in the coming Day of Judgment. No wonder that he used the Hebrew Kabbala in support of Christian theology, or that his many works include an exposition of Genesis. Apocalypticism, after all, involves divine secrets revealed to a few elect: precisely the principle of gnosticism, which is also about enlightenment accessible only to the few.

In Christian belief, Simon Magus, the sorcerer of Acts 8 who bewitched the people of Samaria, was regarded as the founder of gnosticism. His legend portrayed him as falsely pretending to be a messiah, or son of God, or the Holy Spirit, and falling to his death in an attempt to demonstrate his occult ability to fly. But the promise of salvation through the secret knowledge he possessed continued to attract followers. The gnostic quest for salvation on an esoteric plane inevitably mixed with the spiritual aspirations of more orthodox believers. The "unveiling" offered by both gnostic and the more familiar apocalyptic revelations could be pursued as one, and they sometimes were.

A more understandable and accessible kind of *renovatio* was to affect the fortunes of the church and of Christendom more immediately. The sense of corruption, decadence, and decline that fed apocalyptic fires through the Middle Ages was partly grounded in the failings of Christ's church. If the world faced God's wrath and his early Judgment, that was due partly to people's sins, but also to a church that failed to do its job. God's church reflected the wickedness of God's creatures, or, worse, led them astray. Not only had they succumbed to greed, worldliness, and pride, but they were returning to paganism.

Revived interest in antiquity and ancient texts affected theology and the papal court. Inspired by Cicero, God the Father was associated with Jupiter, and the Virgin Mary with Diana, with whose attributes she was sometimes painted. No longer in opposition to paganism, Christianity could be regarded as the fulfillment of its best wisdom. On Michelangelo's ceiling of the Sistine Chapel, pagan prophetesses rubbed elbows with Old Testament prophets; in the frescoes that Pinturicchio painted for the Borgia apartments in the Vatican, the mysteries of Osiris preface the mysteries of Christ. The abomination of desolation stood in the holy place (Matthew 24:15). No wonder that Savonarola identified Rome with Babylon, and Alexander VI (who was to excommunicate him) with the forces of Antichrist.

The new classical orientation of the clerical hierarchy offended devout Christians as much as its worldliness and venality, and pious fifteenth-century Christians sought to restore the church to its primitive faith. As the sixteenth century opened, their struggles to save their souls and renovate the church brought about the Reformation: another way of trying to restore the conditions of primitive Christendom.

A simple interpretation of the Reformation has it born of a reaction against clerical abuses—plurality of offices, nonresidence, nepotism, debauchery and graft, and the buying and selling of offices, masses, and indulgences that liberated souls from purgatory. Simony—the sale of holy things for money, named after Simon the Sorcerer, who offered the apostles money for the power to work miracles—was ubiquitous. The seven deadly sins—pride, covetousness, lust, anger, gluttony, envy, sloth—had taken up residence around St. Peter's shrine. The power of the popes rested on avarice and arms: they hired great architects to build ostentatious temples to poor Galileans, and waged war on behalf of a religion of meekness and peace. Yet they had acted this way for a very long time without setting off more than growls or sniggers. What made the difference?

What Luther denounced was less the pious rackets of the Roman Church than its blasphemous confidence trick in pretending that its rituals and its intercession could absolve people from sin and assure salvation. Confession and absolution could not save from sin: only trust in God could do that, and those who pretended otherwise were deceivers. Christians should live by faith, and faith came from the gospels and the grace of God, not from priests and sacraments. This personalization was an exhilarating simplification of religious life, and, in its perspective, the old church stood for galling complications, and the pope for Antichrist. Gutenberg's age of print, which gave an extraordinary boost to reformed arguments, was also the age of woodcuts. Frequently the papacy was depicted in graphic detail as diabolic: devils excreting popes, popes crucifying Christ, or popes reincarnated as the Great

Beast of Revelation, each of its seven heads crowned with the papal tiara.

But what of notions of the Apocalypse? As late as the nineteenth century a bishop would explain: "The perpetuity of the Catholic Church to the end of time is a dogma. Not eternal perpetuity, since it must end with the world, but indefinite for us who ignore that time."[2] The researches undertaken to establish an approximate date for that end time can never be more than conjectures about an event whose secret God has reserved for himself. So, in the nineteenth century, Christians were still busy trying to track God's secret by calculating when the world would end, and the church was still telling them, as it had since the fifth century, that there was little point in that exercise. Most sixteenth-century reformers agreed with this orthodox church view, at least in principle, but they could do no more against popular sentiment than their Catholic competitors. Both Luther and Melanchton believed that the end of time was not far off, certainly no farther than 1600. And Heinrich Bullinger, chief pastor of Zurich in 1531, delivered and published a whole volume of sermons entitled: *One Hundred Sermons upon the Apocalypse of Jesu Christ* (in Latin in 1557, translated into English in 1561).

Once the seamless garment of the church was rent, a patchwork of creeds replaced it and the cacophony of their discordant messages dismayed reforming leaders as much as it did their rulers. Prophets proliferated. Before the commotion spilled over to the Atlantic rim and beyond, central Europe was a chaos of Christianities, sects, cults, factions, nonconformities, dissensions, and secessions, all of which whipped up the climate of crisis. Luther seemed to preach the priesthood of all believers; but believers who follow their inner light can easily mistake sparks of imagination for inspiration from on high. It was not easy to tell the two apart when Anabaptists ran naked through the streets of Amsterdam crying "Woe, woe, woe, the wrath of God";[3] when the small Saxon town of Zwickau spawned a brood of prophets forecasting the purification of the church and the imminent end of the world; when Thomas Münzer, who believed that souls needed to be purified by suffering and tribulation, recognized in the social rebellion of German peasants the struggle of the saints of the Last Days; and when, after the peasants' disastrous defeat and Münzer's execution in 1525, Hans Hut announced the end of the world and Christ's return for 1528. Hut was executed in 1527, but his disciples attempted to hasten the predicted coming by force of arms. Though nothing worse occurred in 1528 than had happened before (which had been bad enough), 1533 was perilously close.

Centenaries of the Savior's Passion have always offered a deliciously frightening focus for enthusiasts: 1033, 1233, 1733, 1834, even June 12, 1933. In 1433, the scholarly Nicholas of Cusa, though well aware of human ignorance, had predicted the Great Judgment for 1533. As the time drew nigh, Cusa's prediction began to coincide with the expectations of Anabaptists, who probably ignored it: Melchior Hoffman, the itinerant visionary who preached the Second Coming and the millennium for 1593, before he was caged away in a Strasbourg jail; Jan Matthys, the righteous Haarlem baker who sent his apostles out to rid the earth of the ungodly and predicted the Lord's vengeance for 1534; and John of Leiden, who joined him that year in Münster to prepare a New Jerusalem for the Apocalypse.

For all these prophets, as for the simple folk who drank in their message, true Christianity involved restored apostolic poverty—social equality, goods held in common, and rejection of worldly hierarchies, oaths of allegiance, sovereignties, and all tithes and taxes. The highest authority—God's word as revealed in His Gospel—approved their hungriest aspirations, and could easily be taken to suggest fulfillment by force. Clearly, apocalyptic rhetoric used to radical ends destabilized not only church and state but also more modest "reformed" establishments whose interest in salvation did not extend to overturning the social arrangements of this wicked world.

Though he was pretty sure that his times were the last days, Luther considered the book of Revelation "neither apostolic nor prophetic," and relegated it to an appendix of his new German Bible. Calvin did not bother to comment on it. In 1530, the authoritative *Lutheran Confession of Augsburg* denounced millenarianism as "Jewish doctrine." Yet apocalyptic terminology filled the reformers' attacks on Rome, as it did their references to the fearsome Turks, catspaws of Antichrist, who were then taking over the eastern Mediterranean and working their way through the Balkans to Hungary. Luther's break with Rome in itself spurred eschatological expectations.

A recent study of millennialism suggests that millennial language had declined by Luther's time and avers that "mainstream millennial forecasts did die down by the sixteenth century."[4]Yet all parties to the Reformation mobilized eschatological prophecy, prospective and retrospective. The great planetary conjunction of 1484 cast its shadow over the century that followed, the first edition of the *danse macabre* was published in 1485, and Dürer's woodcuts of the Apocalypse appeared in 1498. Anxiety about the Last Judgment had come to stay. Fascinated by the sixteenth century's obsession with Last Days, Denis Crouzet's great study of the French religious wars depicts a time when the apocalyptic is omnipresent and God's ire only too evident in calamities, prodigies, and monstrous manifestations.[5]

From the beginning of the sixteenth century, German almanacs, perhaps reflecting the Balkan advances of the infidel Turk, had been predicting an imminent deluge, probably for 1524 or 1525. In the latter year, Dürer recorded his dream of such a catastrophe. But already in 1524 a high magistrate of the parliament of Toulouse had ordered an ark to be built on top of a nearby hill, to provide escape in the forthcoming flood. Clearly, German traumas had had time to seep into France, where almanacs and predictions agreed that the end was near, and astrology began to generate great eschatological anxiety. France, comments Crouzet, was plunging into the phantasms of a time of adversity and terror.[6]

The religious civil wars that tore the French apart began in 1560 and ended only with the century. Long before the conspiracies, massacres, and pitched battles that marked those dire decades, people had become accustomed to living on the razor's edge between a corrupt world and the catastrophic Judgment that awaited it. The 1530s brought news of the bloodshed at Münster, the 1540s of the slaughter of Vaudois Protestants in Piedmont. Calvin's *Institutes*, first published in Latin, appeared in a French translation in 1541, the year when Ignatius Loyola became general of the recently founded Company of Jesus and one year before the (re)creation of the Roman Inquisition. Loyola was linked by his admirers to the Fifth Angel of the Apocalypse, at the sound of whose trumpet a great star falls from heaven—the evil star representing Luther and his pernicious army of Protestant locusts.[7] But the word of Calvin was spreading too, and the 1550s would see it take hold far beyond Geneva. Crouzet argues from the eschatological panic of the time to the successes of Calvinism, which transcended apocalyptic terrors by offering a new economy of salvation.[8] He may be right; but damnation was more in evidence than salvation of any kind.

As princes died violent deaths or hunted down their subjects, social and political order disintegrated, justice dissolved, and the tide of iniquity and blasphemy advanced, foreshadowing doom. In 1550, Nostradamus published the first of his annual almanacs, and he often thought that the end was near. In 1556, a Swiss medical student at Montpellier noted the apocalyptic prophecies making the rounds there and elsewhere, predicting the end of the world for Magdalene's Day, July 22 of that year.[9] Despite premonitory signs and their feverish interpretation, nothing happened. But all great contemporary astrologers, including Archduke Leopold of Austria, expected bad times in 1559–62, when the earth would be affected by the inauspicious dominance of the moon.

The skies were full of horrors: great winds, strange stars, multiple apparitions of suns or moons, eclipses, warriors battling in the clouds, all predicting bloody troubles. Earthquakes, epidemics, floods, and wandering prophets confirmed these forewarnings. Jean Bodin, whose major work, though "diffuse and containing astrological and other rubbish, was the foundation of political science in France,"[10] denounced "the inveterate error" of counting by the prophecies of Daniel, "which has put down such deep root that today it seems impossible to extirpate."[11] Apocalypticism had entered the language, and millennial references to the crack of doom and the promised end abounded: Charles IX of France, who, in 1572, presided over the massacre of St. Bartholomew in which between ten thousand and thirty thousand Huguenots perished, was the king of the End of Days. God's Judgment was near; God's Judgment was here.

The surfeit of apocalypticism was such that it provoked reactions among a few strong-minded observers. In 1545, Calvin had taken up his pen to attack the *secte des libertins*—free spirits indifferent to religion, and skeptical about the Scriptures and the terrors of their more pious neighbors. Lost among credulous masses desperate to believe in anything, these doubters were visible enough for a broadsheet of 1581 to comment on their sneers. The Last Judgment had been so much talked about, they said, so often predicted, and nothing had happened. Had the Last Day been lost on the way?

More representative of current opinion was "the doctor of our time," cited in a book published in Lyon in 1606, "who had a great covered ship prepared to save himself on the Garonne."[12] Even more so were the terms of the Protestants' rejection of Pope Gregory XIII's calendar reform of 1582. Since 46 BC, the Julian calendar instituted by Julius Caesar had fallen ten days behind.

To make it correspond to the period that the earth takes to go round the sun, Gregory decreed that the day after October 4, 1582, should become October 15. Catholic Europe followed suit. Protestants had good reason to mistrust a pope who had instituted the Counter Reformation's Jesuit militia and the *Index of Prohibited Books*, and who had responded to news of Huguenots massacred on St. Bartholomew's Day by saying a celebratory mass. But one of their stronger arguments against the Gregorian calendar (which the English accepted only in 1752 and the Protestant Swiss in 1812) was that it queered calculations of the end. The recreant pope did not believe in the End of the World.

Orthodoxy is the holding of right opinions. Reformers wanted to correct what the Church of Rome taught as right opinions with righter opinions of their own. In the process, they opened the door to heterodoxy: a host of different and differing opinions based on particular interpretations of the Scriptures, personal visions, and private revelations.

Just as religious beliefs bind communities together, they also help to set them apart by inspiring, justifying, and emphasizing social, political, and tribal conflicts. The wars that tore through early modern Europe bear witness to this divisiveness, and so do its civil wars. After the Edict of Nantes pacified France and, as Henry IV's great minister Sully put it, turned it from dusk to dawn, nowhere was religious enthusiasm more in evidence than in England. Henry VIII had been excommunicated in 1533; Elizabeth, his daughter, would be excommunicated in 1570. The title of an anonymous publication of those days says much about the contemporary mood: *On the Ende of this World and the Second Coming of Christ: A Comfortable and Most Necessarie Discourse for These Miserable and Dangerous Dayes.* For John Foxe, whose *Book of Martyrs* published in England in 1563 traced the heroic sufferings of victims of papist tyranny, the struggle between Christ and Antichrist then coming to a head was due to climax in the reign of that second Constantine, the Christian empress Elizabeth.[13]

Elizabeth, however, lacked neither critics nor competitors. Her reign, as Keith Thomas puts it, "produced a small army of pseudo-Messiahs,"[14] and the list of those who claimed to be Christ or witnesses to his coming is a long one. In 1586, Ralph Durden, imprisoned for identifying the kingdom with the Beast of Revelation, was predicting the downfall of Gloriana's monarchy for 1589. In 1591, an illiterate ex-soldier, William Hackett, proclaimed himself the messiah come to judge the world. He threatened dire plagues upon the kingdom if its people did not repent, and if the queen did not give up her crown to him. His arrest and execution did not discourage other messengers of God. The last Englishman burnt for heresy (in 1612) would be an Anabaptist, Edward Wightman, who claimed to be Elijah, the prophet. But plenty of prophets popped up here and there, such as Lady Eleanor Davis, daughter of the Earl of Castlehaven, who was awakened by a voice from heaven announcing, "Nineteene years and a halfe to the day of Judgment and you as the meek virgin." When the meek virgin vandalized the altar of Lichfield Cathedral by pouring hot tar and wheat paste on it, she was confined in Bethlehem hospital (Bedlam) for one year. Ladies and gentlemen deserved more consideration than vulgar bibliomancers.

By the mid-seventeenth century, England was awash in self-proclaimed prophets. The civil war of those years was about taxes and royal power, but the king, Charles I, was denounced as a crypto-papist, and his royalist supporters as the host of Antichrist. Almanacs predicted not only Rome's downfall but Judgment, millennium, and the end of a "wicked, perverse and crooked generation," of the world itself. The Apocalypse supplied Cromwell's New Model Army of millenarian saints with a guide to action and with the goal of installing the New Jerusalem in verdant England. The continent, too, supplied inspiration of a contorted kind. The influential German theosophist Jakob

Boehme for example (1575–1624), identified Emperor Rudolf II and his brother Matthias, who succeeded him as Holy Roman Emperor between 1612 and 1619, as Antichrist. Of Boehme's murky mystical writings, twenty or more were translated in seventeenth-century England, including an anthology, the *Mercurius Teutonicus* (1649), where Antichrist, the Whore of Babylon, Beasts, and False Prophets in their mystery of iniquity and perverse practices were abundantly described.

Without much need of prompting, Baptists and Anabaptists, Levellers, Diggers, Socinians, Ranters, Quakers, Muggletonians, and all sorts of popular utopian millenarians, the stoutest foes of Antichrist, were busy preparing Christ's kingdom. The spiritual regeneration that the Reformation had sought, sects and sectarians now claimed to represent. Some like William Sedgwick, who incautiously prophesied the end of the world in fourteen days, lived to be dubbed Doomsday Sedgwick.[15] Cromwell's own porter, driven mad by eschatological expectations, preached to the London crowd from the window of his cell. Lodowicke Muggleton and his cousin John Reeve, both tailors, proclaimed themselves to be the two witnesses of Revelation 11:3 ("and I shall give power to my two witnesses and they shall prophesy twelve hundred and three score days") come to usher in the Second Coming. The Last Muggletonian was to die in 1979.

More violent, Fifth Monarchy Men aimed to bring about the fifth monarchy that Daniel (2:44) presents as due to succeed the four empires of Assyria, Persia, Greece, and Rome, "when all Nations shall be converted unto God, and the Saints in them shall be the prevailing party in this World," reigning with Christ for a thousand years.[16] At first, Fifth Monarchy Men supported Cromwell, whose Commonwealth was supposed to prepare the ground for their millennium, but then they turned against him. First hailed as the new Moses leading his people to the promised land, the General was soon revealed as an apocalyptic monster:

Beast, Dragon, or little horn, according to taste. When the saints' unsuccessful risings had been defeated and their leaders beheaded, the sect died out. Not so the communistic ideas of the Diggers, who shunned violence. One Digger leader, Gerrard Winstanley, for whom property and social hierarchy sprang from the Fall, envisaged the millennium as a time when land would be restored to common ownership and all would live as equals under a chilling authoritarian regime. Communism was hardly new in the Christian tradition; nor were authoritarian ideals. No wonder that, with Cromwell gone, Restoration England made speculation about the Second Coming a criminal offense. Even John Donne's "What if this present was the world's last night?" fell out of favor.

We are sometimes told that, by the 1660s, English millenarianism had exhausted itself—though it would soon recover. Even a limited dismissal, though, ignores the publication in 1667 of *Paradise Lost*, where God predicts the general doom and makes quite clear that the earth will burn, "then rise from the conflagrant mass, purg'd and refin'd"; and even more the appearance of *Pilgrim's Progress* in 1678, which opens with the hero, Christian, reading a book, "and as he read he wept and trembled: I am for certain informed that this our City will be burned with fire from Heaven."

The bubble of continental millenarianism, meanwhile, had burst in the bloodbath of the Thirty Years' War, widely regarded at first as the great struggle that was supposed to mark the Last Days. The 1620s and early 1630s teemed with prophecies and revelations of approaching Armageddon. Gustavus Adolphus of Sweden, the Protestant champion, took on messianic proportions and the names he was called—Lion of the North, Elias, and Gideon—carried Biblical, and sometimes apocalyptic, overtones. But Gustavus died in the battle of Lützen in 1632, fighting and devastation dragged on, and no Armageddon resolved the issue. Peace came only with the numbed exhaustion of the combatants, and of the fantasies some had entertained of a millennial kingdom.

One apocalyptic personage who made an easy crossing from medieval into modern times, where he survives today, was Antichrist. Far from a major presence in the New Testament, the Antichrist is above all a deceiver or, as Richard Emmerson has called him, a diabolical parody of Christ. After assuring his Thessalonian correspondents that the day of Christ was at hand, Paul (2:3 ff) warned them against a deceiver, the son of perdition, who pretends he is God as he opposes God. The opportunity to associate "opponents" of God with Antichrist, his messengers, or his disciples was to reach great proportions. For Augustine, heretics, schismatics, perjurers, cheaters, evildoers, soothsayers, adulterers, drunkards, usurers, and slavedealers, "whatsoever is contrary to the word of God, is Antichrist." Thomas Aquinas thought as much.[17] Clearly, as John the Evangelist knew (1 John, 4:3), "even now already, he is in the world." And John's contemporaries, first century Christians living in the midst of persecution, had no reason to doubt it. Caligula, who insisted that he be worshipped as God, was Antichrist; so was Diocletian; but Nero was preferred. Numerology identified him with the number of the Beast, 666; the Armenian name of Antichrist became Neren (Nero);[18] and coins bearing the emperor's effigy (any emperor's effigy) probably represented that mark of the Beast without which (in Revelation 13:17) one could neither buy nor sell.

It was easy to pass from historical figures of unjust persecutors and usurpers to the eschatological figure of Antichrist, the son of iniquity, son or synonym of Belial—the lawless one of Jewish apocalyptic literature. Wild barbarians—Goths, Huns, Tartars—had been denounced as Antichrist, or at least as his acolytes, the hosts of Gog and Magog; and in due course Turks and Saracens would be so identified. According to the version one preferred, Antichrist was a catspaw of the devil (that great

Satan), his auxiliary, or his alter ego. Consistency is no friend of legend, and the apostolic tradition allowed great leeway to a variety of interpretations. So Antichrist's identity altered from generation to generation, according to circumstance and need. Disorder and lawlessness, attributes of Belial, predicted his coming or attested his presence; so did clerical and political rivalries; or the activities of Augustine's long list of sinners, false prophets, and opponents of God. Popes like Gregory IX and Innocent IV denounced emperors like Frederic II as Antichrist, while the emperor's clerks denounced Innocent IV as the Great Dragon of the Apocalypse and demonstrated that the numerical value of his name and title, *Innocencius papa*, added up to 666.

In the fourteenth century, the "Babylonish captivity" of the popes in Avignon (1309–77) and the Roman dictatorship of Cola di Rienzo (1347, 1354) began to connect Antichrist with popes who abandoned their holy city. The Great Schism, when, between 1378 and 1417, four Roman popes faced four Avignonese and Pisan popes, further affirmed the identification. Then, in 1415, John Huss, the Bohemian reformer, was burnt before the Church Council at Constance after the emperor had offered him safe-conduct. For his followers, the Hussites, it would no longer be individual popes but the papacy and the existing structure of the Roman Church that represented the body of Antichrist. When they criticized papal worldliness and vice, when they insisted that Scripture was the sole authority and that every man could read and interpret it for himself, Wycliffite Lollards in England and Hussites in Bohemia stood for reformation before the Reformation. But these were paltry heretics until the early sixteenth-century explosion shattered the unity of the church and made hitherto marginal views central religious issues. For Luther, the Church of the Pope was the Synagogue of Satan. For his English admirer William Tyndale, who translated the Bible into English before he was strangled and burned in 1536, papists had "set up that great idol, the Whore of Babylon, antichrist of

Rome, whom they call pope." Calvin, notoriously unenthusiastic about such matters, attributed interest in them to Catholics. He may have been right; but John Knox, Calvin's disciple, was just as keen to anticipate Antichrist and to discuss him in his sermons. One such, delivered at St. Andrews University in 1572, the year before his death, left a deep impression. "He maid me sa to grew and tremble," remembered one student, "that I could not hald a pen to wrigt."[19]

Iconography reflected the transition from personification to the institutionalization of Antichrist. In 1499 and 1500, Luca Signorelli painted *The Doings of Antichrist* in Orvieto Cathedral: a bearded man, the traditional deceiver, pretending to be Christ, preaches to a large crowd while the devil stands behind him. Within one generation, Lucas Cranach and Cranach's workshop were portraying Antichrist as wearing the papal crown. Widely circulating woodcuts popularized such subversive representations, and so did the annual almanacs in which *der Endechrist* accompanied or preceded the End of Days. Meanwhile, Foxe's *Book of Martyrs* turned the identification into an English stereotype. By 1641, a clergyman could be denounced to Parliament for declaring that the pope was *not* Antichrist.[20] The Presbyterian John Milton (1608–74), the Quaker George Fox (1624–91), the Baptist John Bunyan (1622–88), and the conforming churchman Isaac Newton (1642–1727) were all convinced that pope and Antichrist were one.

Essential to Antichrist's supporting cast were Elijah and Enoch, who bear witness against him, do battle with him, and are killed but rise again on the fourth day to go to heaven for three and a half years, when they return to help annihilate the Son of Iniquity in time for the Last Judgment. In the ninth century BC, King Ahab's Phoenician queen, Jezebel, had promoted the worship of Baal over that of Yahweh. Elijah had confounded the priests of Baal, reaffirmed Jewish monotheism, and taught the idea of salvation bestowed on a "purified remnant" of the Jewish people. Taken to heaven in a whirlwind, he demonstrated the possibility of a life beyond earthly life. Four centuries after this performance, God had remembered him when speaking to Malachi (4:5): "Behold, I will send you Elijah the prophet before the coming of the great and dreadful day of the Lord." Thereafter, alone or in the company of Enoch, father of Methusaleh and alleged author of ominous revelations, he became part of the Antichrist legend.

Late in the fourteenth century, Eustache Deschamps's *Ballad of Antichrist* culminates in the coming of the dire duo that speeds Antichrist's destruction. Over and over, at moments of crisis, prophets and saints had claimed to incarnate the Two Witnesses, or had it attributed to them by admirers. St. Francis and St. Dominic (more often Francis alone) had been cast in that role, and so more generally had other preachers inspired by the Holy Spirit that filled the witnesses to lead the fight against Antichrist. Reformers who could see the standard predictions of last times being realized around them readily recognized witnesses (John Huss and his companion Jerome of Prague, burnt at the stake, were one such case), or claimed to be witnesses themselves, as Richard Farnham and John Bull did in London in 1636, and John Reeve and Lodowicke Muggleton a little later. By then, Protestant exegetes had conflated all martyrs oppressed by Antichrist into the true Two Witnesses. The papacy represented Antichrist, the witnesses were the heroes of the Reformation.[21]

Many such heroes were spawned by the trials that French Protestants had to endure as the liberties granted them by the Edict of Nantes (1598) were gradually whittled away, until in 1685 the edict itself was revoked by Louis XIV. Persecution of Huguenots led to civil war in the rugged hill country of the Cévennes, where "inspired" prophesying encouraged guerilla resistance into the early eighteenth century at a cost of some forty thousand lives. It also encouraged the pastor of the mostly refugee Calvinist community in Rotterdam, Pierre Jurieu, to turn to Daniel and to the Apocalypse to predict the end of the Catholic Church for 1690, at least in France, where the Two Witnesses already awaited their resurrection.

Jurieu's *Accomplishment of the Scripture Prophecies* (1686) enlisted sacred history on the side of forlorn Protestant heroes; and by predicting "great things for the year 1689," it probably inspired the invasion of England by William of Orange, where his coronation put an end to the rule of James II and his Babylonish sympathies. Jurieu's apocalyptic interpretations also influenced a glass manufacturer from southeastern France to recruit fifteen peasant children and train them in prophecy. These youngsters would, in turn, stir up more children to prophesy, fall into convulsions, and speak in tongues. Believing themselves possessed by the Holy Spirit, they passed on their gift by blowing in another's mouth: "Receive the Holy Ghost." As a result, one bishop recorded, "prophets swarmed on all sides, one counted them in hundreds . . . the end of the world drew nigh."[22]

In the 1700s, when the revolt collapsed, some of these *enfants terribles* sought refuge in England, where they and their English followers lived in daily expectation of the millennium. Traditionally, Elijah, while preaching to reconvert those whom Antichrist deceived, had power to work miracles, as he had done against the priests of Baal and as Antichrist did in his delusive way. The French prophets in England asserted that they too, like Elijah, had the power to raise the dead—specifically a Dr. Thomas Emes, deceased, whom they would resurrect on March 25, 1708. There was war against France in Europe (within weeks the Duke of Marlborough would defeat the French at Oudenarde), and that very March the Stuart pretender attempted an invasion of Scotland. So political tensions meshed with prophetic ones: thunder, famine, fire, and brimstone were predicted for the fateful day. Only the first occurred on Whit Tuesday, March 25; nevertheless, great crowds gathered to see Dr. Emes arising from his grave. When he did not, the prophets were unrepentant, and the "prevalency of this new Delusion" surprised Daniel Defoe.[23]

But new delusions were old delusions revigorated. Around the mid-seventeenth century, many of the earliest Quakers, taken by the Spirit, had fallen "into dreadful Tremblings in their whole Bodies and Joints, with Risings and Swellings in their Bowels; Shriekings, Yellings, Howlings and Roarings."[24] Now, a century later, their spiritual offspring began to meet, pray, shake, shout, and speak in tongues and voices. Following a revelation vouchsafed to Ann Lee, a Quaker converted by the French prophets, these Shaking Quakers, or Shakers, were going to emigrate to America in 1774.

As stated in Revelation 13:7, making war against the Saints was a sure identification of Antichrist. When not pursuing Huguenots, the Son of Belial hunted down over-devout Catholics: the Jansenists, who identified with the doctrines of a Belgian bishop, Cornelius Jansen. With Augustine (but also with Luther and with Calvin), Jansen and his followers believed in predestination—the divine decree that infallibly damns some and saves others. They saw it as a just choice inaccessible to human minds, one that bound mankind in a supernatural determinism yet held it responsible for its actions, and opened up the heavens as if they were the abyss.

Neither Jansen nor the Jansenists were Protestant: on the contrary, they hoped to beat the Protestants at their own game by recapturing the pious austerity of the primitive church. Offspring of the Catholic Counter Reformation, they had been alienated by the church's lax moral and sacramental teachings, and they specially disapproved of Jesuits, whom they accused of currying favor with well-placed patrons by affording them easy access to communion and grace on the cheap. The holier-than-thouness of the Jansenists did not make them popular, but it helped attract spiritual athletes like Blaise Pascal. Their preoccupation with casuistry, however, and their hostility to the Jesuits would get them into hot water.

Casuistry is the application of moral principles to particular cases. In popular parlance, however, and sometimes in practice, it had become an art of bending rules and playing with moral principles—something that lawyers do all the time, but that good Christians are not supposed to do, least of all those responsible for teaching Christians to be good. Rationalist churchmen had turned casuistry into a kind of sophistry that Jansenists denounced, and their criticism got them into trouble first with their church, then with their king. Papal bulls condemned their rigor; royal and ecclesiastical officials persecuted them. The worse the persecutions got, the more radical the Jansenist response became. A Jansenist barrage of books and pamphlets demonstrated that the persecution they suffered was a sign of the end. A concert of Jansenist prophets filled the 1700s with dire predictions: calamity, blood, destruction, torments and persecutions, plagues and flames, the coming of Elijah and of Antichrist, cities and monarchies cast down, the earth covered with sores—sinful, abject, desolate. In 1713, one more papal bull, *Unigenitus*, soon denounced as the Beast of the Apocalypse, persuaded those who rejected it that the church had abandoned its redemptive functions and that only a faithful remnant could expect salvation.

In 1730, Louis XV decided to place the power of the state behind enforcement of *Unigenitus*. Apocalyptic predictions were obviously being fulfilled, and the persecuted Jansenists likened themselves to early martyrs of the church and, like some of these (notably the Montanists), began to fall into ecstatic trances, to speak in tongues, or to produce prophetic rantings. By 1731, miraculous phenomena began to attract crowds to the tomb of a recently deceased Jansenist "saint," the deacon François de Paris. The rash of healings, convulsions, fits, and faints at Paris's tomb in the cemetery of St. Médard led to a royal ordinance in 1732 that closed the cemetery to the public. A popular ditty mocked it: "De par le roi, défense à Dieu de faire miracle en ce lieu" [No miracles, the king has spoken: God ain't allowed even a token]. Elijah, too, had had to contend with a misguided king, Ahab (Kings 1, 18), and his idolatrous consort, Jezebel, yet God had given him power to confound the priests of Baal. Several reincarnations of Elijah ended up in the cells of royal prisons— the Bastille, Vincennes—but persecution could only confirm them in their faith. A sinful world panted for redemption.

Three hundred years earlier, Cardinal Nicholas of Cusa had cautiously predicted the end of the world for 1734. Jansenists were more precipitate. They knew that the war of the Beast had begun in 1730 (or maybe 1713), and would come to a head in 1733. It did not, but prodigies and convulsions continued and, before long, orthodox foes of Jansenism also began to suffer, as theological disputes turned into political ones. The Jesuits especially were denounced by their ascetic foes as masters of casuistry no better than devout humanists and much too indifferent to a world sunk in depravity and corruption. The Jesuits, to whom Jansenists were crypto-Calvinists who had abandoned hope in free will and salvation, gave as good as they got. But in the end, if the Jesuits were expelled from Portuguese dominions in 1759, from France in 1764, from Spain and the Spanish empire in 1767, and suppressed by the pope in 1773, Jansenist sympathizers had a lot to do with the vexations they endured.

In Voltaire's *Philosophical Dictionary* (1764), fanaticism was described as an epidemic disease, and fanatics as "convulsives," religion having turned to poison "in their infected brains." But the spiritual and prophetic torments of the fanatics whom Voltaire denounced expressed the unease and frustrations of individuals and of a society deeply troubled by this and other crises. Their distress (*misères*) reflected a wider wretchedness. The end times that they announced really foretold an end—if not of the world, at least of *a* world.

APOCALYPSE AND SCIENCE

The highest wisdom has but one science—
the science of the whole—the science explaining
the whole creation, and man's place in it.

   – LEO TOLSTOY

T OMASSO CAMPANELLA (1568–1639), a Calabrian Dominican, wrote his most famous work in prison. *The City of the Sun* (1623), where property is held in common and the elements of science are inscribed on walls to educate the people, where flying machines and ships without sails appear two and a half centuries before their time, outlines God's kingdom on earth: a fusion of church and society, religion and natural law. Campanella tried to free Calabria from Spanish rule and turn it into the earthly bridgehead of the millennial kingdom. The stars that he observed had announced the collision of earth with the sun in 1603. The year 1600 would be "the hinge of times," when the beneficent sun, burning with love, began to hurtle toward an earth, which bulged with hatred, at a speed he thought could be determined—perhaps by Gallileo, who later converted him to his heliocentric heresy. But Campanella spent that year and twenty-nine other years imprisoned for his ideas, writing poems, metaphysics, theology, and political science fiction. Sinful humanity could be regenerated through a religious reform carried out by a universal ecclesiastical empire, perhaps a *Monarchy of the Messiah* (1605). Collision or no collision, he insisted, "I am the bell announcing the new dawn."

This devout Christian, and all apocalyptists were devout Christians in their ways, did not expect science to work like what we today call science—the application of objective methods to the phenomena of the physical universe. Rather, he expected it to confirm his views on the destiny of mankind and his predictions concerning the end of the world—his apocalyptic and millennial dreams.

We tend to read the history of science forwards, for its premonitions of where what happened led. Professor Frances Yates has sensibly urged that it should also be read backwards, "seeing its connection with what had gone before."[1] If we do that, we discover the intimate connection between science and theology. Much of the progress in mathematics and in the natural and the physical sciences is related to the religious quest for wisdom, especially about God's intentions. Piety and learning went together, and science followed. Compatibility with the Scriptures long remained a criterion of scientific proof, as of common sense.

For Thomas Henry Huxley, in the nineteenth century, science was "nothing but trained and organized common sense." That sounds straightforward enough. But common sense is not common to all across all ages; nor even, as sixteenth- and seventeenth-century Catholics and Protestants might testify, to all in any one age. In 1534 or 1535, Rabelais's *Gargantua* declared that "an honest man, a man of good sense, always believes what he is told and what he finds written down." That was said tongue in cheek. But common sense is simply the consensus to which members of a given society are conditioned; and the consensus of Christendom for a long time was that the natural and the supernatural interpenetrate.

The world of the seventeenth century, as of earlier times, was fluid, imprecise, ill-defined, and easily redefined. Phenomena, people, and objects shifted from shape to shape, leaves turned into birds, men into beasts, and clouds into horsemen or dragons. The logic of the fairy-tale world that expired only in the nineteenth or twentieth century was not our logic, but it was a logic all the same. Visions and miracles were facts, just like trees that could speak, horses that could fly, and other prodigies.[2] Revelation and similar prophecies were puzzles to decypher. The universe was a riddle to be read by plumbing clues that God had planted in the world and in the skies around it.

The jungle of portents was no more impenetrable than the structure of atoms or of DNA is today. The cosmos was a network of magical forces that men could manipulate if they knew how; and "natural magic" linked astrology, alchemy, cryptology, and dreams as Aristotle had linked science, theology, ethics, and metaphysics. Visions, sightings of meteors, comets, rainbows, hairy or bearded stars, lights, fires, and armies in the sky, were *signs* to be decoded by astrologers subsidized by eager astrophiles spurred by fear, rumor, and self-interest. Early modern scientists were magicians intent on discerning, mastering, and harnessing supernatural powers: the occult quality of numbers, the applied astronomy we call astrology, and the applied understanding of correspondences between the world of spirits and the world of men that we call alchemy.[3]

Like a coded message where letters turn to numbers and vice versa, the doctrine of correspondences familiar to popular wisdom, as to Swedenborg or Baudelaire, held that every part of the physical world corresponded to some aspect of the spiritual world. Herbal lore, for example, healing or maleficent, rested on correspondences between the shape or the name of a plant or root and parts or functions of the body. Words too have a hidden meaning as well as an outward sense, and interpreters of scripture or of history searched for it. So did the relationship among stars, planets, and the material world.

The great quest of these early scientists was for perfection.

Imperfection was disorder, confusion, and anarchy: marks of a fallen world and a fallen humanity whose corruption extended to the chemical disorganization of matter that could be redeemed, purified, and set right by formula, ritual, or revelation. Greek and Renaissance gnostics knew that, under proper astral influences, the human soul could achieve a perfect state. Metals too were alive, as beings are, and hence they were mutable; they could be perfected so that, for example, lead turned to gold. The tincture or powder or liquid described as philosophers' stone could transmute metals, cure illnesses, prolong life, and revitalize the spirit. The search for it encouraged alchemists to develop laboratory equipment and procedures, to examine a variety of substances and their interactions, and to discover mineral acids and alcohol, thus laying the groundwork of chemistry, pharmacology, and metallurgy.

Like his student Paracelsus (1493–1541), Tritemius, the late-fifteenth-century abbot of a German monastery and first writer to mention the story of Faustus, was a master of cosmology, numerology, and alchemical lore. Both men were devout (Paracelsus spent his last years as a wandering Bible preacher and healer), both were intrigued by the properties of stars, both were interested in prophecy, and both awaited Christ's Second Coming and his new monarchy. The introduction to the "prognostics" of Paracelsus makes several references to "the great calamity just beginning" and to "the coming visit of God and end of man." These prophecies were still cited in the seventeenth century, and it was on their basis that Gustavus Adolphus of Sweden became "the Lion of the North." But Paracelsus was also an innovative chemist and physician who produced the first clinical description of syphilis, suggesting that it could be treated with mercury, as it was after 1909; who connected goiter with minerals in local drinking water; and who attributed the miners' respiratory disease, silicosis, not to irate mountain spirits but to the inhalation of metal vapors.

Alchemists were practical scientists interested in developing experimental and applied mathematics to public and private advantage. But their magic could be a holy quest that pursued knowledge less by research than by revelation, just as alchemy was viewed as "a study which brings man nearer to the creator."[4] By the seventeenth century, although alchemy had turned into chemistry, an Anglican critic of credulity conceded that many chemical secrets were learned through the revelation of spirits. Robert Boyle, too, the renowned Anglo-Irish chemist and natural philosopher, regarded the study of nature, which helped reveal the Creator's greatness, as a Christian duty. And it was a Christian's privilege to seek out the Creator's designs, essential to learning whether "at that great decretory day the vast fabrick of the world, which all confess must have its frame quite shattered, shall be suffered to relapse into its first nothing . . . or shall be, after its dissolution, renewed to a better state and, as it were, transfigured."[5] More than a century after Boyle another chemist, Joseph Priestley, entertained no doubts. *The Present State of Europe Compared with Ancient Prophecies* (1794) was all about Daniel, Revelation, and opponents of the French Revolution as followers of the Beast.

Well into the seventeenth century, few doubted that prophecy offered a key to surrounding mysteries, and the practice continued as a normal intellectual activity at least into the nineteenth century. Inspired or possessed, prophets, as the original Greek implied [*pro*—for, *phetes*—speaker], spoke for another: God. They could announce and sometimes interpret His will with reference to more or less catastrophic events past or future, and to extraordinary doings such as schism, war, and natural disasters in the present. Many oracles and prophecies past attributed to Sybils, to Old Testament sources, or to semi-mythical ones simmered in the memory of generations.

The store of prophecies on which one could draw was cumulative, self-referential, and self-confirming. Christ was a prophet, too, and evidence of prophecy fulfilled was evidence of the divine inspiration of the Bible. Christianity was a historical religion: a religion about history that turned on history past, events listed, and dates conjectured or established; and on history future, deduced from prophetic clues and Biblical indications. As the earliest Lutheran history, a chronicle revised by Melanchton in 1532 and translated into English in 1550, explained: "God wyll have us so truely warned that as we knowe the histories of al the worlde, we should consyder that the tyme of finishyng be not farre of, and that of this wise we should have wherewith to confirme our faith."[6]

If you knew what had happened, you did not necessarily know what would happen, but you could make a more educated guess. The state of the world just before the coming of Christ, for instance, could help predict the circumstances of his Second Coming. Indeed, as Newton was going to point out in a treatise on the prophecies of Daniel and of Revelation, the value of prophecy lay not in what it foretold, but in offering "convincing argument that the world is governed by providence."[7] Fulfillment of God's plan was progress; so providence and progress overlapped. In pursuit of such crucial goals, prophecy, like alchemy but more so, had to be a science, situated in history, and interpreted by mathematical calculations.

Newton was not the first to think so. In 1593, Sigismund Schwabe, a well-known German preacher and student of Melanchton, published a *Historical Arithmetic* that was designed to prepare its readers for the Last Judgment by combining Biblical teaching and arithmetical instruction: numbering the years from the Creation to the birth of Christ, using Biblical stories to illustrate addition, subtraction, division, and so on. God had supplied effective ways for investigating his world. Calculation provided a providential key, reckoning could lead to godly wisdom, and numerology was linked to prophetic truth.

Star lore makes my point even more clearly. Leonardo da

Vinci (1452–1519), who had little time for the supernatural, made a collection of silly jokes designed to poke fun at contemporary prophets and magicians, of whom "many have made a trade of delusions and false miracles, deceiving the stupid multitude." Yet even Leonardo (who occasionally had apocalyptic visions) differentiated between "fallacious divination by the stars" and "mathematical astrology," which he compared with painting, since both pursuits depended on perspective.[8] Most people's perspective, however, was less discriminating. For Paracelsus, who published *An Interpretation of the Comet Which Appeared in the Mountains in the Middle of August 1531*, foretelling bloodshed, social upheavals, and the rest, medicine and astrology were intertwined, as events on earth and in the heavens must be. That was what his contemporaries thought, and that is what many of our contemporaries think.

Pope Calixtus III (1455–58) instituted the *angelus* in wary reaction to the passage of Halley's comet in 1456. Although repeated bulls prohibited divination and judicial astrology, Leonardo's patron, Pope Julius II, waited for propitious astrological conjunctions to put up his own statue in Bologna or to lay the cornerstone of one of his castles. Pope Paul III (1534–49), an ardent believer in astrology, made sure that his daily timetable, consistories, audiences, and bulls followed the auspices of the stars. What could be wrong with that? "The art of magic," Sir Walter Raleigh held, was "the art of worshipping God."[9] In 1572, when Tycho Brahe discovered a new star, he presented it as heralding the Second Coming. Johannes Kepler, who had been his assistant, checked the New Testament date of the crucifixion against the cycle of solar eclipses and found an error of four years. Both men took a lively interest in the astrological applications of their discoveries. When another new star appeared in 1604, Kepler drew no apocalyptic conclusions, but attributed it to God's finger in the sky.[10] Astrology was one more way of approaching the incomprehensible glory of God. But it had to be done properly.

Stars had their moods, and our word "disaster" exhibits the negative sense of a star's potentially sinister influence: ill-starred or ill-omened. The reading of the stars could be related to health or events, but also to other elements of the cosmos. That was why the ancients applied themselves to observe the regularity and the irregularities of celestial activities. It was Babylonian astronomers who inspired and spurred Babylonian mathematics, in which notations that probably evolved to record business transactions became much more sophisticated in tracking the movement of heavenly bodies.

Men could not understand or control their world, but astrologers could explain natural phenomena according to methods they tried to make as rigorous and exact as possible. Observation and calculation together could establish the influence exercised by celestial bodies and predict likely consequences, even weather forecasts. Calendars could provide a standard of reference for astronomical observations; the clock that Egyptians read in the starry skies was based on particularly bright stars whose spirits ruled over periods of time; and the twelve major constellations that lined the plane of the earth's orbit and the sun's apparent path became the *zodiakos kyklos*, the animal circle of the zodiac. Charts that showed the relative position of sun, moon, planets, and zodiac signs at specific moments in time provided information about the present and predictions of the future. The "hour-watchers" or *horoscopos* who compiled and used them produced the prototype of our horoscopes.

Plumbing the mysteries of nature had always been a religious quest. Used in conjunction with scientific observation, mathematics helped to reveal cosmic harmonies, the secret necessities of relations between creator and creation, God and man, man and nature. Of such cosmological visions, astrology was an integral part. Astrological and astronomical problems went together, as did astronomical and astrological practice from Ptolemy and Campanella to Tycho Brahe and Kepler. Like the latter two, the court mathematicians and astronomers of the great were astrologers too.[11]

Astrology, the daughter of astronomy, provided a map of the universe, of destiny, and of God's plans for men and women. Miracles like the halting of the sun to help Joshua's endeavors, or the eclipse that mourned the passion of Jesus, were not subject to natural law or celestial mechanics. But every irregularity mirrored or predicted trouble. As Gloucester told King Lear, "These late eclipses in the sun and moon portend no good to us." Even the terminal darkening of the sun and moon, when stars fell from the heavens (Matthew 24:29), was more than a preliminary to the coming of the Son of Man. It was the striking symbol that the order of the world had come to an end.

While they awaited that inevitable and proximate event, astrologers brought new precision to the observation of heavenly bodies, the calculation of their movements, and the measurement of time. The year 1202 when Joachim of Fiore died also saw the introduction of Arabic numerals into Europe, including the zero. Equipped with that crucial digit, calculation became easier and more accurate; and much of it, as before, turned about great events, of which none could be greater than the world's ending. In the words of a Tudor mathematician, "there was never any great change in the world, neither translations or empires, neither scarce any fall of famous princes, no dearth or penury, no death or mortality, but God by the signs of heaven did premonish men thereof, to repent and beware betimes."[12]

But there were risks involved. In 1532, Michael Stiefel, a fine mathematician and follower of Luther, published *Apocalypse on the Apocalypse: A Little Book of Arithmetic about the Antichrist*, computing the Day of Judgment for 8 a.m. on October 9, 1533. On that day, the local peasants left their labors and trudged en masse to the village of Lochau, where Stiefel was pastor. When nothing happened at 8 a.m. or later, they seized, bound, and dragged the minister to nearby Wittenberg, where some sued him for damages. Stiefel survived the contretemps, went over his calculations, and twenty years later published another tract, *Eine Sehr Wunderbarliche Wortrechnung* ("a very wonderful re-calculation"), which recognized that he had made a mistake.

But it wasn't so much that mathematics could err. In an illiterate world, numbers as well as letters were mysterious to most—magical and potentially maleficent. Those who counted had grown more proficient but those who watched them count remained suspicious. Astrology was magic, and mathematicians who practiced magic too were easily assimilated with astrologers. Just as simple people equated writing with spells, so clerks and magistrates could look askance at "superstitious algebra" and "the black art of geometry."[13]

Attempts to pursue those signs of heaven by which God premonished men to repent and beware betimes could also produce unexpected results. Before he devised logarithms, invented the notation of decimal fractions, and produced a forerunner of the slide rule, John Napier, laird of Merchistoun, near Edinburgh (1550–1617), had published *A Plaine Discoverie of the Whole Revelation of St. John* (1594), which he dedicated to King James VI of Scotland, shortly to become James I of England. In the *Plain Discoverie*, Napier denounced the pope as Antichrist, which by that time was not sensational news, but also warned against "Papists and Atheists and Newtrals whereof this Revelation foretells that the number shall greatly increase in these latter daies." He also predicted the Last Judgment either for 1688, according to Revelation, or 1700, according to Daniel.

Logarithms had been intended to simplify the complicated calculations needed for astronomy, but Napier is said to have valued them chiefly because they speeded up his calculations of the number of the Beast. Since, like most prudent prognosticators, he passed on before he could check his results, we must assume that he died content.

"Facts do not penetrate the world of our beliefs," wrote Marcel

Proust in *Swann's Way.* "They haven't generated them; they don't destroy them. They can inflict the most constant contradictions upon them without weakening them." But if facts have no effect on beliefs, beliefs do have effect on facts; indeed, they act as facts in politics and society. That is why in April 1583 the bishop of London preached at St. Paul's Cross against the astrologers who predicted the end of the world, based on the conjunction of Jupiter and Saturn: on April 28 a great wind would spring up, they said, and mark the onset of unheard-of calamities before the final consummation.

Greater winds had meanwhile been rising to threaten the firm foundations of the earth itself. In far-off Poland, Nicolaus Copernicus, who died in 1543, had calculated that the earth, like other planets, revolved around the sun. A Pisan mathematician, Galileo Galilei, would soon demonstrate that this absurd idea was less ridiculous than it at first appeared. Heliocentrism, which pushed back the limits of a universe with earth no longer at its center, nowise challenged Scripture. Luther and Melanchton had disliked the views Copernicus expressed, but Clement VII approved them, and Pope Urban VII was much impressed by Galileo's brilliance. More orthodox authorities, however, breasting the crosscurrents of the Counter Reformation, mistrusted "mathematical suppositions" that disavowed entrenched articles of faith and encouraged "petulant spirits" to ignore apostolic tradition. The work of Copernicus, thought to be subversive, was placed on the *Index* in 1616, and that of Galileo in 1633. There they remained for two centuries. But the finite world was coming to an end, and the Judgment of an infinite universe would be more difficult to imagine than that of the limited world. The *Book of Nature* would henceforth be seen, as Galileo put it, to be written in mathematical characters.

Galileo had drawn up a horoscope for his son, and he regularly cast them for his Medici patrons.[14] Within a few years of the Italian's death in 1642, a French mathematician, Pierre Gassendi, was denouncing *The Vanity of Judicial Astrology or*

Divination by the Stars. But the scientific validity of astrology mattered less than its potential fallout. Predictions could destabilize the throne, the church, and the lives of ordinary folk. Astrologers, as Rabelais quipped, were mostly disastrologers. The astral conjunctions they found in the past validated the sensational forebodings they voiced about the future. The politics of prophecy too often proved subversive. In 1631, Pope Urban VIII sagely prohibited all predictions dealing with ecclesiastical and political matters and with the life of the pope or his relatives. Napier's predictions sounded seditious when translated into French for the edification of restive Protestants, or when revived in the 1640s during the civil wars in England.

But prophetic and astrological forecasts were the lifeblood of chapbooks and almanacs, the central popular interest of the sixteenth and seventeenth centuries, and coincidence could easily highlight their sensationalism. The fame of Nostradamus, for one, never faded, and his predictions of distinguished deaths, upheavals, wars, and blood all over the place brought grist to almanac-makers' mills. For 1559, to take just one example, Nostradamus predicted "death, ruin, affliction and banishment of the enemies of Christ's church." That year King Henri II of France was killed and his son, Francis II, would die in 1560. In 1559, also, Elizabeth was crowned queen of England, John Knox returned to Scotland, and the Protestant Lords of the Congregation began to destroy religious houses in their land. The situation was too fluid for comfort, let alone for celestial intervention. Yet celestial phenomena lent themselves to prognostication. Solar or lunar eclipses were visible in Shakespeare's England virtually every other year; and contemporaries knew what they meant from the portents preceding Julius Caesar's death:

> Distemper'd portents quartered in the skies—
> As stars with trains of fire, and dews of blood,
> Disasters in the sun; and the moist star

Upon whose influence Neptune's empire stands
Sick, almost to Doomsday, with eclipse.

No wonder that ministers and monarchs tried to censor or
moderate destabilizing voices. In 1579, during the French wars
of religion, King Henri III prohibited political predictions. But
when, in 1600, Marie de Medici married Henri IV she brought
with her a whole stable of astrologers in the Italian fashion. It
would be only an alliance of church and state that could begin
to muzzle disturbing practices: when the last state astrologer,
Morin de Villefranche, professor of mathematics at the Collège
de France, died in 1659, he was not replaced.[15] Then came the
major comet of 1664–65 and the run up to 1666, an ominous date
that included the number of the Beast. Few were surprised to see
the Great Fire of London virtually destroy England's capital.[16]
That was when Colbert, minister of Louis XIV, founded the
Academy of Science and prohibited astronomers from practic-
ing astrology. Ten years later, in 1676, a royal edict on imprison-
ing mad people bore down hard on freelance prophets. Yet
even so, in 1680, Pierre Bayle's *Letters on the Comet* dedicated
itself to calming the terrors that had been fed by the eclipse of
1676: "Some died of fear, others took refuge in confessionals,"
one contemporary witness noted.[17]

Astronomers and astrologers knew better than those whom
their findings panicked. Theirs was no sinister science. It was,
after all, by following a star that the magi had reached Bethlehem. Meanwhile, occult and technological lore went together,
the latter feeding on the former until it could discard it. In 1623,
Campanella's *City of the Sun* was governed by priests skilled in
astral magic; in 1624, Francis Bacon's *New Atlantis* was served
by technology-minded priests interested, like their creator, in
observation, experiment, and scientific inquiry. By the mid-
seventeenth century, astral and mechanical science were invoked
as one. Comets, as an astrologer explained in 1678, produced

wars and the death of princes by scorching the air, disturbing the blood, and causing choler, which makes for war and disturbs the delicate organs of great persons susceptible to atmospheric changes. Meteors proceeded from natural causes too, yet "are frequently also the presages of imminent calamities."[18] When natural science was enlisted to explain astral influences, could their marginalization be far behind? Or would irrationality continue to function in the realm of reason?

In mid-nineteenth-century England, a seven-year-old boy read the Bible every day and also "a book of incommunicable dreariness called Newton's *Thoughts on the Apocalypse*." The boy, Edmund Gosse, was the son of an eminent zoologist, and Newton was England's greatest scientific figure. Like the elder Gosse, Newton bears witness to the fact that, in the nineteenth century, as in the seventeenth, one could combine serious scientific research with intense apocalyptic preoccupations.

When Newton entered the University of Cambridge in 1660, he declared that he wanted to study mathematics "because I wish to test judicial astrology"—in other words, the business of predicting by the stars.[19] The eight and a half broad columns that the fifteenth edition of the *Encyclopedia Britannica* allots to the scientist allow just over ten rather dismissive lines to the spiritual interests of this fervently religious man. One would never guess that Newton had written more than two million words on alchemy and that he was as steeped in Biblical lore as in the hermetic tradition.

The fact that his observations on the prophecies of Daniel and the Apocalypse of John were published posthumously encouraged eighteenth-century rationalists to laugh them away ("The strongest minds meet their eclipse," quipped Frederic the Great; "Newton wrote his Apocalypse"), and nineteenth-century admirers to disregard them as products of dozy decrepitude. But the *Observations* were products of Newton's prime, not his dotage. Frank Manuel has demonstrated that Newton devoted much of his life to computations, histories, and counts designed to correct contemporary understanding of Biblical chronology. His interest in Daniel went back a long way, to his days when, as a student at Cambridge, he had tried to work out the approximate time of the Second Coming. He regarded the four monarchies that Daniel foretold as the framework of world history, and he calculated that the reign of the papal Antichrist could not last much longer, since 1200 of Daniel's 1290 years had run out already.

Newton's dearest disciple, Nicolas Fatio de Duillier, whose expectations of a Second Coming were more precipitate, became the secretary of the French Huguenot prophets who predicted the imminent destruction of London in a bloody holocaust. He was condemned to stand in the pillory for his role in their disruptive preaching. Newton dissociated himself from him, but never from his eschatological beliefs. Even as president of the Royal Society, he assumed that history was drawing to a close because men like himself stood ready to expound and clarify the prophetic revelations preliminary to the impending apocalypse. He believed in the return of the Jews to the Holy Land, the restoration of Jerusalem and of the temple there, and "the coming of the kingdom for which we daily pray."[20]

But even this true believer thought it prudent to keep his views from public view. By the eighteenth century, discretion had become the better part of scientific valor. If Newton's apocalyptic speculations were published posthumously, it was because rationalists and deists had seized the high intellectual ground, branding his kind of religion as "pannick fear," eschatological research as superstition, and enthusiasm as fanaticism. In 1709, John Trenchard's *Natural History of Superstition* attributed the latter to "Aversion, Pride and Fury in the shape of Zeal," and rage driven by the glory of God. "The Holy Enthusiastick," wrote Trenchard, "longs to Feast and riot upon humane Sacrifices, turn Cities and Nations into Shambles, and destroy with Fire and Sword such who dare to thwart his Frenzy."

Apocalypicism, now, could be explained psychologically and sociologically, as Trenchard did. His more influential and widely read contemporary, Anthony Ashley Cooper, third Earl of Shaftesbury, equated enthusiasm and the vapors that rise "in bad times especially, when the Spirits of Men are low, as either in publick Calamitys, or during the Unwholesomeness of Air or Diet, or when convulsions happen in Nature, Storms, Earthquakes, or other Amazing Prodigys."[21] So Newton had good reason to fear ridicule if he publicized his religious ideas: a religious maniac would not be knighted as he was, let alone taken seriously as a scientist. Those who came after him either conformed to the new intellectual standards or surrendered claim to a respectful hearing in societies where the gauge of intellectual correctness had altered.

ENLIGHTENMENT?

For modes of Faith, let graceless zealots fight,
He can't be wrong, whose life is in the right.

– ALEXANDER POPE, 1733

T HE AGE OF ENLIGHTENMENT, which sought to apply reason to all things, dismissed Revelation as obscurantism; and not Revelation only. Religious beliefs, once resting on broad consensus, had become so diverse that they found room even for disbelief. Good-natured skepticism affected believers too. When, at the mid-eighteenth century, a visionary friar informed Pope Benedict XIV that the Antichrist had come into the world and was three years old, the pope sighed with relief: "Then I shall leave the problem to my successor."[1] The faith of simple people outlived such irony. But it was the sort of faith that drove peasants to sacrifice calves to the Virgin, so that she should protect their herds from harm; and it confirmed the prejudices of the sophisticated.

Disintegration of consensual religion and the waning prestige of magic polarized cultural attitudes and sharpened divisions between elites and masses. Among the educated and those who, modeling themselves on them, regarded reason as the ultimate authority, supernatural or miraculous events had to find rational explanations or be dismissed as superstitions. John Locke, the seventeenth-century icon of eighteenth-century philosophy, advocated *The Reasonableness of Christianity* (1695) without resort to tradition or creed; John Toland, the freethinking Deist, dismissed mystic doxyes in *Christianity Not Mysterious* (1696). Matthew Tindal's *Christianity as Old as the Creation* (1730) rejected revelation and the supernatural. And many who continued to believe in God preferred to marginalize a creator who wrought the universe, but abstained from intervening in its doings. Not long before, religious conflict had turned on rival beliefs; now it became a clash between belief and unbelief.

But hearts have reasons that reason does not know, and hearts continued to swing between trust and terror. All gods are born of fear. Following previous prophets, Paul had advised the Phillipians to work out their salvation in fear and trembling; and his spirit survived in the *Book of Common Prayer,* where fear of the Lord is the beginning of wisdom. "Those are my best dayes," John Donne admitted, "when I shake with feare." The enlightened age, so called, was to furnish as many such best dayes as its predecessors.

> They speak, *earth, ocean, air;* I hear them say
> *Awake, repent,* 'ere we dissolve away!

In the year 1750, when the *Gentlemen's Magazine* printed those verses, London was shaken by two earthquakes in quick succession. John Wesley took them as warnings from God, and other interpreters as punishments for a rebellious and wicked people. Fearing a third and final tremor, incredible numbers walked in the fields, sat in boats on the Thames all night, or thronged the roads out of London.[2] In 1712, William Whiston, Newton's successor as professor of mathematics at Cambridge, had predicted that a comet would soon destroy the world. In November 1750, the third volume of Whiston's memoirs recalled the second woe of Revelation 11:13 to predict the fall of a tenth part of London, the death of seven thousand men, "and the remnant so affrighted that they gave glory to the God of heaven."

Then, in 1755, divine seismics struck again, in Boston. Many "shrieked with Apprehension of its being the Day of Judgment, and some thought they heard the Last Trump sounding, and cryed out for Mercy."[3] When, a few months later, another earthquake struck the Atlantic coast of Spain and Portugal, its ravages were enlisted in rationalist disputations of the day. The whole population of Boston was less numerous than the 30,000 victims of the Lisbon earthquake alone, where fire and a tidal wave had finished what the quake began.

Voltaire was shocked. Only a few years before, he had composed a *Poem on the Natural Law* that represented nature as beneficent and the universe as a temple where the Eternal rules. In the wake of the Lisbon disaster, he decided that the world was incomprehensible, the Eternal deaf or nonexistent, and man the helpless football of fate. His immediate response on hearing of the earthquake had been to write to his banker, eager to cash a letter of exchange on Cadiz, which had also been badly shaken. Once his financial interests had been dealt with, however, moral revulsion came into its own. His letters of late November 1755 are full of references both to Leibnitz, who thought that all was for the best in a world that looked from Geneva like a game of chance where all the dice are loaded, and to Alexander Pope, whose *Essay on Man* had concluded, "whatever is, is right." Within a few days, Voltaire composed the *Poem on the Disaster of Lisbon*, desperately angry and grieving over the fate of humans inextricably entangled in the fundamental absurdity of life:

> Tormented atoms on a heap of muck
> That death devours and that fate trips up
> Strange to myself, estranged from my own kind,
> Who am I? Where am I? Where do I go, what find?

In 1756, war broke out in the Germanies, where much of Voltaire's money was invested, and also across the Atlantic and on it, where Voltaire had armed a vessel, the *Pascal*. War bodes ill for investors, and that year's *Essay on General History* defined history as one long succession of useless atrocities. Rack and ruin: the world is one great shipwreck. Providence does not exist; providential order is an illusion. That year he began to think about *Candide*, a counter-*Pilgrim's Progress*, which is about paradise lost, regained, and lost again, until the final accommodation with mediocre reality. Savonarola had organized bonfires of vanities. *Candide* was a bonfire of illusions. There is no benevolent deity, even if you call it divine design. Whatever is, is not right, and certainly not for the best. "Why was this world created?" asks one character in *Candide*, and the author's alter ego answers: "To drive us all mad."

There were many, however, who knew better than this. Pope's "scene of man" was indeed "a mighty maze, but not without a plan." The world has been created by the will of God, mankind was meant to obey his will, Christ (as a "Witness to the great Dispensation approaching" testified) had been speaking to the World since Lisbon, "and will continue to speak in Earthquakes and other Signs in Times and Nature too." In February 1763, when the Peace of Paris ended the Seven Years' War, a pious Methodist, George Bell, prophesied the end of the world for February 28. John Wesley, who had long surmounted any early belief in the imminent coming of Christ, had to preach to show the "utter absurdity of the supposition that the world was to end that night." Yet many were afraid to go to bed and wandered about the fields "persuaded that if the world did not end, at least London would be swallowed up by an earthquake," as Lisbon had been only eight years before.[4]

England continued to breed visionaries and prophets. The heirs of the mid-seventeenth century sectarians of Cromwell's day, with their belief that the kingdom of God was at hand, were still preaching and praying a century later, ready to seize on untoward comets, eclipses, and earthquakes that bolstered their expectations. Many of their ilk had shifted allegiance to the evangelical movement that the persevering piety of the Wesley brothers and the spectacular preaching of George Whitefield turned into Methodism. John Wesley distrusted enthusiasm, but when even he was liable to entreat God to send down the New Jerusalem as if it were a sluggish elevator, it is not surprising to find chiliasm in revivalist chapels and meetings.

The freedom of religious expression that Voltaire so admired in England meant that trade in beliefs was free. As Robert Southey explained, "one man printed his dreams, another his day-visions; one had seen an angel coming out of the sun with a drawn sword in his hand, another had seen fiery dragons in the air, and hosts of angels in battle array . . . The lower classes . . . began to believe that the Seven Seals were about to be opened."[5] In this overheated atmosphere, which political crises like those of the 1790s or 1830s only accentuated, the offerings of the established church could well seem stale and flavorless. In *Adam Bede*, a novel whose action takes place at the end of the eighteenth century, George Eliot describes the village parson, Mr. Irwin, a lax, tolerant, decent man, as lacking lofty aims and theological enthusiasm. She knew that to less sympathetic, more fervent eyes than hers, clergy of Irwin's sort looked like "men given up to lusts of the flesh and pride of life; hunting and shooting, and adorning their own houses; asking what shall we eat, and what shall we drink, and wherewithal shall we be clothed?—careless of dispensing the bread of life to their flocks, preaching at best but a carnal and soul-benumbing morality."[6]

Those souls who sought more than benumbing morality might well turn to inspired women preachers like Eliot's semi-fictional Dinah Morris, to whom "it seemed as if speech came to me without any will of my own, and words were given to me that came out as the tears come because our hearts are full and we can't help it."[7] Or they would lend an ear to the like of William Clowes, potter and itinerant preacher, who dismissed ritual, routine, and convention as irrelevant to salvation. Conformity fettered the souls of believers "too much with what men call system and order."[8] Vigorous, loud, and unruly in the way of the old-time prophets or the apostles speaking in the last days, women like Morris and men like Clowes captivated hearers with the violence of their denunciations and their appeals.

Not for them the complacency of those content to go through ritual motions of worship. "They believed," Eliot tells us, "in present miracles, in instant conversions, in revelations by dreams and visions . . . having a literal way of interpreting the scriptures, which is not at all sanctioned by approved commentators." Or, as the landlord of the inn in Hayslope more forcefully phrased it, "there's no holding these Methodisses when the maggit's once got i'their head; many of'em goes stark starin' mad wi'their religion."[9]

Religious enthusiasm could be discovered in polite society too. When not working on nebular and magnetic theory, a member of the Swedish Board of Mines named Emanuel Swedenborg (1688–1772) had dedicated himself to showing that the physical universe had a fundamentally spiritual structure. While visiting London in 1743, Swedenborg had a vision. In the course of dinner, the Lord appeared to him surrounded by light and told him, "Don't eat so much!" A second vision revealed that he had been chosen to explain the Scriptures.[10] Further conversations with angels and spirits persuaded the mystic that the New Jerusalem had descended from heaven in 1757, as predicted in Revelation 21:1–2, and the Second Advent was proceeding according to plan. All this was not immediately apparent because it took place on the spiritual plane. It had to be interpreted in terms of correspondences between the angelic realm and the visible world (a mirror image of the invisible), to which divine truths were being progressively revealed.

Swedenborgianism as a kind of gnosticism attracted the critical attention of Immanuel Kant, who had already inveighed against eschatological interpretations of earthquakes, and who in 1766 attacked the dreams of a visionary (*Träume Einer Geistersehers*). Its quest for spiritual regeneration also fascinated several Wesleyan ministers determined to build Jerusalem here on earth (a view that William Blake adopted). Founded in 1787, the New Jerusalem Church did not affect the urban situation in Palestine; but the conjunction of early Methodism and intellectual spiritualism almost inevitably veered toward popular eschatology. And eschatology proved popular with more than the masses.[11] A cultivated woman like Dr. Johnson's friend Esther Thrale Piozzi, fascinated by signs, omens, and Revelation, was apt to interpret current events in terms of apocalyptic prophecy. So was Selina, Countess of Huntingdon; so was the *Gentleman's Magazine*, steadfastly on the lookout for "Signs of the Times"; and so was Joseph Priestley, schoolmaster, scientist, and Presbyterian minister.

Discoverer of oxygen, ammonia, carbon monoxide, and other gases, Priestley was convinced that "everything looks like the approach of that dismal catastrophe," the end of the world. On the basis of revelation and prophecy, he had discerned evidence of the coming end in the rebellion of England's American colonies, and would do so again in the French Revolution, which presented "a near view of the millennium."[12] Taken together, the two revolutions looked like the inauguration of the state of universal happiness and peace "distinctly and repeatedly foretold in many prophecies delivered more than two thousand years ago."[13] Having helped found the Unitarian Society in 1791, Priestley would be voted French citizenship by the Legislative Assembly that same year and then, in 1792, be elected by two departments—Orne and Rhône-et-Loire—to represent them in the French Convention. Having declined the honor, he waited a couple of years before taking refuge in the United States, where his last work was dedicated to his friend Thomas Jefferson.

In France, too, where enlightenment never quelled obscurantism, comets were notoriously associated with apocalyptic turmoil. Even the famous astronomer Daniel Bernoulli (1700–82), whose work on the frontiers of science earned him numberless prizes, opined that "if the body of the planet is not a visible sign of God's wrath, its tail could well be one."[14] Newton had studied the comet of 1680, to whose previous appearance his assistant William Whiston attributed the deluge. In May 1773 (a bumper year for comets and hence for panic fears of the world's ending), the professor of astronomy at the Collège de France, Joseph-Jérome de Lalande, was scheduled to read a paper on comets before the Academy of Sciences. Rumors about his conclusion that should comets come too close to earth, they could provoke tsunamis, caused widespread sensation and alarm, and forced the postponement of Lalande's communication. "The ferment was such," noted a contemporary diary, the *Mémoires de Bachaumont*, on May 9, "that devout ignorants solicited the archbishop [of Paris] to order forty hours of prayers to turn away the enormous deluge that threatened us." Ecclesiastical intervention was prevented by a delegation of members of the Academy, who argued that the move would not only be ridiculous but would increase existing fears.[15]

Meanwhile, the later 1700s had ushered in a new age of mysticism and illumination: gnostic with Swedenborg and the theosophists, therapeutic with Franz Anton Mesmer and his "animal magnetism," magic with that charlatan of genius, the Count of Cagliostro, less speculative with more popular prophets and prophetesses. Among fashionable fanatics, the Swedish ambassador in Paris and son-in-law of the king's first minister, the Protestant Jacques Necker, was an adept of the Swedenborgian sect. Baron August de Staël had a Swedenborgian attaché who made spirits appear in mirrors and read the future in books stained with blood. Since the sect inclined to look upon the

French Revolution as "nothing less that the Judgment Day of tyrants,"[16] the baron's religious mysticism carried into political mysticism so well that it lost him his job. One of Staël's good friends, Johann-Caspar Lavater (1741–1801), pastor and inventor of the science of physiognomy (which he intended to reveal the links between face and soul), was more famous in his time for his religious writings. And Necker's daughter, Germaine de Staël, who thought that Lavater believed himself to be a reincarnation of St. John, praised his mystical works despite "his bizarre opinions on himself and his miraculous vocation."[17]

On a more popular level, Jansenists, convulsionist or not, continued to announce or call for Elijah and other signs of God's forthcoming wrath. Their prophets predicted chastisement, torments, persecutions, calamities, ruins, flames, torrents of blood, and cities overthrown or swallowed up. Elijah awaited, he was at the gate, he would recognize his own: "It's in the last extremity that I shall come to save you." The sharper the economic and political crisis of the 1780s, the more Elijahs and their messengers seemed to proliferate. In 1783, in expectation of the senior witness, Catherine Renaud predicted the overthrow of the kingdom, earthquake, famine, pestilence, war, massacres, and ruin. In 1785, Jean-Baptiste Ruery, a professed descendant of King David who claimed that heavenly sources assured him he was destined to rule as king in Jerusalem, likewise predicted kingdoms overthrown, revolutionary outbreaks, the Jews returning to the Holy Land, and Jesus returning to launch the Third Age. Predictions became more focused by the year. "The Revolution has to come," cried Sister Aile in April 1787: "I see only ambush, I see only precipice, the blood flows around me, I hear the clash of arms, the palace of the king is swept away, his crown is torn off. I'm being thrust into the well of the abyss in the midst of so great a revolution."[18]

At Fareins, in faraway Forez, in the 1780s, the local priest preached a similar message: Elijah's coming, the early conversion of the Jews, Christ's Second Coming and his new kingdom. The French Revolution proved that the *curé* spoke true; but before Christ's reign of a thousand years could be established, the old world had to be destroyed, materialism abolished, churches closed, and priests eliminated in order to usher in the new era of peace, love, happiness, and fraternity. On Trinity Sunday (June 3) 1792, the priest of Saint-Jean-Bonnefonds, near Saint-Étienne, preaching from his pulpit, announced the imminent coming of the Messiah; and, indeed, the Messiah of the year I [of the Republic, proclaimed in September 1792] was born in Paris that August. In November 1794, authorities in Forez reported that villagers of the Montbrison district were leaving their fields and farms to await Elijah's coming in the nearby forests, before moving on to found the Republic of Jesus Christ in Jerusalem.[19]

As we saw, the persecution of Jansenists, which inspired such vivid and enduring apocalyptic reactions, was also to inspire persecution of their Jesuit foes. In 1773, the year in which Pope Clement XIV dissolved the Company of Jesus, pious Catholics in provincial capitals like Lyon and Toulouse began to gather in groups of *Amis de la Vérité*. Did the sympathies of these Friends of Truth lie with Jesuits or with Jansenists? We do know that these respectable women and men, some of them in holy orders, venerated Elijah and prayed for the conversion of the Jews and the renovation of the church. In Périgord and in the backcountry of Bordeaux, a holy woman, Suzette Labrousse, had been attracting attention since the 1760s. She, too, sought to see the church reformed, and expected "the happiest of revolutions [that] would end all misfortunes."[20]

Another devout Catholic who expressed himself less discreetly concluded that the Roman clergy, and especially the hierarchy, represented Antichrist. Emmanuel Lacunza, a Chilean Jesuit who became a refugee in Italy after 1767 when his order was expelled from the dominions of the King of Spain, also sought consolation in Biblical prophecies. His *Coming of the Messiah in*

Glory and Majesty, finished in 1790, published posthumously in 1812, reasserted the conversion and restoration of the Jews, the Second Coming, and the millennium. It was, of course, placed on the *Index of Prohibited Books* as soon as it was published; but ideas of this sort were made to survive official disapproval, especially when events appeared to bear them out.[21]

For Labrousse and those who thought like her, revolution would be the prelude to God's regeneration of the world. The priests who mulled over their readings of Isaiah and Daniel, Ezekiel, and Revelation, who expected God's ire to strike the new Babylon and looked out for the scriptural evils that would precede Christ's rule on earth, knew that the cataclysm to come would purify religion and perfect mankind. That would not surprise those familiar with the calculations of Cardinal Pierre d'Ailly, Canon Roussart, Dijon Academy rector Pierre Turel, or the Londoner Peter Pearson, all of whom forecast the end of the world, or at least of Christendom, for 1789. When something very like what had been predicted actually occurred, it set a lot more folk rummaging for old prophecies that would confirm new ones. Nostradamus was cited; so was the fourteenth-century Franciscan, Jean de Roquetaillade. In an eclectic mood, a priest in Angers, in western France, used his parish register to demonstrate how one prophecy after another was coming true: earthquake in 1755, outpouring of God's wrath in 1790, revolution, famine, and war close at hand before the stars went out in 1799 and the world ended.[22]

But where one world seemed to end, another was preparing to be born. When, at the beginning of our century, Albert Mathiez, the young Marxist historian, studied the religious aspects of the French Revolution, he was impressed by the "messianic hope of regeneration" surrounding 1789 like a halo and greeting even Necker, the financier recalled after the fall of the Bastille, as the Messiah of France. In the preface he contributed to Mathiez's studies, that fine medieval historian, Gabriel

Monod, confirmed the younger scholar's judgment: the Revolution had been a Revelation and revolutionaries had lived in expectation of the millennium.[23]

Consciously or not, revolution and romanticism (or pre-romanticism) colored the age with hope, terror, crisis, and change, cascading, rushing, stimulating, and astounding, impossible to ignore or to dismiss. For William Blake, who expected the world to be consumed by fire, the French Revolution was a portent of the Apocalypse. Wordsworth, too, glimpsed "characters of the great Apocalypse,/ The types and symbols of Eternity,/ Of first, and last, and midst, and without end." In Coleridge's shorthand note, revolution, millennium, and redemption went together. "Old things seemed passing away," remembered Robert Southey, "and nothing was dreamt of but the regeneration of the human race."[24]

Some participants in the revolution expected regeneration to come when reason was applied to human affairs. Others, however, wanted to "hasten the inevitable fulfillment of God's plans by all available means." Thus Henri Grégoire (1750–1831), a priest from Lorraine, member of revolutionary assemblies, and constitutional bishop of Blois, married Enlightenment *and* chiliasm. Believing that Jews must convert before the Second Coming, he decided that equal rights for Jews would hasten the millennium. Grégoire's life, which spanned three monarchies, one republic, and one empire, was incredibly busy. But he never ceased to work for the Jews and also for blacks, believing that equal treatment for everyone would advance God's plan for mankind and prepare all humans for the millennium.[25]

Lavater had calculated that the Messiah should return in 1794; others referred to the revolution unfolding as the fifth trumpet of the Final Judgment, and to the revolutionary Terror as the scourge of God. Partisans of the revolution confirmed them. Like the Great Beast of Revelation, "they opened their mouth in blasphemy against God, to blaspheme his name and his tabernacle and they that dwelt in heaven" (Revelation 13:6). The guillotine was carried in processions as holy images had been carried a few years before, the Christian calendar was set aside in a symbolic act of 1792, the revolution itself was described as "holy," and members of the Convention were told that they were the creators of a new world: "Say that there shall be light," urged Boissy d'Anglas, "and there will be light."[26]

Just as the French Revolution had its saints, so it had its seers and prophetesses. Catherine Théot (1716–94) claimed to be the Mother of God and intrigued even Robespierre, who probably saved her from the guillotine, and whose foes certainly accused him of being one of her followers. After predicting that her death would be marked by frightful occurrences, Théot died in prison on the day when the great powder magazine at Grenelle blew up. Her followers concluded that she would rise again, but she did not.

Women prophets and preachers have been active since Old Testament days, and they were numerous in England. Bible-reading folk there were well aware of Peter's words on the Day of Pentecost, recalling the prophet Joel: "And it shall come to pass in the last days, saith God, I will pour out my spirit upon all flesh; and your sons and your daughters shall prophesy, and your young men shall dream visions, and your old men shall dream dreams" (Acts 2:17).

For educated men and women, rationalism went with religious indifference, and fervor looked like uncouth fanaticism. But ordinary people found wonders enough in heaven and signs in the earth: blood, fire, and vapor of smoke, as Joel had predicted and Peter had repeated, to awe and inspire. Devils were being cast out all over the land, as cottage religion and cottage evangelists never forgot the apocalyptic message. That suited many who judged the established church too lukewarm, and even chapel Methodism too conformist. When he drifted into Lichfield Church, the itinerant carpenter and preacher Hugh

Bourne, leader of the Primitive Methodist Connexion, found the lightness, sin, and gross idolatry oppressive, a sign of the times and of imminent judgment: "I trembled for the place and for the people."[27]

Protestant England had long been familiar with the image of the pope as Antichrist, one with the Beast of Revelation whose destruction would herald the reign of the saints. A revolution that overthrew the Romish Church in France and threatened it elsewhere was one more signal that the last days were nigh. The fall of the papacy, the destruction of the Turkish Empire, and the return of the Jews to the Holy Land could not be long delayed. Jesus had ordered the apostles to be his witnesses unto the uttermost ends of the earth. This evangelistic spirit inspired the foundation of a host of missionary societies: Methodist in 1786, Baptist in 1792, the London Missionary Society in 1795, the Church Missionary Society and the Religious Tract Society in 1799, the British and Foreign Bible Society in 1804, and the London Society for Promoting Christianity among the Jews in 1809 being just part of a longer list. By the end of the Napoleonic Wars, in Protestant countries, forty-one societies were spending millions to propagate the gospel in 141 languages. The French Revolution, as the Reverend Thomas Malthus apprehended, was a blazing comet destined either to inspire or to scorch up and destroy the shrinking inhabitants of the earth. Tremendous events were bringing on the fullness of times. Missionary endeavors would hasten the expected end.

So would more traditional apocalypticism. As the London *Times* pointed out, sects, mesmerists, somnambulists, prophets, and prophetesses preceded the French Revolution and prepared the public mind for momentous changes.[28] The changes in question were more specifically addressed in a proliferation of pamphlets such as *The World's Doom* (London, 1795), which detailed prodigies that many of late had witnessed: "Armies both horse and foot, have been seen passing over the moon . . .

spectres, clad in terrible array, have come into the world to denounce bloody vengeance upon the wicked and the oppressor." Perhaps the new Babylon was not Paris, but London?

Since 1791, a retired naval officer, Richard Brothers, had known that Babylon *was* London, and God, who conveyed the message, would destroy it, either by fire (Brothers dissuaded him from doing that) or by earthquake. By 1795, however, Brothers could no longer avert the divine wrath inspired by Britain's opposition to revolution in France, which proceeded from the judgment of God. He had tried to warn the government, parliament, and the king, but had been rebuffed. Now Brothers announced that, on June 4, the king's official birthday, London and much of the rest of the world would be annihilated. "Numberless people even of Rank and Character run in Flocks to increase the Presumption or feed the Phrenzy of this extraordinary man," noted Mrs. Piozzi.

Times were hard, prices high, people restive, food was scarce, and the government insecure. Brothers was arrested, charged with "unlawfully, maliciously, and wickedly writing, printing and publishing various fantastical prophecies, with intent to create dissensions and other disturbances within this realm," declared insane, and placed in a madhouse, where he remained until 1806. But many fled London to escape threatened destruction, and more were alarmed when on the evening of June 4, a violent thunderstorm, wind, hail, and lightning brought "terror and dismay."[29] The bad weather continued, and the end of 1795 even saw an earthquake, but public curiosity had shifted to other matters. What did not abate was the inclination (as one member of parliament and disciple of Brothers was to put it) "to read the modern history of Europe in the prophetic records of the Old and New Testament." When, in 1800, Francis Dobbs, MP, quoted Daniel and Revelation to denounce the proposed Act of Union between England and Ireland as inexpedient and impious, he found consolation in the knowledge that the Messiah would come to prevent it that year or next.[30]

There may have been a vague reference in Dobbs's words to the prophecies of Joanna Southcott (1750–1814), a farm servant who joined the Methodists in 1791, by Divine Command, and soon became the recipient of revelations concerning the destruction of Satan and the coming of the millennial kingdom, as well as current events like the war in France, naval mutinies, and rotten harvests. Joanna was the woman whose coming would free the world of sin and preserve the faithful through the tribulation. Having identified herself as the Woman Clothed with the Sun of Revelation 12, and the bride of the Lamb, who looms in Revelation 19:7–8, she began to seal those who hoped to be among the 144,000 elect (Revelation 7:3–4). By 1814, the sixty-four-year- old virgin had convinced herself, her followers, and even the medical man who examined her that she was pregnant with a supernaturally conceived child. Before she could "bring forth the man child who was to rule all nations with a rod of iron" (Revelation 12:5), she died. And though her body was held for four days awaiting resurrection and parturition, nothing ensued. Happily, experience has little hold on faith, and Southcottians survived for the rest of the century. During the difficult years (1903–28) when he was Archbishop of Canterbury, Randall Thomas Davidson was often pressed to consult her prophecies for the country's sake.

But if prophets differed about England's fate, few differed about France. In 1793, the German pietist, physician, and semi-Swedenborgian mystic Johann Friedrich Jung-Stilling, who announced Christ's Second Advent and the speedy coming of the millennium, had presented the French Revolution as a forerunner of Antichrist. So, among many others, did a pamphlet of 1795 locating the Antichrist in the Convention and expecting the Beast to rise up out of the sea in 1796. By 1799, the name of Antichrist had become clear, and it was (in the Corsican dialect) N'Apollione, the Destroyer, "coming forwards followed by a cloud of locusts from ye bottomless Pit." That was Mrs. Piozzi, who recorded how many found the First Consul to be "the Devil Incarnate, the Appolyon mentioned in Scripture."[31]

It is appropriate that the first sentence of Tolstoy's *War and Peace* should refer to Napoleon as Antichrist, for nowhere was this view more popular than in Russia. Exiled in St. Petersburg after 1802, Joseph de Maistre, ambassador of the dispossessed King of Sardinia, saw the revolution as a political expression of Satanic revolt. He insisted on its (and Napoleon's) apocalyptic role, and exhorted his friends to hold themselves ready for a huge event in the divine order: "Formidable prophets are fore-telling that *the time is here.*"[32] That became very clear when, in May 1812, Napoleon invaded Russia and the Russian church denounced him as Antichrist. Tsar Alexander's mission became a religious one: to conquer Antichrist.

The tsar was not a particularly religious man, but an impressionable one. He had gradually fallen under the influence of a pious friend, Prince Aleksandr Golytsin, whom he appointed procurator of the Holy Synod, or minister of religion. Golytsin urged Alexander to read the Bible, and Alexander was dazzled. The Grand Master of the Imperial Court, Aleksandr Koshelev, was keen on occultism. He had studied Swedenborg, Lavater, and Jung-Stilling, and had corresponded with Quakers and Moravian Brethren whose evangelical religion of the heart suited his sentimental mysticism. After the great fire of Moscow had "shed light in [the tsar's] soul,"[33] Golytsin became head of a department of Spiritual Affairs and Popular Enlightenment (a historian of religion in Russia called it the ministry of religio-utopian propaganda), and an Imperial Russian Bible Society was founded, as a branch of the British and Foreign Bible Society, to translate, publish, and distribute the Scriptures in all the major languages of the empire.

Once the forces of Antichrist had been driven back and the tsar's armies had marched into Paris/Babylon, the tsar encountered another of those inspiring figures with which his course seems littered. Baroness Julie de Krüdener (1764–1824) was the author of a successful sentimental novel, *Valérie* (1803), a friend of Madame de Staël, Chateaubriand, and of Benjamin Constant who prayed with her. First widowed, then converted or inspired by the eclectic gospel message of the Moravian Brethren, she shifted her interests from society to sanctimony. She sought out Jung-Stilling, and she met Pastor Jean-Frédéric Oberlin, the saintly social reformer, who was, to a degree, both a Rousseauist and a Swedenborgian, as well as an all-round decent man. An apocalyptist with a vast fortune and a social conscience, Krüdener envisaged the Parousia as a grand explosion of love, and the millennium as a time when masters would wash the vegetables for their supper and fetch water from the well, while "all servant-girls will walk about in silken dresses."[34]

Like so many contemporaries, she regarded the travails of the last decades as signs of an imminent end: "The judgment day is approaching; it is close at hand, and the world dances on a volcano!" she wrote in 1814 to an equally mystical friend, the Romanian princess Ruxandra Sturza, who was close to Alexander. Napoleon hovered uneasily on Elba, while Krüdener predicted that calamitous times were about to return "and everyone feels forebodings." In January 1815, she foretold that Napoleon would leave his isle and that the year 1815 would prove a memorable one: "The wars, the desolation will be terrible!" Sturza passed the prophecy on to the tsar. On April 1, Napoleon landed in France, and soon Julie and Alexander prayed and sobbed together. She assured the tsar that he was the White Angel who would prevail over the Black Angel. When that was done, he could embark on his true great task: the founding of a single European religion.

After Waterloo, even while his new-found enthusiasm was beginning to cool, the tsar let Mme de Krüdener inspire him to insist on a new union of the nations based on the gospel: the

Holy Alliance. Alexander, as the Spanish envoy to Paris declared, had no character, but an extremely ardent imagination. Lord Castlereagh, the English foreign secretary, thought the Holy Alliance a "piece of sublime mysticism and nonsense," and he was probably right. But Alexander's fellow-monarchs signed it (Britain did not). Along with the Congress system of regular international conferences that accompanied it, Julie de Krüdener's sublime mysticism had created a precedent, first for the League of Nations, then for the United Nations.

Sainte-Beuve published two essays on the lady in the *Revue des Deux Mondes*, one in 1837, the other in 1849. His Julie is an elegant, vain, dissipated socialite and a voguish author. He attributed her religio-mystical enthusiasm to "faith and illusion, that is sincerity," but also to a beautiful woman's middle-aged shift from worldliness to other-worldliness and from one kind of tender-heartedness to another—piety being the last of our love affairs.[35] One might add that great wealth makes both piety and prophecy more acceptable. Nevertheless, when she died, not quite sixty years old, the flagging prophetess was about to set up a colony for repentant sinners.

APOCALYPSE IN
WORLDLY TIMES

On a des devins quand on n'a plus de prophètes,
des sortilèges quand on renonce aux cérémonies
religieuses, et l'on ouvre les antres des sorciers
quand on ferme les temples du Seigneur.

‒ FRANÇOIS-RENÉ DE CHATEAUBRIAND

One has fortune-tellers when one has no more prophets,
spells when religious ceremonies are abandoned, and the
lairs of witches open when the temples of the Lord are closed.

MOST TEXTBOOKS agree that the nineteenth century was a heyday of secularism: science, technology, reform, and education banished, or at least marginalized, superstition. But secularization had its limits. What one calls superstition, another calls belief, and the marvels of modernity often served to spread and publicize marvels familiar to pre-modern days. This dissemination applied especially to what Tolstoy described as "the most powerful weapon of ignorance: the diffusion of printed material."[1] Penny handbills and broadsheets circulated widely, offering information and misinformation accessible to all, now made more attractive by lurid illustrations. Murders, monsters, massacres, and miracles offered both thrills and edification, as when a penny rag of 1835 explained that year's comet in reassuringly scientific terms while publicizing its fearsome implications.[2]

Comets were favorites of the popular press, which doused the fires of fear with astronomical information and fanned anxiety with reference to menaces it disdained. We have encountered the panic that rumors of a destructive comet caused in 1773. Doomsday predictions surged again in 1816, 1832, 1857, and 1861, to be explained away but never put to rest. Earnest appeals to reason reveal widespread nervousness and seem to revel in it. A broadsheet about the comet of 1843 attests to traditional fears that it engendered: "We have been hearing a lot about the end of the world; such rumors might well be justified by this swift and gigantic comet." "Don't be afraid," runs a ballad of that year. "Some say it's done: the Heavens have poured their wrath on us and all will end. To work [God's] will, destructive fires will burn all the earth."[3]

Disaster lore was not limited to the skies. Print continued to broadcast prophecies and calculations of religious enthusiasts whose millenarianism increasingly coincided with progressive aspirations. One of these, whose millenarian expectations called for the end of vice, misery, and ignorance and the spread of true religion, righteousness, happiness, and peace, was James Bicheno, a dissenting minister and schoolmaster in the English Home Counties, who attributed the number of the Beast, 666, to Louis XIV, interpreted Daniel's prophecies to pinpoint 1789, 1819, and 1864 as crucial years, and expected the millennium to begin this last year. But Bicheno was far from alone. Preparing for imminent events, Lady Hester Stanhope (1776–1839), a niece of William Pitt the Younger, in whose house she proved herself a brilliant political hostess, left London for the Lebanon in 1810 to be nearer to the expected Advent. Until her death, she always kept two Arab steeds in her stables, one for the Messiah and one for herself.[4]

In 1815 and 1816, the eruptions of an Indonesian volcano, Mt. Tambora, filled the world's skies with volcanic dust and reduced incoming sunlight, so that 1816 was full of incomprehensible climatic disturbances. An abnormally cold spring and summer affected crops and health throughout the West, produced famine, and encouraged more grim forecasts. One millennialist, William Ward, concluded that the coming of the Lord had been visibly advanced and might be expected between 1830 and 1833 (or 1835). Another Ward, John, "the True Believer," who published more than forty millennial pamphlets, was convinced that the millennium had already begun, and dated his publications year 6 of the millennium, year 7 , and so on. I cannot tell which of the two was the enormously popular Zion Ward, found guilty of blasphemy at Derby in 1832 "and with a fellow prophet imprisoned for two years." But E.P. Thompson cites him in the context of a "revival of messianic movements during the excitement of Reform Bill agitation and its aftermath."[5]

The great Reform Act of 1832 was the first of a series of measures that gradually expanded electoral rights to ever more numerous portions of the British public. It came in the wake of a similarly moderate measure in France and, like it, disappointed more people than it pleased. But it also came in the middle of a great plague that struck Europe with fear and trembling: the cholera. When cholera came to England, yet one more sign of God's approaching judgment, prayers became as prominent as prophylaxis. A day of fast and repentance was appointed to avert "the coming storm," which it apparently did, though "the destitute and reckless class" in England, Scotland, and Ireland counted over 50,000 dead (in 1848 a worse outbreak killed nearly 100,000).[6] This was the atmosphere when, in 1838, at the beginning of Queen Victoria's reign, Sir William Courtenay, the popular lunatic, rode around Kentish villages denouncing the injustice of the new Poor Law of 1834 as a breach of divine law, and preaching from the most apocalyptic passages of the epistle of James that "the coming of the Lord draweth nigh" (5:8). Having killed a constable sent to arrest him, Courtenay marshaled his followers to resist the troops that had been sent against them, sounded a trumpet to be heard in Jerusalem, and announced that, if killed, he would rise again. He died along with a dozen others, but failed to return as promised.[7]

The old-time religion now had a novel religion to bolster its awesome message. Romanticism had invented ruins, the religion of beauty, and the religion of religion. The Romantics suffered from contemporary society: its materialism, rationalism, functionalism, capitalism, and liberalism. Their rejection of these qualities coincided with that of contemporary pietism, which also deprecated material concerns and emphasized higher aspirations and revelations. Ancient myth and epic were sources of inspiration, but so were the Scriptures and the esoteric interpretation of their eschatological predictions. One representative of this trend was Friedrich von Hardenberg (1772–1801), better known by his pseudonym, Novalis, who concluded that only magic could interpret experience. Brought up in a pietist household, he delved into the writings of Jakob Boehme and of Paracelsus, and into the texts attributed to the probably mythical founder of Rosicrucianism: Christian Knorr von Rosenroth. Rosenroth's *Proper Exposition of the Aspects of the Book of Revelation* (1680) was a cabbalistic elucidation of apocalyptic numerology that concluded with the fall of the idolatrous Roman Church and the establishment of Christ's millennium in 1860.

Novalis is better remembered by the blue flower that one of his heroes dreamt about, and which became a symbol of Romantic love and longing. But his contemporary influence was more directly religious. He urged his readers to consult Revelation in this, the final, age, which was to be followed by "a coming history and a coming humanity." And a historical essay that he wrote in 1799 preached a new unified religion: "It will come, it must come, the holy time of eternal peace, where the new Jerusalem will be the capital of the world."[8] *Christianity or Europe* was published in 1826, a quarter-century after its author's death. But, circulated in manuscript, it affected many a sensitive soul and spurred heterodox dreams of a Christianity that would bring together all followers of Christ, regardless of their church.

This Biblical inspiration affected the future folklorist and mythologist Joseph von Görres (1776–1848), who started out as an ardent republican and supporter of the French Revolution and ended up as ardent a Catholic, believing the world to be in its last age and prophesying "the final resurrection and supreme judgment" of "the dead and dispersed elements of the present."[9] More notably, it affected the Schlegel brothers, August and Frederic, sons of a hymn-writing pastor with literary aspirations and great propagandists of the Romantic school. Fascinated by Genesis and by Revelation (as by Jakob Boehme), Frederic von Schlegel (1772–1829) delved into apocalyptic chronology and numerology, pursuing sacred signs and numbers that would reveal the coming of end days and of the Judgment, which he impatiently expected.[10] His *Lectures on Universal History* attributed European conflicts to Antichrist; and his letters reflect growing belief in imminent catastrophe, after which the new world order would mark the end of secular history and a glorious revival, perhaps in 1836.[11]

Those familiar with early nineteenth-century Europe, secular or religious, will recognize themes familiar to those times. Romanticism, which often calls for rejuvenation and revival, is also about the twilight and the trials that precede them. This duality comes out well in Caspar David Friedrich's *A Walk at Dusk*, painted in the early 1830s, where a shadowy character, perhaps the artist himself, stands between a megalithic gravestone, symbol of death, and the waxing moon, symbol of Christ's resurrection. Once again, the Romantic cult of terror and of mysticism, of Satan and his train of violence, monsters, and darkness, drank deeply from the more lurid passages of the Bible. Romantic imagery illustrates these strains, now tenebrous, now flaring. One thinks at once of William Blake, fed on Bunyan and on the Apocalypse: not a Romantic, certainly, but one of their inspirations. Yet there were other artists, less well known today, like Philippe-Jacques de Loutherbourg—who died in 1812, a member of the Royal Academy in England, alchemist, and illustrator of the Bible—whose industrial paintings look like volcanic eruptions. William Turner was haunted by disasters, avalanches, storms, and Biblical scenes, while John Martin, another illustrator of the Bible, portrayed cataclysms on a cosmic scale: *The Last Judgment* and *The Day of His Wrath*. James Ward always knelt to pray before laying brush to monumental canvases depicting catastrophic storms, rivers of fire, and radiant clouds; Francis Danby made his reputation with Biblical scenes like *The Opening of the Sixth Seal*; and Benjamin Robert Haydon, desperate at his inability to capture his visions, cut his throat in 1846, leaving his diary open at Matthew's description of the Last Judgment.

English and Irish painters had few continental imitators but many admirers. Martin's *Deluge* won a gold medal in Paris in 1834, and his dark engravings and illustrations of Milton and the Bible affected artists like Gustave Doré and the American Thomas Cole. Their intense contrasts of light and shade, their violent and supernatural subject matter, fitted the mood of pre- and post-revolutionary Storm and Stress, fed on Satan's rebellion and its occult fallout.

Nor did apocalyptic references lose their appeal with time. One of the most popular religious paintings of the nineteenth century, William Holman Hunt's much-copied *Light of the World* (1853), illustrated a verse from Revelation. The year after its exhibition, Robert Mackay's *Rise and Progress of Christianity* referred to the time's "crazy infatuation with prophecies."[12] As if to confirm Mackay's impression, George Eliot, long enchanted by apocalyptic vaticinations, would begin *Romola* in 1860: all about Savonarola's Florence, prophets, and false prophets.[13]

Like the Florentine revolution of the fifteenth century, the

French Revolution of the eighteenth had been an apocalyptic event. And Napoleon, an Antichrist to some, was a messiah figure for others. In this perspective, Waterloo looks like a hiccup in an ocean of expectations, some religious, some adapting the idiom of religion to more secular millenarianisms. Politics and faith interlaced, as the claims to the French throne of spurious but persistent claimants were asserted by a variety of prophets. In 1816, at Gallardon not far from Chartres, a peasant called Thomas Martin was visited in his field by a gentleman who turned out to be the archangel Raphael. Martin was to tell first Louis XVIII, then Charles X, that their brother's son still lived and, under the name of Naundorff, was the legitimate King of France. In the fraught early 1830s, when cholera and rebellion vied for the attention of troubled Frenchmen, Martin's obscure but apocalyptic prophecies were resurrected or invented to predict more plagues and calamities: "the time draws near . . . gloom, evils . . . day of execution . . . scourges about to strike, the massacre will be general throughout France."[14]

A covey of strange prophets, such as Pierre-Eugène Vintras, who had to be condemned by papal briefs of 1843 and 1851, would spring up in the wake of "Martin l'Archange," announcing the reign of the Holy Spirit and producing curious miracles such as bleeding hosts. By the 1840s, Louis Reybaud's Jérome Paturot would find that wherever he set foot, he stepped on a messiah.[15]

Paris and its neighborhood were not the only seedbeds of prophecy. In Forez, again, small groups of Jansenists and *jansénisants* maintained their prophetic beliefs in the coming of a new Elijah and the triumphant advent of the Holy Spirit. At Saint-Jean-de-Bonnefonds near Saint-Étienne, where in 1792 the local priest announced the Messiah's imminent appearance, believers in his coming were known as *béguins* (bigots?). In the 1840s, their stubborn faith was rewarded by the appearance of an elderly peasant from the nearby Haute-Loire, Jean-Baptists

Digonnet, who proclaimed himself messiah, Christ, and God, predicted the imminent end of the world, and became known as *le petit Bon Dieu des béguins.* Three times arrested, Digonnet and his followers were tried in Assizes in July 1851, and the *petit Bon Dieu* eventually died in a Catholic hospice in 1857. But a shrinking band of believers kept his cult alive until the Second World War.[16]

Episodes of this sort can easily be dismissed as irrelevant, though nervous authorities in nervous times did not think so. But perfectly respectable magistrates like the Jansenist judge P.-J. Agier, or that other Jansenist and believer in Martin's revelations, Louis Silvy, a counselor in the Cour des Comptes who acquired and preserved the ruins of Port-Royal, studied the Scriptures to establish the Coming and noted that millenarian opinions "had much spread of late." Right they were. The healing Marian medal struck in 1832, following the Virgin's appearance to Catherine Labouré, depicted Mary in a pose evocative of the Woman Clothed with the Sun. Ten years later, when millions of such medals were in circulation, a manuscript of the eighteenth-century missionary Grignon de Montfort was discovered allegedly warning that the Second Coming was to be preceded by an Age of Mary. The Age of Mary had obviously arrived, and the Virgin who appeared to two shepherd children at La Salette in 1846 was pretty clear about it: "Here is the time of times, the end of ends."[17]

Madame de Staël's book on Germany, *De l'Allemagne* (1807), which was basic to the spread of Romanticism in France, included influential chapters on German religiousness and mysticism. It would be hard to say how far, or how fast, this volume turned a generation detached from spiritual concerns back to an Apocalypse briefly relegated to the back burner. Revelations abounded, and John of Patmos came back into fashion. Both Pierre-Simon Ballanche, the philosopher who reconciled Christian faith with revolution and Romanticism, and Félicité de Lammenais, the fervent priest, were millenarians. "A new era begins, a new age is rising," declared Ballanche in 1831; and that same year, Lammenais proclaimed that: "the last era of humanity begins."[18] New Age was in the air. Pierre-Jean Béranger, the most popular poet-songster of the century's first half, welcomed the world entering its Fourth Age, that of humanity, thanks to the influence of new prophets come to fulfill the work of Columbus and of Jesus.

For Lammenais, also, the end of times was nigh: "Hold yourselves ready," he warned, "the times are drawing near."[19] His *Paroles d'un croyant* (Words of a Believer, 1834) provided an updating of earlier prophecies offered in the spirit of primitive Christianity: punishment of the powerful and the rich, and glorification of the poor and the oppressed in a context of blood, great terrors, cries of horror and suffering. Such payoff reflected the reactions of a sensitive soul exasperated to see Jesus crucified in Rome, and relieved at last to see the angel of the Apocalypse raising his sword against those sons of Satan, the Roman clergy.

If Lammenais sometimes expressed himself in apocalyptic terms, the republicans and the socialists involved in the revolutions of 1848 *were* apocalyptic. In February 1848, a few days after King Louis-Philippe abdicated, a pamphlet addressed to republican Catholics called for the establishment of God's kingdom on earth, as Christ desired.[20] Republican eschatology also announced a new era; the best-known Christian Democratic periodical of 1848 was called *L'ère nouvelle*; and Christian representatives in the Assembly of 1848 described the new republic as a New World or the New Evangel Era. "The times of a new heaven and a new earth are near," wrote a workers' paper in January 1849. "That's when the Good News will be announced." Pauline Roland, high priestess of the recently founded Social Church, announced "the Good News," as did sympathetic Social Christians (or Christian Socialists) like the abbé Chantôme, a follower of Buchez who expected a new Pentecost very soon.[21]

How much of this was Christian spirit, and how much Christian vocabulary unavoidable in cultures steeped in the Scriptures? Probably a bit of both. Romantics had drawn heavily on Christianity. Their progressivism retained apocalyptic fear and trembling, adapted to the redemptive value of suffering. Nations suffered like Christ, peoples suffered like Christ, and the People suffered like Christ—and would triumph like him. The spirit of the Sermon on the Mount inspired the new Christianity of the Romantics, as it would inspire the post-Christian romanticism of the nineteenth-century socialists. But the spirit of Patmos inspired contemporary nationalists as well. When, around 1848, Poles, Italians, and Serbs asserted for themselves the role of Christ among the nations, they alluded to the Resurrection and to the Second Coming. But the reference had been around for some time, notably in speculations and claims made by Polish refugees from Russian repression after their rising of 1831.[22]

In 1839, for example, a vision of the Virgin and a revelation of the Holy Ghost told André Towianski, a Lithuanian refugee in Paris, to act as one of the messengers of the Apocalypse, preaching the end of time and the hour of divine grace. Three peoples—Jews, French, and Slavs—would play leading roles in this process; but it was the crucial role that Towianski attributed to Napoleon, natural in a Polish patriot, that probably persuaded Louis-Philippe to expel him from France and, soon after, to deprive Towianski's main disciple of his chair of Slavic literature at the Collège de France. Poet and mystic, Adam Mickiewicz (1798–1855) considered himself designated by God to be the forerunner of his homeland's liberation. Poland's resurrection would usher in the millenarian reign of world happiness waiting around the corner. Mickiewicz's explanation of the long *Pilgrimage of the Polish Nation* (1832) and of its significance for Christendom had been prefaced by the Count of Montalembert, for whom Poland, "the Christ of nations," was "the [sacrificial] victim chosen from Above to wash off with its blood the sins of modern society, and to buy that liberty for which the world thirsts."

In 1842, a two-volume work on *The Official Church and Messianism* presented Towianski's (and Mickiewicz's) expectations to the French public and evoked a searing rejoinder. *The New Montanists at the Collège de France* denounced the would-be prophets of a new, dangerously radical redeemer: Towianski, Mickiewicz, but also Edgar Quinet, Jules Michelet, and, for good measure, Georges Sand. Montanus was the second-century prophet who had announced the imminent descent of Jerusalem onto the Phrygian plain. But the list of "Montanists" associated with the politics of social reform and social justice made clear that salvation now involved liberation: liberty both national and social. Lammenais, who wrote a "Hymn to Poland," had assured his friend Montalembert that the republicans of their day would have been the most ardent disciples of Christ in Christ's day. And Mickiewicz found occasion to tell the pope himself that God's spirit nowadays dwelt within the Paris workers, struggling to be free as Poles wished to be free.

The Jews: An Interlude

Somewhat strange in a Pole or Lithuanian, but naturally enough for a Bible-reader, Towianski had looked to Jews, along with French and Slavs, to advance the eschatological progress he hoped for soon. Jews had a crucial role to play in the Second Coming: restored as a nation to their ancient homeland, they would recognize Jesus as messiah and king. And so tradition linked the onset of the millennial age to the restoration of a Jewish kingdom in Zion. The belief, known as Restorationism, that the 1000-year reign of Christ on earth could not begin until this happened, went back a long way—quite possibly to the first century. So Christians who denounced the Jews for denying Christ also believed that they would be converted, either just before Antichrist appeared or just before the Second Advent. Traditional exegesis had Elijah (or Enoch and Elijah) serving as agents of this conversion, and the conversion itself signaling the coming of Christ. That was one reason for the violent hostility shown to Jews whose stubborn refusal to convert delayed the Second Coming; but it also explained the interest and sympathy shown to a people whose future actions were indispensable to the final salvation of the world.

The latter version went down well in England, where the English had been apprised since the sixteenth century that they were God's chosen people, and perhaps a remnant of Israel's ten lost tribes. "Caucasian," a term dear to the United States Immigration Service, probably originated with nineteenth-century British Israelism, which believed that descendants of these tribes had migrated over the Caucasus Mountains to become Anglo-Saxon peoples. Like Richard Brothers before him, Sir William Courtenay had presented himself as King of the Jews; and at least two seventeenth-century prophets had proposed to lead the Jews back to Jerusalem. Less deranged than they, Joseph Priestley, the apocalyptic chemist, had addressed several letters to Jews. Nothing much came of these efforts, but beliefs of this kind weighed in the passing of the English Toleration Act of 1689, as in the Naturalization Bill of 1753, passed in May and repealed in December, which Whigs supported in the hope that it would encourage conversion by the Jews.

Jansenists also tended to look upon the Jews with sympathy. Author of a *Hebraic Bible* (1753), the Oratorian priest Charles-François Houbigant, despite dismay at the excesses of Jansenist convulsionaries, professed conversion of the Jews and their temporal reign in a flourishing Zion just before the end of the world. He placed that in the twentieth century, with Antichrist appearing in 1932, to be finally vanquished by Elijah, precursor of Jesus Christ. When, in 1791, the National Assembly emancipated the

"Jewish nations" (Henri Grégoire, who in 1788 had pressed the Jewish case, was one of their champions), believers announced that their regeneration was at hand. Jews would return to Palestine, the desert would bloom again, new cities would spring up, and the weather would change, ready for the new heaven and earth to come. Napoleon's Palestine campaign of 1798, and the Sanhedrin (or high council of rabbis) that he called together some years later, seemed to lend credence to such hopes as well as bolstering rival images of Napoleon himself, an Antichrist to many, and, to others, a Messiah.[23]

The London Society for Propagating Christianity among the Jews was founded in 1809, and the millennialist color of its propaganda fitted well with the evangelical wave that swelled through Britain in the early part of the century. The leadership of the society comprised the fine flower of English politics, money, and religion. It included the stout opponent of the slave trade, William Wilberforce, and his ally Zachary Macaulay, editor of *The Christian Observer* and father of the famous historian; Lord George Bentinck, second son of the Duke of Portland and future patron of Benjamin Disraeli; and Anthony Ashley Cooper, later seventh Earl of Shaftesbury, leader of campaigns to shorten the working day, keep women and young boys out of mines, educate poor children, found Young Men's Christian Associations, and other excellent causes.[24]

But what good causes brought together, political and religious differences could sunder. Reasonably enough, Lord Ashley and other Restorationists opposed Jewish emancipation precisely because they wanted Jews to convert and return to Zion. When, in 1830, a bill was introduced to allow Jews elected to Parliament to take their seats without a Christian oath, the London Society split: some of its most eminent figures led the fight for the bill in Lords and Commons, while others like Bentinck and Ashley (both of whom had championed Catholic emancipation shortly before) led the opposition to it.

The division was more about competition between Whigs and Tories, and protection or free trade for the land. But Jews were a convenient football, and they were kept out of the House of Commons until 1858, and out of the Lords till 1866, when at last the oath that members of parliament were required to swear no longer included the words "on the true faith of a Christian." Long before then, the London Society had refocused on a goal on which all members could agree: Jerusalem. Lord Ashley was married to a daughter of Lady Emily Cowper, mistress of the powerful British foreign minister, Palmerston, before she became his wife in 1839. In 1837, responding to the requests of Ashley and Thomas Baring, a member of the banking family that had helped finance Britain's war effort against France, Palmerston instructed the British consul general in Alexandria to install a vice-consul in Jerusalem, accredited (as Ashley jubilantly noted in the *Quarterly Review*) "to the former kingdom of David and the Twelve Tribes."[25]

The kingdom of David, as usual, was a pawn of broader political games in which, in 1840, Britain faced down France over Egypt (and Syria and Palestine) and won. It was in that context that Palmerston developed a pragmatic Restorationism of his own, informing the British ambassador in Constantinople that "there exists among the Jews dispersed over Europe a strong notion that the time is approaching when their nation is to return to Palestine." Supporting this stand, the London *Times* reported that remnants of the ten tribes had been discovered "on the south-west shores of the Caspian, enclosed in a chain of mountains," and that the 1260-year delay was "not very far from its termination." It proposed a kingdom of Jews to be ruled by Prince George of Cambridge, married—why not?—to a daughter of the King of France.[26] All this would come to nothing, but another benign evangelical conspiracy did better.

German pietists also entertained eschatological hopes of Jewish conversion. Heinrich Johann Richter (1799–1847), the great organizer of missions to Borneo, South Africa, and the North American Indians, who founded the Rhine-Westphalia Society for the Conversion of Israel, died before the auspicious day that he expected to dawn in 1847. But a like-minded compatriot had better luck. Christian Karl Bunsen, a liberal Prussian diplomat and theologian married to an Englishwoman, had served as Prussian minister to the Vatican between 1824 and 1838, then as minister to England, 1841–54, where he wrote his best-known work, *Signs of the Times* (1855). It was this ardent Restorationist who persuaded Ashley, Palmerston, the Archbishop of Canterbury, and his own king, the romantic Frederic William IV, to back the establishment of an Anglo-Prussian bishopric in Jerusalem. The first bishop, a Jewish convert named Michael Solomon Alexander, would be ordained by the Archbishop of Canterbury in 1841. "So the beginning is made," wrote Bunsen to Ashley in July of that year, "please God, for the restoration of Israel."[27]

The restoration of Israel would take a little longer. But prophecy believers in Britain and the United States "helped lay the intellectual groundwork for the Zionist movement launched by Theodore Herzl at the 1897 World Zionist Congress in Basel." There were Jewish foundations for Zionism, and some of them were also millenarian and messianic. But one cannot discount the evangelical impulse either. In 1891, for example, a petition signed by over four hundred eminent Americans, including Cyrus McCormick, J.P. Morgan, and John D. Rockefeller, urged President Benjamin Harrison to advance "the purpose of God concerning His ancient people" by supporting the cause of a Jewish state in Palestine. An Israeli forest is dedicated to one of the petition's organizers, William Eugene Blackstone, regarded as a founder of Zionism.[28]

But if the Israelitish tradition proved influential, especially among Anglo-Saxon readers of the Bible, a rival tradition dominated the Continent. Its source was the same as that of the

Restorationists: the need for Jewish cooperation in the fulfillment of eschatological prophecy. From this, conclusions hostile
to the Jews could as easily, indeed more easily, be drawn as sympathetic ones. Conversion of the Jews was a necessary step
toward the millennium, the defeat of Antichrist, and the Lord's
return in glory. But, notoriously, the Jews refused to convert—a
stance that explains the exasperation of those who massacred or
otherwise took revenge on this stiff-necked people.[29]

The straightforward resentment of Jewish hostility to Christ
and to Christ's people became complicated when Christian
commentators made Antichrist himself a Jew or, at least, identified his hosts as Jewish. When, in the mid-fourteenth century,
Sir John Mandeville invented the colorful travel tales that left
their mark on Chaucer and on Shakespeare, he reflected the
popular identification of Gog and Magog with the lost tribes of
Israel pent up behind Alexander's fabled Caspian Gates, to be
released in the last days to slaughter Christians. Since Gog and
Magog spoke only Hebrew, Mandeville explained that the Jews
of Europe were already learning Hebrew "to leden him in to
cristendom for to destroye the cristene people."[30]

Augustine had maintained that Elijah would return in the last
days and help convert the Jews.[31] Luther, who did not like Jews
at all, had no particular need for them in his scenarios of the end,
where Turks, a clearer and more present danger, replaced them
as Satan's acolytes. When Luther identified the pope with
Antichrist and Rome with Babylon, anti-Semites were set free
to focus on more worldly social and economic reasons for hating
the Jew. But the French Revolution, which revived millennial
dreams, also reminded Catholics of their Jewish nightmares;
and defenders of an embattled church were to keep the image of
anti-Christian Jews firmly in their sights.

Within a few years of 1789, the Jesuit abbé Barruel, an exile
in London, had revealed the masonic origins of the devilish
revolution. But Barruel had not insisted sufficiently on Jewish

responsibility for revolutionary horrors (no wonder: there were practically no Jews involved). A well-intentioned correspondent remedied that when he explained that Templars, Illuminati, rationalists, philosophers, and members of subversive reading societies were nothing but catspaws of an age-old Jewish conspiracy that lay behind the overthrow of the Bourbon monarchy, as it had also lain behind the American Revolution. The Simonini letter, so-called after the name of its spurious writer, was probably a forgery of Fouché's police; but it was right on target. In 1807, Napoleon's calling of the Sanhedrin demonstrated his role as Antichrist and false messiah in cahoots with Jews. The serviceable legend of a Jewish conspiracy never looked back.[32]

The papacy itself, at first unimpressed by such meretricious hoaxes, could not long ignore the link between Jews, who were bad, and the revolution that liberated them, which was even worse. In February 1798, after Pius VI had been moved out of Rome, the slums of the city rose against the occupying French, killing what soldiers they laid hands on, but also slaughtering the Jews who had been liberated from the ghetto. Leo XII (1823-29), the puritan avenging angel of reaction, made Jews particular targets, ordering them back into ghettos, forbidding them to own real estate, requiring them once more to attend special weekly sermons designed to convert them. The austere Gregory XVI (1831-46), his successor, though no better, was forced to negotiate a Rothschild loan and hence to ease Jewish conditions a bit. Pius IX, who introduced railroads and gaslights, also eased control of the Jews. But 1848 turned papal liberalism into dark reaction: Italy first, Christendom next, became arenas of apocalyptic struggle between the forces of good, led by the pope, and the forces of evil, represented by states Pius disapproved of (Italy first, then philosemitic Britain, Prussia, and France), but also by nationalists, radicals, masons, and their allies the Jews. The papacy in Italy, and the Catholic Church in France, Italy, and Germany felt themselves under siege from the forces of modernity, and they reacted by demonizing them. Published in 1869, on the eve of the Vatican Council of 1870, Gougenot des Mousseaux's *The Jew, Judaism and the Judaization of Christian Peoples* revived medieval views of Jews as agents of Satan and prophesied the coming of a Jewish Messiah/Antichrist. The author was blessed by Pius IX for his courage.

French eschatologists like the Paris priest Pierre Lachèze had published more or less standard works on *The Apocalypse* (1840), *The End of Days* (1841), and *The Return of the Jews and the Apocalypse* (1846), predicting the restoration of the Jerusalem temple for 1892 and Doomsday in 1900. But such scenarios continued the Restorationist vein. Des Mousseaux, and his epigone the abbé Chabauty writing in the 1880s, compulsively linked masons, Jews, the Jewish Antichrist, and Satan's coming world dominion. The Judeo-masonic peril had a great future that would be realized in the writings of Édouard Drumont and culminate in the policies of Vichy.

One champion whom Drumont's *France juive* (1886) aroused to defend "this marvelous people . . . this energetic and vigorous race" to whom Christianity owed its religious doctrines was a Spanish theosophist married to a Scottish earl. Maria Mariategui Sinclair, Duchess of Pomar, Countess Caithness, was a keen observer of signs that pointed to the imminent Second Coming and a firm believer in the identification of the lost tribes of Israel with the ancestors of the British people: the Irish probably descended from Simeon, the Danes from Dan, and the Normans from Benjamin. Long a recipient of revelations from on high, Lady Caithness regarded the coming end as good news, with the Jews and their British descendants among its foremost harbingers. But connecting one detested people with another could only inflame Drumont's ire further; and far more people read Drumont than ever heard of Lady Caithness.[33]

Norman Cohn has shown the relation between the spate of publications set off by des Mousseaux and Drumont and the rise of a venomously political anti-Semitism in the West. He has also described the rise of the enormously influential fable of the Protocols of the Sages of Zion, produced at the turn of the century by the Russian mythomaniac and mystic Sergei Nilus. Obsessed by the imminence of Antichrist's coming, Nilus first published *The Great in the Small: Antichrist Considered as an Imminent Political Possibility* in 1901, and kept improving it edition by edition. The third edition of the work contained the alleged *Protocols* of secret meetings of Jewish leaders conspiring to achieve dominion of the world. To a French student of the Russian Orthodox Church who visited him in 1909, Nilus explained that, at that very moment, the *Protocols* were being fulfilled: "The mysterious sign of the coming Antichrist appears on all sides . . . the imminent advent of his kingdom can be felt everywhere." The sixth revised edition of *The Great in the Small* was published in 1917 under the title *He Is Near, at the Door . . . Here Comes Antichrist and the Reign of the Devil on Earth.*[34]

But this work is not about anti-Semitism, which is a long-running plague; it is about end-of-the-worldism, which is another. We have seen that Jews sometimes attain high visibility as harbingers of the end; most of the time, however, all they get is walk-on parts or silence. Gérard de Nerval, for example, strikingly representative of Romanticism in his appreciation of the exotic and fantastic, of irrationalism and occultism, translated *Faust* in the 1820s and brought back wild theories about Solomon and Sheba from the Orient, but showed no interest in Jews. In the spring of 1853 he went to see his friend, Heinrich Heine, whose poems he was translating into prose, and told him he had come to return the cash advance he had received for the work because the times were accomplished and the end of the world was at hand. Heine sent for a cab, and Nerval spent the following months in Dr. Dubois's clinic.[35]

It is not clear whether other mid-century eschatologists were deranged.[36] But plenty of works by clerics and nonclerics testify to sustained interest in the millennium and the Second Coming. Some millenarians, repelled by Napoleon III's failure to support the pope, even cast him as Antichrist. What is clear is that the Franco-Prussian War of 1870–71 gave the old religion, replete with apocalyptic images, a philip. As early as 1871, a priest from war-scarred Lorraine, J.M. Curicque, brought out a new edition of his *Prophetic Voices* that cited all the familiar signs of doom: blasphemy abounding, Sundays profaned, comets, meteorites, sightings of flying serpents and armies battling in the skies, ciboriums crying tears, stigmatics, bleeding hosts, visions, apparitions, prodigies, miraculous cures, holy images emitting odors, pearling blood or tears, not to mention thorns growing out of St. Theresa's miraculously preserved hut.[37] The throng of visionaries and prophets inspired the Bishop of Orleans, Félix-Antoine Dupanloup, to issue a *Letter on the Prophecies* (1874) warning against those who interpreted the Apocalypse in the light of Nostradamus: "A whole generation gluts itself on chimeras . . . trembles before calamities forecast, as before the coming of the year 1000."

But prophecies soldiered on, and many carried political overtones. At Pellevoisin in the Indre, in one of those small "Vendées" that withstood the French Revolution, and where the village priest had been guillotined in 1793, a maiden's visions of the Virgin set off a flow of pilgrims to her shrine. Estelle Faguette's sanctuary of the 1870s still stands close to the grave where Georges Bernanos rests today. Other women have been forgotten. But at Fraudais, in the Loire-Inférieure, Marie-Julie, stigmatist and visionary, repeated messages received from the Virgin and St. Michael predicting the victory of evil, terrible woes, the burning of Paris, and the coming savior. At Francoulès, near Cahors, Pauline Périé prophesied great woes followed by religious and royal restoration. And at Bouleret (Cher), Josephine Réverdy foretold great massacres, great public calamities, a great pope, and a great king of Naundorff's family.[38]

There were more like these women. As late as the 1890s, a voguish visionary, Henriette Couédon, was repeating the same dire message: rains of fire, earthquakes, famine, floods, schism, great pope, great king; but also the Jews cast out of the country to go and found a Jewish kingdom in the Holy Land. An angel had charged Couédon with a mission: to warn her fellows of the evils that threatened and to predict the return of the monarchy to France. Drumont wondered whether she was carrying out a mission, or simply "echoing preoccupations that floated in the air": fear of another uprising like the Commune of 1871 and hope of a royal restoration to replace the rickety Third Republic. *La voyante de la Rue de Paradis*, named for the street where Couédon lived in Paris, reflected some of the obsessions of her fashionable public, as her country counterparts echoed the sermons of provincial priests scandalized by a papacy besieged and an observance threatened. But Couédon also predicted the murderous fire of the Charity Bazaar in May 1897, and this foreknowledge impressed even skeptics like Émile Zola. As a recent chronicler of *Visionaries in France* has commented, the terrible fire "would be interpreted as the beginning of a necessary expiation, a sign of divine Providence."[39] One might add that the *voyante's* prophecies also fitted the predispositions of rabid anti-Semites like Édouard Drumont, who was well aware of the Jews' allotted role preceding the end of time; and that other eschatological scribbler, Gaston Méry, the city editor of Drumont's daily, *La libre parole*, who fought a duel on Couédon's behalf and founded a journal devoted to sorcery and to her: *L'écho du merveilleux*.

The Catholic Church of the 1870s was embattled on several fronts; and Germany, where Bismarck's offensive against political priests in school and pulpit created the *Kulturkampf*, was one of these fronts. As elsewhere, conflict produced not just outbursts of fanaticism on both sides but the usual visions and apparitions—notably in the village of Marpingen in the Catholic Saarland, which provided German believers with a shrine to compete with Lourdes and La Salette.[40]

The German novelist and playwright Gerhart Hauptmann was awarded the Nobel Prize for Literature in 1912. Two years before, he had published the story of *The Fool in Christ: Emanuel Quint*. It is about a peasant weaver of that name who thinks he is Christ. But the fictional Quint was not alone. Hauptmann explains that, about 1890, many Germans came to believe in the Last Judgment and "the approach of a millennium which was to change the earth into paradise."[41] Evidently, passion for prophecy was not restricted to Catholics. The cathedral of Metz, in German-occupied Lorraine, had been damaged in the war with France. When William II ordered its restoration, soon after his accession to the throne in 1888, he had its main portal adorned with his own likeness as Daniel the prophet. When, a decade later, the kaiser entered Jerusalem through a special opening made for him near the tower of David, he was riding a white horse, clad in a white mantle, with a gold crown on his head.

If William had strange ideas, he also had strange friends. One of his favorites, Helmuth von Moltke, nephew of the great soldier of identical name who defeated France, became chief of the General Staff in 1906 and, in that post, helped lose the First World War within its first few weeks. The younger Moltke was a close friend of Rudolf Steiner, the occultist founder of Anthroposophy, who "saw the descent of Christ as the redeeming cosmic event."[42] Steiner's rather confusing cyclical cosmology (it superposed "epochs" and "ages") had contemporary humanity living in Kali Yuga: the last, shortest, nastiest age in each Hindu world cycle. This dark age was due to end around the beginning of the twentieth century, and its successor would see the development (or redevelopment) of mankind's clairvoyant capacities.

Clairvoyance would have served Moltke well. The most recent historian of his role in German military planning has described his vision of the future as "dark, dominated by the belief in the inevitability of a coming war . . . Cosmic cycles of a millennial nature would bring the *Parousia*"[43]—the coming of Christ in glory. Moltke was far from exceptional in believing that a final showdown between the Triple Alliance and the Triple Entente was unavoidable and that, if Germany was to win, the showdown should come sooner rather than later. But his alleged belief in a Second Coming complicates the equation. Was the war that Moltke and his emperor nudged forward in 1914 meant to be Armageddon or, given the certainty of cosmic cataclysm, could its coming just be expected to happen? And how much of this thinking was shared by the messianic William II? We shall never know if the outbreak of the war that changed the modern world was spurred by eschatological dottiness, but serious historians doubt it.

Leaving the United States to a later chapter, Britain, that great Bible-reading nation, remained the home of eschatology. Signal evidence may be found in the British general who led the great 1918 drive northward out of Egypt to Damascus, by way of that natural battleground, the plain at the foot of the mountain of Megiddo, and who became Allenby of Armageddon.[44] Equally warlike, William and Catherine Booth's Christian Mission (to be renamed the Salvation Army in 1879) represented a fierce vision of the last days, in which the struggle against evil called for rigid discipline in the forces of good. In 1865, Sabine Baring-Gould's "Onward Christian Soldiers" reflected this apocalyptic view, as did the Salvation Army's crimson and blue flag bearing the motto "Blood and Fire!" and its own war song, "Come join our Army, to battle we go, Jesus will help us conquer the foe."

A less explicitly belligerent prophet was almost as effective. Older than the Booths, John Nelson Darby left the established church around 1830 to prepare for the approaching coming of

Christ. He joined and came to lead the Plymouth Brethren, who were dedicated to ascetic anticipation of the Parousia: "The expectation of Christ's return is the exact measure, the thermometer reading . . . of the life of the church." What Darby expected to the end of his days in 1882 was the proximate rapture of believers rising to meet Christ in the air, followed by the tribulation of remaining humans whom Antichrist would rule for seven years, after which the saints would return and Armageddon would usher in Christ's thousand-year reign on earth.

Plymouth Brethren were not very numerous, but their austere dedication helped them affirm themselves in many walks of life. Thus, Philip Edmund Gosse, the distinguished naturalist, taught his son Edmund to expect the return of Christ at any moment. "My father," remembered Edmund Gosse in *Father and Son* (1907), "awaited with anxious hope 'the coming of the Lord,' an event which he still frequently believed to be imminent. He would calculate, by reference to the prophecies of the Old and New Testament, the exact date of this event; the date would pass without the expected Advent, and he would be more than disappointed—he would be incensed. Then he would understand that he must have made some slight error in calculation, and the pleasures of anticipation would recommence." The boy proposed staying home from school, so that father and son could be together at the Second Coming. "Let me be with you when we rise to meet the Lord in the air!" It was no go. Even his father's faith had limits.[45]

Sir Robert Anderson, Scotland Yard's chief of criminal investigation around the turn of the century (he was involved in the pursuit of Jack the Ripper) and an enthusiastic student of prophecy, was also a Darbyite and firm believer in the Second Coming. His book, *The Coming Prince*, first published in 1884, was last reissued in 1986. But perhaps the best- (and least-) known member of the Brethren was Orde Charles Wingate, third-generation scion of a family of soldiers, "suckled on the strong milk of the Old Testament." Both Plymouth Brethren, Wingate's father and mother were passionate devotees of God and the Bible. The boy grew up amid "fierce shafts of revelation from the book" to keep him warm in a house otherwise "dark, gloomy, frugal in both food and affection"—a description borne out by Gosse's experience. But Wingate's mother also taught him that he must help the prophecies of the Bible come true and assist the Jews in returning to Palestine.[46]

Before he died in an air crash at the age of forty-one, Wingate had done his best to carry out his mother's mandate. While serving as intelligence officer in Palestine between 1936 and 1939, he organized *kibbutznik* night patrols to repel Arab raids on Jewish communities, and thus honed the methods of irregular warfare that helped him to liberate Abyssinia and cut Japanese communications in Burma. By 1944, when Wingate's plane crashed there, eschatology had been marginalized by current events. It came into its own with a bang in 1945, but it is worth noting one more version of nineteenth-century world-endness.

In 1859, the Frenchman Eugène Huzar published a work that would be read at least into the next decade: *The End of the World by Science*. History is cyclic, argued Huzar, and cycles invariably end in disaster because men challenge God, as Adam did and also Prometheus, brought down by hubris. Now, as in earlier days, the quest for science, fruit of the tree of knowledge, will prove self-destructive; and the greater the progress, the harder the fall. The advanced scientific civilization of the nineteenth century, Huzar concluded, runs fatally to its doom.[47]

Views like Huzar's had little currency in enlightened circles. Darwin also published his *Origin of Species by Natural Selection* in 1859, and John Stuart Mill his *Essay on Liberty*. That same year, John Brown, the American abolitionist, was hanged after his abortive raid on Harper's Ferry. Addressing the Association of German Scientists soon after, a young zoologist from the University of Iena, Ernst Haeckel, equated Darwin, evolution and progress: "Progress is a natural law that no human power . . . can ever succeed in suppressing . . . The future belongs only to progress."[48]

But evolution and progress made some people uneasy. The time of the end described in Daniel 12:4 was one when "many shall run to and fro and knowledge shall be increased." Schools, roads, railroads, postal services, mass-circulation newspapers, and unheard-of powers destructive and constructive suggested (once again) that the end was near. Tennyson espied "all things creeping to a day of doom." Ruskin's *Modern Painters* described elements of progress and decline as "strangely mingled" in the modern world. That was clear enough in the effect of the Second Law of Thermodynamics, which William Thomson, later Lord Kelvin, formulated in 1852. Sun and earth had been much hotter a million years before; they would be vastly colder a million years hence. Diffusion of heat would gradually reduce universal energy to a state of entropy, when no more thermal energy would be available for mechanical work and humans would be fated to die out.

Though generous enough in the delays proposed, especially when compared with those of most apocalyptists, Kelvin's forecasts, and those of other serious scientists who elaborated on them in the 1860s and 1870s, popularized visions of bleak last days to come. The world of Joseph Conrad, and of Thomas Hardy, was "blighted" or about to be. In 1895, Brooks Adams's *Law of Civilization and Decay* articulated this vision and lamented the degeneration of the times. Morose expectations became commonplace. In the prologue that he wrote in 1896 to Bousset's now-classic *Antichrist Legend*, A.H. Keane, vice-president of the London Anthropological Institute, made this gloomy expectation clear:

We all know how the rage for expounding [the books of Daniel and Revelation] breaks out at intervals, and especially how it has tended to assume the character of a virulent epidemic towards the close of each successive century of the Christian era. Symptoms are not wanting that as the present century approaches its end the intermittent fever will again reach its centennial crisis, and the advertising columns of the periodical press show that prophecy-mongering about the Antichrist and "the crack of doom" is already in the air.[49]

The world was growing old and weak, the stars were darkening, the firmament was contracting, and the sun was losing strength daily and sinking closer to the earth. Readers of Nostradamus expected the end of the world in 1886. Natural catastrophes seemed to confirm his forecast. In August 1883, the Indonesian island of Krakatau exploded with the force of ten thousand bombs of Hiroshima vintage. The blast was heard halfway across Australia, smoke rose 25 miles high, and 40,000 people were drowned in the tidal wave that followed. Closer to home, in February 1887, a serious earthquake in Nice was interpreted as a premonitory sign. On the Caribbean island of Martinique, the volcano Mt. Pelée had erupted in 1851 and 1892. When it exploded again in 1902, it destroyed St. Pierre, a town of 30,000.

That was the physical background for several publications in 1886: Barbey d'Aurevilly's *Les diaboliques* illustrated by Félicien Rops, Stanislas de Guaita's *Au seuil du mystère*, Jules Bois's *Noces de Satan*, Drumont's *France juive,* and Nietzsche's *Gay Science*, with its madman crying out that God is dead. Léon Bloy, who never ceased to await the Second Coming, thought that anything one could write or say about that final consummation was less than nothing, yet produced an *Apocalypse*: "I thought that it might be useful, in view of the evident approach of the world's last days and under the threat of universal exterminations."[50]

Fortunately, in 1894, the astronomer Camille Flammarion had extended Kelvin's delays: the end of mankind was rescheduled for 10 million years away, the end of the sun would come 20 million years beyond that.[51] The longer respite was easier to face: one could regard more distant expiration dates more philosophically. By sheer coincidence, one would think, Mahler's Second Symphony, "The Resurrection," was first performed that year. It culminates in a Last Judgment early in the final movement, complete with four last trumps when "the shuddering earth opens its graves and releases [the dead] begging for mercy." A choral finale of divine redemption follows. There was hope after all. Or was there?

PURSUITS OF
THE MILLENNIUM

Go to now, ye rich men, weep and howl for your miseries
that shall come upon you. Your riches are corrupted . . .
your gold and silver is cankered; and the rust of them shall
be a witness against you, and shall eat your flesh as it were fire.
You have heaped treasures together for the last days.

– JAMES 5:1

IN THE TWENTIETH CHAPTER of the book of Revelation, an angel comes down from heaven, binds Satan for a thousand years, casts him into the bottomless pit, then shuts and seals it "that he should deceive the nations no more, till the thousand years be fulfilled." The *millennium* is that thousand years of peace, prosperity, happiness, and good government, during which the saints and Christ will reign on earth. *Millenarism, millennialism,* or *chiliasm* (from the Greek *khilivi,* 1000) is the belief in the coming of the millennium; and a *millenarian* is one who holds that belief.

In the fifth century, the Council of Ephesus decided that the millennium began with the birth of the church, but the notion of God's people preparing for that glorious advent, speeding its coming or helping to perfect it, persisted. The surrounding world was too blemished, the existing church too imperfect, rulers too delinquent, the signs of predicted doom too evident, for the orthodox doctrine to take hold. The prospect of a world regenerated, a new heaven, a new earth, an end of present suffering and anxiety was hard to resist. Hope for the day when the righteous would live and reign with Christ endured; restless, ardent, sometimes frantic, the imagery of Revelation went on being taken literally, or employed as references, suggestions, and figures of speech.

Since Norman Cohn's *Pursuit of the Millennium* (1957) and E.J. Hobsbawm's *Primitive Rebels* (1959), millennial ideas have been related to deprivation, protest, and the quest for radical change. Published in 1964, E.P. Thompson's *Making of the English Working Class* interprets nineteenth-century millennial movements as a pre-political "chiliasm of despair," introductory to the modern era of cooperatives, trade unions, and political action. Cohn's millenarians are disoriented, Hobsbawm's and Thompson's are wretched and discontent; all are presented as desperate and destructive in fancy or in fact. Since the works from which such chiliasts draw their inspiration were written or rewritten in truly terrible times—Daniel's during the megalomaniac Antiochus Epiphanes' persecutions of the Jews, Ezra's after the destruction of the temple, John's under Nero or Domitian or Vespasian—they naturally reflect fantasies of divine intervention leading to retribution and reward.

In the nineteenth century as in the first, millenarian extremism was a reaction to a sense of extremity, millenarian radicalism grew out of radical situations, and prophecy helped focus imagery that was vivid but imprecise. Closely linked to millenarianism, prophecy was suspect to civil authorities that feared its subversive effects, not least the expectation of an end to earthly government. Yet the Christian church itself is founded on prophecy. Christ, a prophet, came in fulfillment of Old Testament prophecies and, like his Old Testament predecessors, proved himself a disturber, an agitator, a critic of established authorities (scribes and pharisees) and of the [dis]order he denounced in a corrupt world. No wonder that Frederic Engels found in the history of early Christianity "notable points of resemblance with the modern working class movement."[1] The epigraph at the head of this chapter illustrates how readily revendicative rhetoric can shade into millennial speech, just as rebellion against conventional religious authority could shade into rebellion against conventional authorities.

What revolted above all was the discrepancy between reality and ideal; between what Christian society should be and sometimes claimed to be, and what went on around. Amid rampant disorder, longing for order could generate rampage and riot; with injustice abounding, attempts to reassert justice produced vengeance and retaliation. Justification could be found in the Scriptures: "Do not rich men oppress you, and draw you before the judgment seats?" asked the apostle James (2:6) before he concluded: "He shall have judgment without mercy, that showed no mercy."

"Seek and ye shall find" applies to the Scriptures as to the Yellow Pages. But while the New Testament is more benign than the Old, it does not lack for hard-boiled texts. In societies where Christianity saturated patterns of thought and speech, it was inevitable that rebels and radicals should use Christian terminology to express their criticisms and their claims. Worldly goals could be presented in religious terms because that was how they presented themselves to thinkers and speakers: vehicles for messages of the defeated, dejected, desperate, and disaffected. Millennial expectations and political radicalism fitted each other's needs. At the end of the eighteenth century, Richard Brothers preached that the proud and lofty shall be humbled, and the righteous and poor shall flourish. But his imagery of a river of blood running through London recalled Jansenist prophecies of blasphemous Paris burning and, even more, of the contemporary revolution as a scriptural predictor of the end. Brothers was confined to a lunatic asylum for fanatical prophecies intended to cause disturbance and dissension. One of his and Joanna Southcott's followers, Peter Morison, a visionary Liverpool cotton printer, was arrested for prophesying that, by the end of 1806, "there would be no hedge, nor even a brick standing . . . the clergy would be lost forever and would be like dung— for they were dumb dogs that did not bark—and all the property belonging to the rich would be taken away and given to the sealed people."

Riches were a property of the great Beast and therefore anti-Christian. Rank was a cause of woe. Milton described Antichrist as Mammon's son; John Bunyan described him as a gentleman. Respectability and a good reputation could be marks of perdition. "Woe unto you," Jesus had said, "when all men speak well of you" (Luke 6:26). Significantly, in *Pilgrim's Progress*, Mr. Worldly Wiseman directs Christian to find Mr. Legality in the village of Morality. There, Legality's son, Civility, would rent him a house at reasonable rates where he could live "with honest neighbors, in credit and good fashion." And thus it was that fervent Christians conjured up compensatory notions of retribution and redemption, while the insulted and the injured, harkening to them, looked to the millennium as to a comfortable antechamber where, reincarnated as saints, they could await the Last Judgment.

The sufferings of the oppressed designated them as elect. They would come into their own when the world was turned upside down. Medieval history, modern history, Jewish history, and Christian history are full of expectant, credulous, turbulent hewers of wood and drawers of water: husbandmen, tillers, shepherds, cowherds, swineherds, peddlers, weavers, *pastoureaux,* tafurs, flagellants, free spirits, beghards, *béguines*, Hussites, Taborites, Johannites, vessels of the Holy Spirit, incarnations of Elias, Enoch, the Messiah, and God himself, jostling toward apocalyptic emancipation.

The trouble was that most of these brow-beaten folk were less interested in the millennium per se than in the extermination that would precede it: the overthrow of oppressors, the annihilation of clergy and Jews, the end of the rich and fat. Their ecstasies and eruptions brought not peace but a pickax. From the twelfth century to the sixteenth and the seventeenth, while eschatological excitement ran high, crusades turned into massacres, and spiritual aspirations turned into social and political insurrections. When destiny long-postponed approached realization, the destiny was vengeance. Cohn quotes from pamphlets of the Münster Anabaptists for whom "the Third Age was to be the age of vengeance and triumph of the saints."[2] That's where the glory of too many saints lay: in wreaking vengeance. Rampant hate becomes more baleful when Biblical authority stands behind it.

But sixteenth-century Anabaptists followed fifteenth-century traditions. For the para-Hussite Taborites, who expected the Apocalypse in February 1420, when only Taborite settlements would be spared, massacre cleared the way to the millennium. Purge the corrupt earth of sinners, and Christ would descend in majesty while his saints soared up to greet him. Hans Böhm, who was burnt for heresy in 1476, proclaimed the village of Niklashausen the center of imminent world salvation, and preached not only repentance but also a tax-and-tithe strike, the expropriation of clerical property, and the restoration of agrarian communism. Thomas Münzer, the apocalyptic priest of the German Peasants' War, called for a war of extermination of the unrighteous by the righteous which would clear the decks for the Last Days at hand. Convinced that the struggle of the saints had begun, he placed himself at the head of peasant troops that were cut to pieces in 1525, and added his own life to those of the righteous dead. More pacific Anabaptists, like the Hutterites, also believed in common ownership of property. So did the seventeenth-century Levellers who, identifying social revolution and the advent of God's kingdom on earth, wanted to "level men's estates"; and the agrarian communist Diggers, for whom the kingdom of heaven was simply land returned to the common treasury of the original dispensation.

The idiom of such folk wasted away no more than their ideas. Makers of almanacs, the people's steadfast reading, were as familiar with the Bible as their customers, and much given to its turns of phrase. Thomas Hardy, the London shoemaker tried for high treason in 1794, was a "Jacobin," but explained himself in the language of the book of Kings: "What portion have we in the house of David?... Israel rebelled against the house of David." In 1801, English laboring men conspiring together were taking oaths based on Ezekiel and on their belief in the day "when iniquity shall have an end ... Remove the diadem, take off the crown ... exalt him that is low and abase him that is high." Like them, Gerrard Winstanley and his Levellers had also quoted the terrifying prophet: "I will overturn, overturn, overturn it: and it shall be no more, until he come whose right it is" (Ezekiel 21:27). "The sword, the sword is drawn ... for slaughter it is furbished." The same apocalyptic tone resounds in 1848: typically, the Chartist *Reformer's Almanac* prophesied, "Woe to the plundering Aristocrats ... the day of vengeance shall come ... the day is near."[3]

We shall find apocalyptic communism and communitarianism reproducing themselves in America's new-found lands, mostly in pacific guise after the example of Hutter, Menno, and Hans Hut. But as late as the end of the nineteenth century, Engels could remind his readers of the social revolutionary content, or at least possibilities, of revivalist Christianity. "The Salvation Army," he wrote in 1892, "which revives the propaganda of early Christianity, appeals to the poor as the elect, fights capitalism in a religious way, and thus fosters an element of early Christian class antagonism which one day may become troublesome for the well-to-do people who now find the ready money for it."[4]

George Bernard Shaw did not agree with this analysis, and wrote *Major Barbara* to say so. But because he liked pugnacious Christians, Shaw extolled the revolutionary content of the army's high-spirited joyousness. In the preface of the play that he finished in 1906, he praised "the transfigured men and women carrying the gospel . . . calling their leader General . . . and their whole body an Army: praying . . . for strength to fight. . . preaching, but not preaching submission . . . There is danger in such activity," he concluded; "and where there is danger there is hope."

Shaw had been born in 1856 into an Anglo-Irish gentry family, useless but cultivated, and little interested in religious practice. One generation younger, D.H. Lawrence, the son of a miner and a schoolteacher, had a much better sense of how religion worked in working-class families. So when, in an essay of the 1920s, he insists that Revelation, which he calls the least Christian book in the New Testament, "has had and perhaps still has more influence, actually, than the Gospels," he knows what he is talking about. The great epistles invite resignation; the Apocalypse provides denunciations, thrills, satisfactions: "It is very nice, if you are poor and *not* humble . . . to bring your grand enemies down to utter destruction and discomfiture, while you yourself rise up to grandeur." Of course, "this business of reigning in glory" is "only an expression of frustrated desire to reign here and now." And what would that be like? "The weak and pseudo-humble are going to wipe all worldly power, glory and riches off the face of the earth, and then they, the truly weak, are going to reign. It will be a millennium of pseudo-humble saints, and gruesome to contemplate."[5]

Norman Cohn described those who watched and worked for the millennium as "the unprivileged, the oppressed, the disoriented and the unbalanced."[6] His millenarians sound like paranoiac fanatics acting out shared delusional fantasies. But one can be paranoiac about real threats and evils too; and piety could drive protest as hard as errancy might do. The fascination exercised by promise of a happy humanity in a perfect world need not generate bloodthirsty chiliasm. It can as easily turn to the Sermon on the Mount, with its evocation of the birds of the air, the lilies of the field, benevolence, selflessness, and peace.

When he explained *The Restoration of the Jews* (1800), James Bicheno, whom we have met before, speculated on what the millennium would be like: vice, misery, and ignorance would end; true religion, righteousness, happiness, and peace would spread everywhere. Swords would be turned to ploughshares, spears into pruning hooks, every man would sit under his own vine (the prophet Micah's fig trees would sound too exotic), and none shall make them afraid. From gospel to social gospel is but one easy step. W.H. Oliver, a student of early nineteenth-century prophets and millenialists, makes the point that texts of this sort (Isaiah 2:4, Micah 4:4) were acquiring a social connotation.[7] And Biblical terminology did not necessarily mean belief. Often quite the contrary.

It is a tribute to the hold of Jewish and Christian vocabulary and imagery that most of the new, secular creeds of the nineteenth century used Christian references to announce their own apocalypse—the regeneration and the golden age that would follow the application of their sociopolitical recipes. One did not need to share "John's passionate and mystic hatred of the civilization of his time" to wish to change it.[8] The New Christianity preached by the Count of Saint-Simon, for example, presented him as the New Messiah, denounced the pope as Antichrist, expected God to annihilate harmful institutions, and insisted that Christianity was love, and that man's earthly goal was to apply it "for the amelioration of the lot of the poorest and most numerous classes in society."

Claude-Henri de Rouvroy, comte de Saint-Simon (1760–1825), had fought in the American War of Independence, had grown rich by speculation during the French Revolution, and had then become poor again. He became famous by preaching the coming of a New Age in which producers, inventors, and artists would lead mankind to the realization of Christian moral principles in a juster, more fraternal creation. For his followers, Saint-Simon was the third Messiah after Moses and Jesus; but they still awaited the female Messiah who would open the way to the world of scientific, industrial, technological, and moral progress. Lady Hester Stanhope was approached, but she declined the honor. On the other hand, and despite its eccentricities, the Saint-Simonian creed of progress made many converts; not least the future Napoleon III, the men who were to create France's banking system and its railway network, and Ferdinand de Lesseps, who cut the Suez Canal and almost did as much in Panama.

Utopia, no place, could be established some place, and it would spread from there to cover the world. The ideal state was spiritual, of course. Why not material, too? For Augustine, chiliasts like Papias, the second-century bishop who believed in the thousand years during which Christ's kingdom would be established on earth in material form, had had too "sensual," too substantial a vision of the reign of Christ; and the church agreed with Augustine. But the Christian people let church talk wash over them and retained visions of last things that were concrete, sensible, and imminent. Their heterodox and non-Christian heirs took over not only the visions but the language as well.

A long Christian revolutionary tradition suggested that the kingdom of God could be created not somewhere else, but in our own world changed by our own efforts.[9] In 1776, Tom Paine's *Common Sense* intimated as much: "We have it in our power to begin the world over again. A situation similar to the present has not happened since the days of Noah . . . The birthday of a new world is at hand."[10] Paine was agnostic before the word was coined; but is it too much to hear in these sentiments an echo of the Wesley brothers' hymn:

Begin the great millennial day;
Now, Saviour with a shout descend,
Thy standard in the heavens display,
And bring the joy which ne'er shall end?[11]

The Communist Manifesto warned against the temptation to lump together Christianity and socialism. "Christian Socialism is but the holy water with which the priest consecrates the heart burnings of the aristocracy."[12] If warnings were necessary, the inclination must have been there. And it is true that Christian Socialists like Frederic Maurice and Charles Kingsley, both clergymen and both professors first at King's College, London, then at Cambridge, wanted to tap "the communism implied in the church's origins and existence" to promote social justice, reconciliation, unions, and cooperatives.[13]

But more than gentlemanly hearts burned over social injustice; and Friedrich Engels, always more sensitive than his famous friend, noted the proclivity of socialists, communists, and social reformers of all kinds to find their inspiration in the Scriptures: "Le christianisme c'est le communisme."[14] That was quite literally so for Wilhelm Weitling (1808–71), the German journeyman-tailor who, according to his biographer, was one of the most important figures of pre-Marxian socialism. The Bible was fundamental, he said, a return to original Christian sources was the ideal, and figures like Thomas Münzer and John of Leiden provided favorite references. Like them, Weitling expected to revivify evangelical Christianity, regenerate mankind, bring the ruling classes to their knees by violence, and become the Messiah of a millennial earthly kingdom of peace and justice. In 1843, his *Gospel of a Poor Sinner*, which presented Jesus as the precursor of communism, led to his trial and imprisonment for blasphemy in Zurich. Soon after, his conspiratorial activities drifted toward open aggressiveness, when he proposed turning the League of the Just, which he had joined while an exile in Paris, into a League of Outlaws that would invade Germany and free it from oppression. Despite alluring echoes of Schiller's *Robbers* and their romantic social banditry, his ideas did not endear him to more up-to-date revolutionaries, who rejected a Christian communism that they denounced as utopian. Weitling emigrated to the promised land of nineteenth-century utopias, and died in New York in 1871.[15]

Be they Christian or not, however, many socialists tended in their discourse to messianism and millenarianism. They called for a return to "God's kingdom" as projected in the Gospels and in primitive Christianity, and for a move beyond "bourgeois clericalism," which they denounced as selfish, unjust, and oppressive. Socialism, the "forty-eighter" Louis Blanc insisted, was evangelism in action. "The spirit of 1848," as Pierre Pierrard has said, would be a bundle of religious and utopian currents.

No one better reflected the mingling of millennial aspirations with radical reform and Biblical language than Robert Owen (1771–1858), the most influential utopian socialist of his day. A rationally benevolent despot, Owen rejected orthodox religion. But the enlightened regime of the mills he founded at New Lanark in 1813, and even the failure of the colony he bankrolled at New Harmony in Indiana (1825–28), publicized his ideals of subordinating machines to men and women, of nature harnessed by nurture, and of restoring to many the dignity of purpose they had long been denied. Apostle of hygiene, education, and rational management, Owen preached his message in apocalyptic terms. History, as he presented it, was a secularized version of the struggle between light and darkness, God and Satan.

Like his younger contemporary Joseph Smith, who also set out to build Zion in the Western hemisphere, Owen called on men and women to come out of iniquity and enter a new world as a preliminary to ultimate perfection. Before humanity was freed from obscurantism and oppression, old things had to pass away entirely and all had to become new: "Not one stone of present society shall be left upon another."[16] Nor was the New Age far off. "Man may now be made a terrestrial angel of goodness and wisdom . . . and inhabit a terrestrial paradise . . . The earth will gradually be made a fit abode for super men and women, under a New Dispensation, which will make the earth a paradise and its inhabitants angels."[17]

Owen lost four-fifths of his considerable self-made fortune in the dissensions and collapse of New Harmony, and his New Dispensation never materialized. But he inspired trade unionism and the consumer cooperative movement, and his life remains a monument to good intentions made concrete. "Every social movement," wrote Engels, "every real advance in England on behalf of the workers, links itself to the name of Robert Owen."[18]

We have to put this assessment in perspective. It was eschatological millenarianism, both in its long tradition and in its contemporary nineteenth-century manifestations, that inspired secular millenarianism and provided its war cries, not least the idea of a radical solution to the age-old struggle between good and evil. Owen spoke of socialism as the "Millennium in practice," and he used the phrase for the title of one of his pamphlets. His periodical, *The New Moral World*, for a while carried the subtitle "Gazette of the Millennium." That was roughly when Owen's younger contemporary, Shelley, who formed his mind and honed his style on the King James Bible, was writing about the world's great age beginning anew. Man regenerated in a world made new: the themes of John of Patmos and of new Lanark's Owen coincided with those of romanticism *and* socialism.

Pierre Leroux, the journeyman-printer and Saint-Simonian who, in the 1830s, wrote a book on the democratic origins of Christianity which introduced the word "socialism" to France, had probably learned it from the Owenites. They were, after all, responsible for its first recorded use, in the *Cooperative Magazine* of 1827. Leroux employed "socialism," he explained, to challenge "individualism," which was then coming into use.

Salvation henceforth should be not individual but collective. And it may well be that Marx and Engels called themselves "communists" because "socialism" had become too closely identified with Owen and with Christianity to serve the purpose of one more millenarian manifestation: their own.

The secular adaptation of religious terminology was accompanied by the transposition of Biblical concepts not just of last times but also of sacrifice and redemption. Parallel religions, now, would be social religions. Democracy, as Edgar Quinet put it, would represent the New Testament accomplished at last. Ballanche, who compared himself to the solitary prophet of Patmos, glorified "the plebeians" as the essence of suffering humanity. Charles Fourier, who called himself the Messiah of Reason, "prophète postcurseur de Jésus," charged with the social revelations his predecessor had neglected, presented his gospel of harmony as a fulfillment of earlier ones.[19]

One of Fourier's disciples, Désiré Gabriel Laverdant, converted to Catholicism in the 1840s, and set out to demonstrate that Christian and utopian socialist beliefs were one, the latter being simply a continuation of "Judeo-Christian millenarianism." As his *Social Catholicism* explained in 1851, the idea of a terrestrial reign of justice preparing mankind for the heavenly kingdom went back to the origins of Christianity and had been introduced into second-century Gaul by St. Ireneus, bishop of Lyon. Fourier was the heir of Ireneus, of Papias, of the apocalyptic John. And the ulterior aim of Fourier's followers was "nothing less than heaven on earth."[20]

Many shared that aim, not least Étienne Cabet (1788–1856), the communitarian pacifist who was elected deputy in 1831 and exiled to England a few years later for his leftism, where he wrote *Voyage to Icaria* (1840). *Icaria* sketched out the reign of God on earth: a communist society with common ownership of everything. It must have made stodgy reading even then, but its motto, "From each according to his capacities, to each according to his needs," had a great future. Then, in 1846, Cabet's *True Christianity Following Jesus Christ* presented Christ himself as a communist. In 1848, his followers moved to the United States to found an Icaria of their own at Nauvoo, where disputes and schisms matched those that tore New Harmony apart. Even so, the last Icarian colony, at Cloverdale in California, dissolved only in 1895.

It has become hard to ignore the occultist and eschatological interests of Romantic writers. But literary scholars tend to relate these themes to their quarries' search for fantastical inspiration, when the hold of the Bible provides a more obvious explanation. Auguste Viatte, for example, author of an intriguing and oft-quoted book on *Victor Hugo and the Illuminati of His Day* (Montreal, 1942), mentions the popularity with illuminist writers of the 1820s and 1830s of a verse from the prophet Joel: "Your sons and daughters shall be prophets and your young men shall see visions" (2:28). But the book of Joel has only three chapters and it is chock-full of gruesome predictions about the day of the Lord that is nigh at hand (see 1:15 and 2:1). Bible readers were brought up to read well beyond particular verses. Would those who remembered the romantically appropriate predictions of an obscure prophet ignore the romantically apocalyptic imagery that framed them? Or equally lurid and appealing passages elsewhere in the Old Testament and the New?

Allumbrados, Illuminati, or Enlightened Ones aspired to or claimed Christ's "illuminating" grace, which could vouchsafe visions of the divine and permit direct communication with the Holy Spirit. They also looked to a classless society, though hardly a democratic one, and their high spiritual aspirations and benevolent social views appealed to many contemporary intellectuals. Like Balzac, these thinkers had been touched by the ideas of Swedenborg, and often also by Joachimite predictions of the Third Era, that of the Spirit, when the institutional church would be relayed by a new church, freer, more contemplative, more lovingly compassionate.[21] That was the church that Lammenais had dreamed of, but also the socialist Leroux, for whom the end of the world had to be understood as the end of the world of inequality and injustice. His lover George Sand shared these views. Her Joachimite *Consuelo* (1842) and its sequel, *The Countess of Rudolstadt,* were inspired by the Hussite movement; her *Spiridion* (1839) recounts the spiritual quest for a new religion that would relate religious and political progress; and her *Miller of Angibault* ends with the proposed foundation of an utopian community.

The humanitarian theology of so many Romantics had inspired the analogy of suffering nations and suffering Christ; it was going to inspire a powerful current of Christian populism that assimilated suffering people and suffering Christ. Poet, occultist, and utopian socialist Alphonse Esquiros (1812–76) published *The People's Gospel* in 1840. Its revolutionary and violent interpretation of the Scriptures led to his imprisonment. No wonder. "If the word became man in the person of Jesus, it will one day become people in all men; that will be the Last Coming."[22] The harvest was not over: Jesus Christ would return "armed with a scythe." God's kingdom was for the poor; the Last Judgment for the oppressors; and, as his *Histoire des Montagnards* (1847) averred, those who fought evil with terror were also doing God's work. Marat too had come to bring not peace but a sword; and Marat would be saved as Lucifer and Satan would be saved—by love.[23]

The same message had appeared in another book published in the same year as *The People's Gospel*: Alphonse-Louis Constant's *Bible of Liberty* (1840). There St. John was glorified as the bard of the revolutionary Apocalypse, and socialism aborning represented the New Jerusalem of his Revelation. The Second Coming would see Christ reincarnated in humanity, Adam and the rebel angels absolved, and the Apocalypse accomplished in "a revelation of man-people-God."[24]

The Enlightenment had taken an interest in the people as noble savages; a sentimental age promoted this concept to sacrificial victim. As usual, the general darkness carried premonitions of an Age of Light; in revolutionary lore, as in eschatology, suffering preceded salvation and redemption. Out of the people's sufferings, deliverance must come; out of its trials, redemption; out of its sorrows, salvation. And since the source of redemption is love, its instrument must be woman: sometimes a feminized angel or Holy Spirit, but most often that ideal mother, Mary, not punitive but merciful.

On August 15, 1838, on the "day of the Assumption of the Virgin Mary and [the] first day of the Year Evadah," when the old world ended and the new began, the times were at last accomplished. Abel Ganneau, who called himself the Mapah—composite of the first syllables of *maman* and *papa*—had begun to preach the oneness of Adam and Eve in an androgynous Evadam. In that new entity, woman, both slave and mother, acted as God's chosen instrument in the emancipation of the weak: "God is the people." But it was woman's mission to reveal this role, and to bring to realization the implications of Pierre Leroux's insistence on the equality of the sexes, and of partners within that ideal being, the couple, that prefigured human relations yet to be perfected.

Bizarre though the Mapah's message sounded, it fitted a major motif of the time. Pierre Leroux was a feminist. Both Esquiros and Constant were feminists, too, and both associated woman not only with redemption but with the oppressed. That was why, having collaborated with Lammenais in a paean to suffering Poland, then published works on *The Assumption of Woman* (1841) and *The Mother of God* (1844), Constant linked saving victims in *The Emancipation of Woman or the Testament of the Pariah* (1846).

The overlong title carried echoes of a book published by one of Constant's friends and disciples, Flora Tristan. A battered

woman, militant Fourierist, admirer of the Mapah, and unsuccessful labor organizer, Tristan was the passionate observer of
the marginalized and the oppressed, one who liberated herself
and then set out to liberate others. A book she wrote in 1837,
about a journey to her native Peru, was called *Peregrinations
of a Pariah*. Another, *Walks in London* (1840), described her
encounter, while visiting Bethlehem Hospital (Bedlam), with a
Frenchman who thought himself the messiah and tried to hand
his mission on to her. Tristan was not convinced, but sympa-
thized with an inspired soul whose views on world renewal
matched her own. Tristan died in 1844 at the age of forty-one.
Constant, who lived a good deal longer, turned to Satanism and
occult studies, changed his name to Eliphas Lévi, and began to
write on magic. This proved a much more influential enterprise,
as his effect on Villiers de l'Isle Adam, Catulle Mendès, Huysmans, and Léon Bloy attests.[25] But just as his occultism was
characteristic of his time's fascination with mysteries and mystery, so his belief in woman as redeemer was characteristic of
its socio-theological speculations. Ballanche, Auguste Comte,
Jules Michelet, John Stuart Mill, to name but the best known,
worshipped his maternal muse. It was by no coincidence that
the nineteenth century proved the heyday of the Marial cult.

What Enlightenment and revolution had cleft asunder,
Restoration and Romanticism brought back together again. The
Angelus hails Mary three times every day; her feast days punctu-
ate the liturgical year in February, March, and every month from
July on; after 1813, when May became the month of Mary, pious
souls paid special attention to marial sanctuaries that grew in
number by clerical policy, freelance visionary enterprise, and
popular interest in appeasing God's wrath. But God himself and
God's church were evolving, becoming less threatening and
more merciful. The principle of religion had for long been fear,
and that was what eighteenth- and nineteenth-century rationalists explained; it would henceforth be forgiveness. The public

sensibility that did away with torture at the end of the eighteenth century, that fought slavery, capital punishment, the brutalization of women and children, and cruelty to animals in the first half of the next century, could not but reflect and affect the image of divine authority. Gradually, reluctantly, this image softened in general and, as it softened, the gentler, more tender virtues took precedence over rigorous, inflexible ones, the ruth of mercy tempered the ill-tempered and capricious despot of ancient Israel, and the New Testament came into its own at last.

What was the role of Romanticism in this trend, and of the romantic cult of regenerative torment and redemptive love? The doctrine of sentimental messianism, as Bénichou has called it, reflects a convergence of traditional religion and romantic dreams. Original sin was humanity damned for its aspirations. Prometheus, like Satan, fell because he aimed too high, challenging God's injustice, indifference, and selfishness as Job never dared to do. They would be redeemed, as Judas was redeemed, "that miserable disciple who is today in heaven, loving much because much has been forgiven him," and as the platoons of fallen angels who flit through the apocalyptic poetry of the times.[26]

"Leave to the millenarians," Edgar Quinet advised contemporary Christians, "the fantastic, fabulous, mythological portion of your theories." But Mariolatry also had its millenarian side. And the fantastic, fabulous, mythological beliefs that Quinet associated with Christian millenarianism were equally associated with the progressivism of the time and with what a very serious student of the Joachimite legacy has described as an explosion of prophetism (Joel again!), not just Christian, but "metaphysico-social, paraChristian, post-Christian, and even antiChristian."[27] Edgar Quinet thought that religious revolutions preceded political ones and, clearly, they often have. In his own day, religious and political changes seem to have gone hand in hand. It is hard to tell which one drove the other.[28]

But the fantastic and the fabulous had a more momentous aspect still. For the millennial myth encompassed not promises of happiness only, but the banishment of evil from mankind and the world. The rationalists and secularists who adopted and adapted Christian notions would prefer, as Quinet preferred, to dismiss the imagery of evil Satan bound and cast into the bottomless pit, let alone that of his return in force for a new struggle. Their more visionary fellows created their own fables: a mythology of evil redeemed by love. In its last verses, Victor Hugo's "The End of Satan" has God's daughter, the angel Liberty, abolish Gehenna and rehabilitate Satan, revived as the archangel he used to be. "Sinister night" is ended by God, "and none is left." Finally God proclaims "Satan is dead; arise celestial Lucifer!"[29]

Mere poetry? Perhaps, but representative of contemporary literature and contemporary ambitions: evil is not essential, merely one more bane like ignorance or illness that can be ousted by reason and by love. Original sin is a myth, the Fall a legend, and evil a social disease, not an ineradicable part of human nature but subject to the laws of progress as God and religions are.[30] Therein lies the profound meaning of Quinet's adjuration: in the New Dispensation, exculpative dogmas replaced punitive ones. God was progress, progress was God; Liberty, Equality, Fraternity, compassion, and mercy would save mankind without supernatural intervention.

The term *justification*, so important in Christian theology, derives from the Latin *justum facere*, "to make righteous." The new road to righteousness was as clear as the old: justification by works; but, above all, justification by faith—that the Christian revolution would be surpassed by the human revolution. An apocalypse as fantastic, fabulous, and mythological as the old had come to vie with John's visions.

TIME'S NOBLEST
OFFSPRING

Westward the course of empire takes its way;
The four first acts already past,
A fifth shall close the drama of the day;
Time's noblest offspring is the last.

   — BISHOP GEORGE BERKELEY

W HEN HE DESCRIBED *The New Industrial World* (1808) in which God's designs for man would be accomplished, Charles Fourier, the utopian socialist, compared himself with Columbus, who had, he said, also been ridiculed for having announced a new world. But Columbus was not ridiculed for announcing a new world. He "discovered" a new continent by chance, when he set sail to find a new route to Asia, its markets, and its unconverted souls. Materialist interpretations of his motives and those of his royal patrons have long ignored his apocalyptic motivation. When, in 1930, a Canadian archivist, Edmond Buron, published Pierre d'Ailly's fifteenth-century *Imago mundi* with Columbus's marginal notes, the find was largely ignored. Then, in 1979, Bernard McGinn reminded us that "Columbus thought his mission to open up a new path to Asia coupled with Spanish rulers' reconquest of Jerusalem would herald the age of universal conversion preceding the End of the world." And, a few years later, Pauline Moffitt Watts quoted the letter that made this goal clear: "God made me the messenger of the new heaven and the new earth of which he spoke in the Apocalypse of St. John after having spoken of it through the mouth of Isaiah; and he showed me the spot where to find it." That was why Columbus named his landfall islet San Salvador.[1]

Like many contemporaries, Columbus was fascinated by the prospect of the world's end approaching, and curious about the delay left before Judgment came. Instructed by d'Ailly's *Imago mundi* and by the calculations of Alphonso X, the Wise, he reckoned that the end of the world was "about 155 years away." But first "the gospel of the kingdom shall be preached in all the world for a witness unto all nations; and then shall the end come" (Matthew 24:14).[2] It was up to him to help God's work along by carrying the message of salvation to those as yet unsaved, and by providing the means to free Jerusalem and rebuild the temple. The gold of the Indies would finance that crusade: "Gold is most excellent," he wrote to Ferdinand and Isabella; "whoever has it may do what he wants in the world, and may succeed in taking souls to Paradise."[3]

We know that Columbus, who took the Orinoco for one of the four rivers of the earthly Paradise, neither located paradise nor helped to create a New Heaven. But he did offer Europe and his princes *un otro mundo*, a new and other world.

We may wonder about the weight of his eschatological considerations; certainly, serious scholars have given them a wide berth. But coming in the wake of Muslim expulsion from the Iberian peninsula itself, the conquest of America for God (and the Spanish crown) could easily look like a millennial mission. Spanish missionaries in the New World knew that they worked for the final conversion of unbelievers before the end of times.[4] They could start, as Puritans in the North did too, by converting American natives, who most thought were descended from the ten lost tribes of Israel. Imaginative readers interpreted Revelation 7:4–9 as intimating that the ten lost tribes would reappear just before the Seventh Seal was broken. Identification of Israel and the Indians was evidence of the imminent end, and the more reason to bring them the Gospel.[5] A Joachimite Franciscan friar like Geronimo de Mendieta regarded Spain as the New Israel, Philip II as the world emperor destined to convert mankind on Last Judgment's eve, Mexico as the millennial kingdom, and Indians as God's children to be preserved from the violence and exactions of the Europeans.

Franciscans and Puritans could sometimes agree on the ten lost tribes, though Puritans envisaged themselves as offspring of Israelites more often than they considered unregenerate natives in that role. They also viewed America as the Israel of its time. North American colonists knew they had come out of Egypt, *and* out of Babylon. The new order of ages—that *novus ordo seclorum* enshrined in the continent's most revered document, the dollar bill—was burgeoning north of the Gulf of Mexico. John Cotton left England in 1633 to create the Saints' kingdom in New England, but he died before the Second Coming, which he had calculated would occur in 1655. Still, he left a pious legacy: the weekend, designed to keep the Sabbath holy from Saturday afternoon to Sunday night.

Quite a different legacy would be bequeathed by one of Cotton's *bêtes noires*: Roger Williams, the nonconformist clergyman driven from Massachusetts Bay for protesting Puritan treatment of the Indians, and holding that magistrates had no right to interfere in matters of religion. In 1636, he founded Providence in what soon became Rhode Island: a democratic community dedicated to freedom of conscience, safe harbor for Catholics, Quakers, and Jews, and the separation of church and state. Yet this Christian democrat looked forward to Satan's chaining as keenly (though less precisely) as Cotton did. Liberty was a natural right, he argued (in *Bloudy Tenet Yet More Bloudy*, 1651); his persecuted church became the Woman in the Wilderness whom the earth helps when dragons like the Puritans of Massachusetts Bay make war upon her; and the struggle against state churches became assimilated to the struggle against Antichrist.

Those apocalyptic Massachusetts clergymen, the Mathers— father, son, and grandson—would labor similarly millenarian vineyards. Richard Mather (1596–1669) sailed for America in 1635 to preach the Puritan message prohibited at home. Increase Mather (1639–1723), who believed in inoculation against small-pox and in witches, but not witch trials, interpreted the comet of 1680 as a portent of "Droughts, Caterpillars, Tempests, Inunda-tions, Sickness"—God's warning shot across the bows of human-ity adrift "before his murdering pieces go off."[6] Cotton Mather, Increase's son (1663–1728), became a friend of Robert Boyle the chemist and a member of the Royal Society of London—more an admirer of God's wonders than of his cataclysms. He supported missions to Indians and schools for slaves, wrote four hundred books, and fathered fifteen children (two of whom survived him). But his most characteristic work must be the *Essays to Do Good* (1710), humanitarian before the word was coined, suggest-ing that reward works better than punishment, and community projects better than repression. Comets and brimstone were being edged out. Perhaps that is why Cotton Mather, more insis-tently than his father, believed that before the world was de-stroyed by fire, the saints would be caught up in the air to escape the destruction and torment of the final conflagration.

Rapture does not appear in the Bible or in the *Encyclopedia Britannica*, but the principle behind belief in it can be found in Paul's first epistle to the Thessalonians (4:16–17): "For the Lord himself shall descend from heaven with a shout, with the voice of the archangel and with the trump of God; and the dead in Christ shall rise first. Then we which are alive shall be caught up to-gether with them in the clouds, to meet the Lord in the air. And so shall we ever be with the Lord."

Curiously, through the words and works of hellfire preachers, the horrors of end days were being adjourned. As a working minister, Jonathan Edwards (1703–58) was much concerned to refute increasingly popular Arminian doctrines that rejected predestination, soft-pedaled original sin in favor of free will, and preached that Jesus Christ died for all, not only for the elect. As "America's premier philosopher-theologian," Edwards was fascinated by the Apocalypse, scrupulously noted all signs of the times, and calculated and recalculated its coming. Having allowed for preliminaries like uniting disunited Protestants, winning over the Catholics, converting Mohammedans and Jews, and enlightening the heathen, he concluded that Antichrist's rule would end when the papacy ended in 1866, and that old serpent, the Devil, would finally be vanquished in the year 2000, when the millennium would begin.

All this would come about "by a gradual progress of religion": preaching the Gospel, reviving prayer, inculcating virtues, and so on. Yet millennia last only one thousand years; and the millennium over, mankind could be expected to return to its vomit: depravity. If the wickedness of the old world had "called for its destruction by a deluge of waters, this wickedness will as much call for its destruction by a deluge of fire." Was there then no escape? There was. At the eleventh hour, rapture awaited those saints who would leave the world to be devoured "by fire from heaven, or by fire breaking out from the bowels of the earth, or both."[7] The fervent believer in the Apocalypse gave priority to respite and reform that would usher in the millennial golden age.[8] But if he cared about what would come after, many put first things first: societies to end drunkenness, slums, crime, poverty, cruelty—anything that would make the country more Christian and bring the millennium nearer.

Here was a new dispensation, and one which, often unconsciously, fitted the temper of an improving age. The coincidence of secular and religious belief that could be observed in nineteenth-century Europe seems to have begun in North America a century earlier. And with this, differences of opinion concerning the relation between millennium and Christ's Second Coming became the touchstones of differing systems of belief. The original creed of Ephesus and of St. Augustine was that the millennium began with Christ's Advent, and that his Second Advent would come in its own good time. To *amillenarists* like these, revelation had been accomplished and the reign of Christ occurred in the heart of Christians. Most eschatologists, however, awaited a literal fulfillment of Scripture prophecy.

That very sobering prospect affected more than religious fanatics. Learned and common folk alike expected warning, great upheavals, trials, judgment, and then consolation. The question was how it would happen, and in what order. *Pre-millenarians* expected Christ to return to earth and *then* set up his millennial rule; *post-millenarians* believed he would return *after* the church had established the millennium. In pre-millenarian scenarios, the kingdom of God comes abruptly, violently, with little human input. For post-millenarians, human effort affects the world's progression toward the messianic kingdom. Christ would return after his church had won many converts and reformed the world.

The world could not be reformed, argued pre-millenarians. It was growing worse, and would get worse still until Christ came with a great shout to set up his rule. Pessimistic millenarians who saw the world going to pot had been dominant so long that few felt the need to discriminate between one kind of millennialism and another. Now, with things apparently looking up, postmillenarians came into their own, interested in improving the world and reforming society. Millenarianism need not represent protest and despair only, but hope of political and social change. Post-millenarians and pre-millenarians alike sought opportunities for missionary enterprise to evangelize, convert, and save souls in time for the Second Coming. All wanted to cleanse,

prepare, awaken; all wanted to confront the forces of evil and recognized the need to make war on them. Only some believed it
possible to establish heaven on earth, while others, placing their
faith in sudden divine intervention, sought a haven until its coming: a sanctuary in the midst of sin and gloom.

An instance of the difficulty that the uninitiated might have
in telling the two persuasions apart can be found in the Shakers,
or Trembling Quakers, who trembled and shook in spiritual
exaltation when the spirit moved them, just as seventeenth-
century Quakers had quaked in their ecstatic fits. Probably inspired by the French Prophets' antics, the United Society of Believers in Christ's Second Appearing originated in Lancashire
before the middle of the eighteenth century. Their eccentricities
led to persecution and, in 1774, their leader, Ann Lee, daughter
of one Manchester blacksmith and wife of another, brought a
group of faithful over to the American colonies, which were then
in the preliminary throes of rebellion against the British crown.

The United Society also called itself the Millennial Church,
and Lee was progressively deified by her devotees as that "female
principle" whose incarnation completed the "male principle"
represented by Jesus, and so fulfilled the Second Coming. Her
sayings sound sensible enough: "Do all your work as though you
had 1000 years to live, and as you would if you knew you must
die tomorrow"; and "Live together every day as though it was
the last day you had to live in the world."9 The gospel that she
preached was also logical: the judgment of God was "nigh at
hand" and demanded withdrawal from the world. So Shakers
organized themselves into "families," holding goods in common, avoiding tobacco and alcohol, and monitoring relations
between the sexes, for the millennium might be progressively
achieved by refusal to procreate, which would mean fewer gen-
tiles and more chaste regenerate saints. This objective did not
quite work out: the unregenerate went on procreating, and the
saints attracted few recruits. They were reported to dance in

extravagant postures, whirl, sing, groan, fall, twitch, hoot, crow, hiss, and, as if this were not enough, their reclusiveness and pacifism in times of war aroused suspicion of conspiracies.

Over the years, eccentricities waned, the "shaking" was replaced by formal, ritual dances, and the disciplined industry of Shaker settlements produced furniture, baskets, seeds, and other goods to sell or barter in the marketplace. Ingenious sisters and brethren invented and seldom patented rotary harrows, threshing machines, circular saws, and, not least, the clothes pin. They were the first to package and market seeds and medicinal herbs. And the simple lines of their functional furniture reflected the belief that work well done was in itself an act of prayer. These domestic goods also ensured their survival, for Shaker artifacts in museums have outlived their gristmills, sawmills, and woolen mills, as they have the membership of the sect. Conscientious isolation from society made Shakers better citizens of the society they renounced; market economy proved harder to resist than persecution; and the world in which they sought only temporary shelter proved in the end more resilient than their faith.

Less eccentric and more philoprogenitive were the artisan German pietists who, in 1842, sailed to America to settle first in New York State and then in Iowa, where they called their settlement Amana, a name culled from the Song of Solomon (4:8). Amana villagers developed a mixed economy, both agricultural and industrial: canning, textiles, furniture, and, more recently, household and electrical equipment. By the 1930s their original Christian communism had turned into a joint-stock corporation, but prosperity endured. Piety, industry, and communal effort seem to go well together.

Even communities that have done less well seem to disprove the popular notion of religious enthusiasts as trying to compensate for wretchedness, insecurity, and alienation. The seventeenth century followers of Johannes Kelpius awaiting Advent in

1694 at Woman-in-the-Wilderness near Germantown, Pennsylvania; the eighteenth-century Seventh-day Baptists of Ephrata, Pennsylvania (one of whose members translated the Declaration of Independence into seven languages at the request of Congress); the nineteenth-century followers of George Rapp all impressed beholders by their plain living, hard work, scrupulous practices, fine craftsmanship, and respect for neighbors; and all sought to model themselves on Acts 4:32–35: "The multitude of them that believed were of one heart and of one soul: neither said any of them that ought of the things which he possessed was his own; but they had all things in common . . . Neither was there any among them that lacked; for as many as were possessors of lands or houses sold them, and brought the prices of the things that were sold and laid them down at the apostle's feet; and distribution was made unto every man according to need."

Mystics, alchemists, pacifists, communists—prosperity brought their societies to an end more often than celibacy or internal dissensions. The Rappites of Harmony, Indiana (sold to Robert Owen in 1824), and later of Economy, Pennsylvania, lasted into the twentieth century. The community of Ephrata, which made it into Voltaire's *Philosophical Dictionary*, is still around, at least for curious tourists. The Owenites of New Harmony, Indiana, did not do so well, perhaps because they lacked religious discipline. Yet even they left a rich legacy of schooling, women's rights, liberation and education of slaves, free libraries, and Working Men's Institutes. The U.S. Geological Survey, the creation of Owen's son, David Dale Owen, was based in New Harmony until 1846, when the Smithsonian Institution provided it with a permanent home. Thus, apparent eccentricity did not preclude success; and even eccentricity was probably more apparent to twentieth-century observers than to contemporaries.

For all these groups, as for the Shakers, heaven began on earth. Many compatriots agreed with them on that score, especially when the revolutionary war promised a truly new found land. Victory at Saratoga in 1777 and at Yorktown in 1781 precipitated showers of sermons that drew on Israel's prophets to predict "the kingdom of the Redeemer . . . established on the ruins of the kingdom of Satan," and the millennium around the year 2000.[10] French intellectuals like Jean-Louis Carra and English preachers like Richard Price hailed the revolution: the third and final stage of history prophesied the one, "ordained by Providence to introduce these [last] times" vowed the other.[11] Eschatological terminology came naturally on all sides. Scholars, prophets, patriots, doomsayers, and apostles of progress shared Biblical references, images, and vocabulary, in a firm belief that the world was fated to end in total change.

Radical change came, but there was still a long way to go. New England and upper New York were full of visionaries, clerics, and common folk estimating the millennium's coming. Ralph Waldo Emerson attempted a brief listing: "Madmen, madwomen, men with beards, Dunkers, Muggletonians, Come-Outers, Groaners, Agrarians, Seventh-Day Baptists, Quakers, Abolitionists, Calvinists, Unitarians and Philosophers . . ."[12] Asa Wild of Amsterdam, New York, had talked to the great Jehovah and had learnt that one-third of the people currently alive would accede to Christ's kingdom. By the Ohio River, one John Dilks predicted the millennium for 1832. The Reverend Robert Reid of Erie, Pennsylvania, more prudently expected it in 1895. A Pittsburgh theologian was more conformist and less specific: "We ourselves in this age of the world are on the eve of . . . a great and terrible day of the Lord." America, writes Ernest Sandeen, was drunk on millenarianism.[13]

In September 1823, in upstate New York, the eighteen-year-old Joseph Smith at prayer was told by an angel that the time was at hand and preparations should begin for Christ's millennial reign. Before he was killed by a mob in Carthage, Illinois, Smith had assured his followers that they would live to see this great event. But Christ would not come until his saints had created conditions worthy of him. That was what Smith tried to pre-arrange on the banks of the Mississippi and what the Mormons' next leader, Brigham Young, set out to build beyond the Rocky Mountains: a Zion of latter-day saints.

By the 1840s, when the Mormons' westward migration was on its way, one of the great disappointments of the century had occurred, one not unrelated to the spread of numeracy in an increasingly democratic Jacksonian America. A Massachusetts burgher, William Miller (1782–1849), had converted from deism to Baptism, begun to study the Bible and calculate its codes, and been ordained a minister in 1833. In 1836, Miller published his conclusions as *Evidence from Scripture and History of the Second Coming,* predicting that it would occur in the twelve months following March 1843, then shifting the fateful date to October 1844. Tens of thousands withdrew from their churches to await the predicted Advent. The faithful who, at Miller's behest (and that of the prophet Habakkuk, who bade them "tarry, wait for it!"), had waited for the Bridegroom when he failed to turn up in 1843, and had gone out to meet him on October 22, 1844, having abandoned homes, crops, animals, given away their money, and closed their stores ("This shop is closed," one sign read, "in honor of the King of Kings who will appear about the 20th of October"), were bitterly disappointed. "We wept and wept," remembered one of them, "till the day dawn."[14]

Following the Great Disappointment, the Millerite movement collapsed. Many Adventists drifted to Shakerism, but found Shaker principles of celibacy difficult to follow. In mid-1847, one Millerite "left the society, announcing that he preferred to go to hell with Elektra his wife than live among the Shakers without her."[15] Others focused on Revelation 6:12, which extolled the patience of the saints, and on Revelation 6:6, which stressed the importance of preaching the gospel "to every nation and kindred and tongue and people." It turned out that 1844 had been a crucial date indeed, not for ending the world, but for "cleansing the sanctuary," first in heaven, and eventually on earth, when the three angels of Revelation 14 were ready to announce God's coming. For that, there was no fixed date. Believers were simply exhorted to be ready, for "the almost complete fulfillment of various lines of prophecy . . . indicates that Christ's coming is near, even at the doors."[16] Meanwhile, since the human body is the temple of the Holy Spirit, abstinence from alcohol and tobacco was mandatory, from coffee, tea, and meat highly recommended, and the Sabbath was to be observed on the seventh day: Saturday. Hence the name Seventh-day Adventists, adopted in 1861.

The year 1861 also saw the outbreak of the American Civil War; and Julia Ward Howe, visiting the army of the Potomac, wrote "The Battle Hymn of the Republic," which glorified John Brown, the abolitionist hanged in 1859 after his unsuccessful raid on Harper's Ferry. The lyrics of Howe's hymn are full of apocalyptic evocations:

> Mine eyes have seen the glory of the coming of the Lord:
> He is trampling out the vintage where the grapes of wrath
>   are stored;
> He hath loosed the fateful lightning of his terrible swift
>   sword;
> His truth is marching on . . .
> He has sounded forth the trumpet that shall never call
>   retreat;
> He is sifting out the hearts of men before his judgment
>   seat . . .

Howe was a friend of Ralph Waldo Emerson, who had once told a Millerite, "The end of the world does not affect me; I can live without it." She was no millenarian; which makes her use of apocalyptic language all the more telling of the hold such imagery retained over American imaginations. Just as the first

Great Awakening (1730–60), with its emotional preaching, has been credited with a role in the creation of the Republic, so the second Great Awakening (1800–30) helped the rise of Jacksonian democracy. But its post-millenarian emphasis on moral responsibility, and hence on social ills like slavery, poverty, prostitution, and alcoholism, invited Americans to reform the nation and themselves.

Harriet Beecher Stowe, daughter, sister, wife of ministers, and author of *Uncle Tom's Cabin* (1851), a tale that moved Queen Victoria as deeply as it moved millions of contemporaries, believed in the Second Coming, and "in 1858 even suggested that it might be imminent."[17] When little Eva reads aloud from the Bible and Uncle Tom listens, it is from Revelation that she describes a sea of glass mingled with fire. And the novel ends on an apocalyptic note: "Read the signs of the times . . . who may abide the day of his appearing? For that day shall burn like an oven . . .Christians! every time you pray that the kingdom of Christ may come, can you forget that prophecy associates in dread fellowship the day of vengeance with the year of the redeemed?"

The nation could only live up to its millennial calling by abolishing slavery. In 1865, the Thirteenth Amendment to the Constitution did that, and Walt Whitman portrayed the earth confronting a new era: "No one knows what will happen next, such portents fill the days and nights; Years prophetical!"[18] There were those who knew what was to happen next: 1866 was the year of Antichrist, when Alfred Nobel discovered dynamite and Fyodor Dostoevsky published *Crime and Punishment.*

Neither dynamite nor Dostoevsky, however, were representative of the half-century past, which had unraveled under the sign of progress. Faith in the possibilities of perfection animated the Christian communist community of Oneida, set up in 1848, which turned into a joint-stock company in 1881 when it waxed prosperous. It inspired the followers of Pastor Jean-Frédéric Oberlin (1740–1825), the millennialist friend of Julie de Krüdener and Alsatian parish reformer, who got roads and bridges built by local peasants, introduced lending and savings banks, established schools and kindergartens, and promoted new agricultural techniques. Named after him, Oberlin College, founded in 1833, was coeducational from the outset and practical in the courses it offered in agricultural management and engineering. Like Oberlin's, evangelical activism was about usefulness. Christians were benevolent. Benevolence increased the happiness of neighbors, of God, of all. Progress was converted to Christianity and living in brotherly love. Evangelism in its spiritual and social aspects prepared the millennium, where this progress would come true. And a typical American reformer like Henry George, whose *Progress and Poverty* (1879) left its mark on George Bernard Shaw, H.G. Wells, and the English Fabians, "shared millennialist assumptions about the possibility of a perfected society based on Christian ethics and salvationist prophecy."[19]

Perhaps the most visible, certainly the most representative, figure of the post-millennial movement must be the great revivalist preacher Charles Grandison Finney (1792–1875), professor of theology at Oberlin and then its president. Finney believed that the millennial age was about to dawn, in the United States at least, and that divine grace was of little consequence in this respect.[20] Conversion could come by human agency, individuals could attain moral perfection, and societies whose members were "consecrated to God in this life" would be prepared for perfection. The first step to the millennium was to convert people to Christ, but not just their souls needed uplift. Rather, it was necessary to improve the conditions of their life and work, educate them, coeducate them, free them from slavery, assure just wages and just prices, regenerate them as individuals, and then society would move into God's kingdom. "If the Church will do all her duty, the millennium may come in this country in three years," Finney wrote in 1835. A minister who talked to him in Rome, New York, was even more sanguine: "So far as my congregation is concerned, the millennium is come already. My people are all converted."[21]

In a way, the Civil War was post-millenarianism's greatest triumph. Like many triumphs, however, it marked the beginnings of its own decline and the return in force of rivals indifferent to social reforms that did not address the vital problem of original sin, to improvements that were no more than patches on gangrene, and to political activists who postured on volcanoes that were about to erupt. The world's ills would be resolved catastrophically and only that way, when the Lord came back; and that dread day was not far off. Signs of end times were clear for all to see (they always are), and godless intellectuals brought further grist to apocalyptic mills. In the wake of William Wordsworth ("One impulse from a vernal wood / May teach you more of man / of moral evil and of good / than all the sages can"), the Emersons and Thoreaus were representing nature as the source of all knowledge. Yet wrathful nature, red in tooth and claw, was but an expression of God's mounting anger, while unbelieving Bible critics picked away at His Word itself. In 1835, David Friedrich Strauss, the German theologian, had published a scandalous *Life of Jesus* that presented supernatural elements in the Gospels as creative legends and Christ himself as a myth. By the 1840s, freethinking pagans were dissolving Christian doctrine in their godless philosophies. Pre-millenarians made the most of it.

Plenty of publications sought to enlighten embattled evangelicals—*Signs of the Times* (1854), *The Last Times* (1856), and many more like them—but their basic ballast was provided by Bible students like John Nelson Darby (1800–82), so named because his uncle fought under Admiral Horatio Nelson at the Battle of the Nile (1798). He had been ordained in the Church of England, then rejected church orders and outward forms to join a puritan group of Brethren who, in the 1830s, became the Plymouth Brethren (whom we encountered earlier), into whose community Edmund Gosse and Orde Wingate would later be born.

It does not seem as if Darby invented much that was new. What, after all, was left to discover after so many centuries of Bible study? But his reflections, his writings (thirty-two volumes of collected works), and his zealous preaching over three continents provided pre-millenarians with a clear structure and time-table for their faith. What Darby discovered in Bible history was that God deals with mankind in a series of dispensations not unlike Joachim of Fiore's successive ages. The most recent dispensation had ended with the crucifixion, the next would begin with the rapture. The rapture was crucial because, as one historian of American fundamentalism has noted, it starts the end time clock ticking.[22] It would be followed in quick order by Antichrist, tribulation, Armageddon, millennium, Satan's comeback and final defeat, resurrection, and the Last Judgment.

We have heard all this before; but now it was presented in rigorous order, against a troubling background of triumphant meliorism, rampant scientism, aggressive Darwinism, and Biblical criticism that treated God's words and those of his prophets as if they were no more than literature. In this context, an interpretation that was simple, clear, and assured would be compelling. The divine authority of Scripture required literal fulfillment of the prophecies. The end was very near; but it was not predictable, so Millerite arithmetic and fallible calculations were irrelevant. Only one thing was known for certain: the Bible was never wrong. Biblical inerrancy became an article of faith for Plymouth Brethren, and more broadly among American fundamentalists. So did dispensationalism, which has become the standard interpretation for hundreds of Bible institutes and seminaries, and for evangelists like Billy Graham and Hal Lindsey.

The Bible was never wrong, but its human interpreters could make mistakes: hence the rival interpretations, reinterpretations, and schisms that mark the history of Christian sects and sectlets, which agree on fundamentals yet divide on details some hold crucial. In 1918, in Jerusalem, General Allenby would meet a remarkable American, Mrs. Spofford; in 1881, she had led a band of Spoffordites to await the coming of the Messiah, who would reach his capital in a flaming golden chariot.[23] Others could do as well without going so far afield. In 1888, Miles Moss, a Kentucky preacher, proclaimed himself the Moses whom the archangel Gabriel had detailed to lead black people back to Africa. In Georgia and South Carolina after 1889, a shower of messiahs and Christs performed miracles and prophesied the end. All blacks would become white, all whites would become black, all mockers would turn into 'gators, cooters, snakes, and dogs. Two Christs were committed to an insane asylum, while two messiahs were arrested as late as 1915 for obtaining money under false pretenses.

In far-off Canada, meanwhile, another apocalyptic script worked itself out as the dominion established by the British North America Act of 1867 sought to integrate the western lands and territorial rights of the Hudson's Bay Company. The expected influx of English-speaking settlers and officials alarmed local Indians, and equally the Métis half-breeds of Indian and French descent, who faced difficult times already. In the Red River valley of what is today southern Manitoba, the buffalo had gone, the fur trade had declined, steamboats and railroads gnawed at the voyageurs' transport business, farming was insecure, and the appearance of government surveyors threatened to destabilize the situation further. In 1869, the Métis stopped surveyor parties, seized the Fort Garry (now Winnipeg) headquarters of the Hudson's Bay Company, and established a provisional government to negotiate acceptable terms of union with Ottawa. The new province of Manitoba would be born in 1870.

The leading figure in all this agitation was Louis Riel (1844–85), who fled when Fort Garry was recaptured by government troops, but later made his peace with Canada and was twice elected to the dominion parliament before leading another rising and another provisional government in defense of Métis land claims. English-speaking Canada in the 1860s and 1870s was Protestant and evangelical, its clergy as prone as that south of the border to bear witness to approaching end times. The fall of Babylon— that is, papal Rome—to Italian troops in 1870 provided a major sign and encouraged men like David Anderson, bishop of Rupert's Land, to believe that the end of days could coincide with the end of the decade. Riel, a pious Catholic, had grown up surrounded by eschatologically minded Protestants, amid echoes of Millerite disappointment and its Adventist sequel. News of the pope's humiliation placed Métis and French-Canadian problems in apocalyptic perspective: the papacy should, and would, move to the new world; Riel would be its prophet.

His eschatology divided history into three ages: that of the Jewish church, that of Rome, and, finally, that of the French-Canadian and Métis priesthood, when the papacy would be transferred to Montreal's Ville Marie before finding a new dawn in western Canada, probably in Riel's birthplace of St. Boniface. The Métis would be redeemed, Catholics and Protestants reconciled, world peace established after terrible wars, while true religion would triumph at last and Christ would return to earth. Now that Rome had fallen, the spirit of God had moved to Montreal; it had entered Riel (who renamed himself David), and Riel imparted it to his followers by breathing on them.

On the eve of clashing with governmental forces, the prophet noted that the battle was being joined "squarely at the time God has marked in the order of things to come. With my own eyes, I saw all the signs of the times . . . before me lies . . . the time announced with all the signs . . . just as we are told in scriptures." The rebel banner carried a large picture of the Lady of Lourdes and, during the last battle, at Batoche, David held up a large figure of Christ, while two men supported his arms in the form of a cross. But the rising was crushed, and the prophet was taken prisoner, tried, and hanged for treason. The priests who confessed him reported that he called himself another Elias and a new St. Peter. He continues (or continued for a long time) as the patron saint of French-Canadian nationalism.[24]

Half-breeds and recently liberated slaves may be dismissed as credulous, but their more numerous fellows continued to play variations on established themes. Thus, in the 1870s, Charles Taze Russell, a Pennsylvania draper and self-taught Adventist, attracted many fellow-students of Bible prophecy when he explained that the Second Coming had taken place in 1874, that true believers could expect to change from fleshly to spiritual bodies in 1878 (a date shifted to 1881, then dropped), and that the kingdom of God on earth would materialize in 1914, after the battle of Armageddon. Believers in Russell's message were to shun earthly religions and nation-states, read the Bible, warn as many as they could about the impending end, and watch for its coming. *The Watchtower* (1879) turned into the Watchtower Bible and Tract Society and then, in 1931, into Jehovah's Witnesses.

As the terminological progression suggests, Russell's Bible Students survived several crises: 1878, 1881, 1914. When the kingdom of God failed to show up in 1914, rapture was postponed to 1918; then to 1925 by Russell's successor, "Judge" Joseph Franklin Rutherford (1869–1942), who was certain that "our generation will see the great battle of Armageddon" and that "millions now living will never die."[25] With other Watchtower directors who considered religion (the religion of others) "a snare and a racket," and brawling nation-states catspaws of apocalyptic beasts, Rutherford was imprisoned in 1918 for inciting insubordination, disloyalty, and refusal of duty in the American armed forces. After the conviction was overturned, he was free to mold the cult he led into an expansive international organization that attracted millions. Beliefs based on his teachings, and on the multitude of tracts that missionary Witnesses distributed from door to door, would inspire stubborn resistance to Nazism as well as the death of faithful Witnesses in Nazi concentration camps. But after the last end-of-world date, 1975, had come and gone, Rutherford's successors gave up (public) calculations. Enough to watch and pray.

The intellectual pressure of liberal theology and other godless enterprises had led to the establishment of an Evangelical Alliance in England in the 1840s and an American offshoot two decades later. But too many evangelicals appeared unsound about the Second Coming, and a series of Bible conferences sought to make amends. One of these, held at Niagara Falls in 1878, approved a creed whose last article, while admitting that "the world will not be converted during the present dispensation," noted that it was "fast ripening for judgment," predicted a "fearful apostasy in the professing Christian body," and affirmed "that the Lord Jesus will come in person to introduce the millennial age."[26] Another Niagara conference, in 1895, agreed on the fundamental tenets of scriptural belief: inerrancy, salvation by faith alone, and the imminent Second Coming. The evangelical Bible was still the King James Version, until Cyrus Schofield published an amplified text in 1909 which contained his interpretive notes in a dispensational and pre-millennial vein. The Schofield Bible, whose sales now approach the ten million mark, is still in print. Then, in 1910, the Bible Institute of Los Angeles, subsidized by Lyman Stewart, the millionaire president of the Union Oil Company of California, began to publish a series of cheap paperbacks entitled *The Fundamentals: A Testimony to the Truth*. In 1919, the World Christian Fundamentals Association was founded, and millenarians became fundamentalists.

Nineteenth-century revivalism spawned yet one more development significant for the future. On January 1, 1901, Agnes Ozman, a student at Bethel Bible College in Topeka, Kansas, was visited by the Holy Spirit and began to speak in tongues.[27] Many millenarians felt that, for the last days, the Scriptures predicted a recurrence of the charisma or divine powers that the first Christians had received on the day of Pentecost, when "they were all filled with the Holy Ghost and began to speak with other tongues, as the Spirit gave them utterance" (Acts 2:4). In Ozman's wake, first Bethel students and teachers, then their converts, had experiences similar to hers. All believed in the efficacy of an abrupt emotional crisis of conversion—a very American kind of instant sanctification—marked by the peculiar grace of speaking in tongues, prophetic utterance, healing, and exorcism. One black convert, William Seymour, took his faith to Los Angeles and, in 1906, his Apostolic Faith Gospel Mission on Azusa Street launched the world beginnings of Pentecostalism.

Some early Pentecostals were known as Holy Rollers because, in the tradition of Quakers and Shakers, their assemblies were marked by convulsions, shouts, ecstatic cries, and torrential tears. But ostracism for bizarre behavior damped neither ardor nor activism. As Russell Hitt points out, most major Pentecostal denominations—Assemblies of God, black Church of God in Christ, Four-Square Gospel—trace their beginnings to the Azusa Street revival. So do Pentecostalist churches overseas, for Pentecostalists, like other apocalyptists, believe that their prophecy has to be preached throughout the world "before the end."[28] And so does the current Charismatic movement that has affected the Roman Catholic Church and other denominations not usually associated with untoward enthusiasm.

The First World War, which revolutionized Europe and the rest of the world, confirmed fundamentalist mindsets, but had little impact on them. As one professor of the Philadelphia School of the Bible remarked, pre-millenarians expecting the worst were "not surprised at the present collapse of civilization; the Word of God told us all about it."[29] Christian pacifists had to face hostile mobs. Sturdy rejectionists like the Bible Students, who regarded the war as a conflict between nations under demonic control, went to jail for their conscientious objection to active service, and a few were even executed.[30] Beyond fundamentalist ranks, however, the four long years of mayhem and destruction stimulated interest in prophecy and the saving advent of Christ. And, during them, the Balfour Declaration of 1917, which pledged British support for efforts to establish a world Jewry in Zion, followed by Allenby's capture of Jerusalem in 1918, encouraged believers who, like the signers of the 1878 Niagara Creed, linked millennium and the Lord's return with Israel's restoration to its land.

Meliorists, meanwhile, Christian or secular, saw their dreams destroyed. Typical of their reactions, Christabel Pankhurst, the Joan of Arc of British feminism, had to abandon her hope that votes for women would pacify and regenerate the world. Even feminists could not best Satan, or the evil lodged in the heart of man; so Pankhurst turned to Adventism and began to preach the Second Coming and its portents: the return of the Jews to Palestine, Antichrist, Armageddon, and the rest. As the chairman of the Adventist Testimony Movement wrote in a foreword to her *Pressing Problems of the Closing Age* (1924), every sign of Christ's return was already present. Now, Pankhurst could assure her readers that "the final chapter of this Age's history [was] opening."[31] Between 1924 and her death in 1958, every crisis would prove her point: the Great Depression, Mussolini (a new, last Caesar and sinister man of destiny), Hitler (a worse one), another war, atomic energy (nature in convulsion) . . . History was hard put to catch up with Pankhurst's apocalyptic imagination, but it managed.

Then, in 1925, a great blow fell upon true believers. That year, the Tennessee legislature, under pressure from supporters of Biblical inerrancy, had outlawed the teaching of doctrines that denied the divine creation of man. When John Scopes, a high school teacher charged with violating the statute by teaching evolution in his science class, was tried and convicted, the case attracted national and international attention. In fact, the Scopes trial had been more or less arranged as a test case between the American Civil Liberties' Union and the Fundamentalist Association. William Jennings Bryan, who led the prosecution, and Clarence Darrow, the prominent trial lawyer who led for the defense, had a great deal in common. Scopes himself had grown up in the same small town—Salem, Illinois—where Bryan had been born; Darrow had cheered Bryan in the 1896 Democratic Convention. Both men supported the cause of labor and of woman suffrage, and both opposed capitalism, capital punishment, and war.

Three times a candidate for the presidency of the United States, Bryan had long championed "liberal" causes like income tax and prohibition. As Woodrow Wilson's secretary of state, he advocated arbitration to prevent war; as a pacifist, he resigned his office when Wilson became too belligerent for his taste. But Bryan was also a firm believer in the literal interpretation of the Bible and argued that it was "better to trust the Rock of Ages than the age of rocks." The jury agreed with him and with Tennessee law, and Scopes was found guilty and fined $100. The law under which he was sentenced was going to be repealed in 1967; but evolution brooked no law, and fundamentalists judged it better to go their own way until the Second Coming should prove their point.[32]

The Scopes trial had been a Pyrrhic victory. Fundamentalist beliefs had been ridiculed before sniggering millions. Just as the American Civil Liberties' Union and the Fundamentalist Association had intended, one orthodoxy had encountered another in the Scopes case and defeated it. Some of Scopes's prosecutors were less interested in Biblical inerrancy than in state and local rights ("The hand that writes the paycheck rules the school," as Bryan put it); and some of Scopes's Darwinist defenders were grinding racist axes of their own. No matter. People then, and history since then, registered the occasion as a moral victory over obscurantism.

Bryan died within weeks of his blemished victory. In a bileful and condescending commentary, one of his sharpest critics, H.L. Mencken, warned that urban America would be wrong to dismiss him and his followers as preposterous, hence harmless. Traveling back from Tennessee, Mencken recorded the omnipresence of those whom he dismissed as bigots: "Heave an egg out of a Pullman window and you will hit a fundamentalist almost anywhere in the US today. They swarm in the country towns . . . They are thick in the mean streets behind the gasworks. They are everywhere learning is too heavy a burden . . . even the vague, pathetic learning on tap in little red schoolhouses. They march with the Klan, with the Christian Endeavor Society, with the Junior Order of United American Mechanics . . . with all the rococo bands that poor and unhappy folk organize to bring some light of purpose into their lives. They have had a thrill, and they are ready for more."[33]

Mencken was taking aim at people who had given him a serious scare, who had or seemed to have colored the contemporary mood, and who, he feared, were not defeated yet. Soon, the Great Depression appeared to prove him right, evoking arguments about God's punishment of apostate America and signs of Christ's imminent return.[34] But Mencken was wrong. "Heave an egg"? With egg on their faces, humiliated fundamentalists began to draw in their horns. They had been as socially activist as other Christians, had played their part in the politics of a society where Christianity and patriotism naturally went together A pre-millenarian evangelist like Dwight Moody had actively engaged in social work, helped to run the Chicago Young Men's Christian Association, founded a seminary for girls, and tried to alleviate the hardships of the poor. Yet the social gospel came to look increasingly like a threat to Christian belief. Before his death in 1899, Moody concluded that social problems could only be solved by divine regeneration and, fundamentally, by the Second Coming. A man like William

Jennings Bryan had continued to regard the social gospel as "applied Christianity," and to insist that "Christian men *must* take an interest in politics."[35] The Scopes affair and Bryan's passing confirmed the temptations of separatism.

Russell of the Watchtower Society had supported labor and opposed big money. Rutherford had been a committed Bryan populist and even campaigned for him in 1896. After all, altruism came from God, and altruism was activist. But the efforts of zealots like Anthony Comstock trying to suppress medical quackery, mail swindles, fraudulent banking schemes, and obscenity in literature gave Christian altruism a bad name: Comstockery. After 1919, the prohibition amendment to the Constitution divided and criminalized the nation. After Scopes, a new separatism encouraged withdrawal from reform, public life, public schools, local and national affairs, and even abstention from voting.

None proved as extreme as Rutherford. In 1929, he declared the secular state demonic. His Bible Students were not to salute national flags or stand up for a national anthem; Mother's Day was denounced as a feminist plot, Christmas and birthday parties were banned as pagan. The main Witness periodical, *The Golden Age*, founded in 1919, denounced the American Medical Association, the germ theory of disease, and smallpox vaccines. The modern world, its snares and its delusions, were to be shunned.

Not all fundamentalists went so far, but separatism remained a fundamentalist tenet. "The world, to which we do not belong, can do its own reforming without our help," wrote Arno Gabelein.[36] "We practice separatism from the world and all of its entanglements," the Reverend Jerry Falwell's *Fundamentalist Phenomenon* declared in 1981: "We refuse to conform to the standards of a sinful society. We practice personal separation as well as ecclesiastical separation."[37] If the dreams Columbus dreamed were to be realized, that was up to a saving remnant.

THE TWENTIETH CENTURY

We are living through a nocturnal epoch—end of
humanism, individualism, formal liberalism of modern
civilization; beginning of the epoch of new religious
collectivities, in which opposed forces and principles
will define themselves, all that dwelt in the underground
and unconscious of modern history will reveal itself.

– NICOLAS BERDIAEFF

A
S THE NINETEENTH CENTURY ENDED, William
James, professor of philosophy (and many other
things) at Harvard, sat down to prepare the
Gifford Lectures on *The Varieties of Religious Experience* that
he would deliver in Edinburgh in 1901. Almost as a matter of
course, he touched on the view "so widespread at the present
day," the "notion in the air about us, that religion is probably
only an anachronism . . . an atavistic relapse into a mode of
thought which humanity in its more enlightened examples has
outgrown."[1] Religion had for centuries explained the nature of
the universe, of nature, of mankind, and their destination. Now,
natural sciences offered that kind of information in more convincing terms, while the social sciences questioned the essential
truth of religions. A Frenchman, Théodule Ribot, thought that
religion was evaporating. James thought that it was turning into

religious philosophy.[2] Irreligious philosophy more likely, most educated bystanders would have opined.

By James's day, young intellectuals were reading the aphoristic essays of Friedrich Nietzsche. Before he lapsed into insanity on a Turin street, the young German philologist and historian had denounced the anachronism of Christian religion, "a piece of antiquity intruding out of distant ages past," and of Christ, "a sage who calls upon us . . . to heed the signs of the imminent end of the world . . . Can one believe that things of this sort are still believed in?"[3]

Son and grandson of Lutheran pastors, Nietzsche had demonstrated that rationalism and optimism had killed tragedy. He could have said the same of Christianity, killed or badly wounded by its rationalizing interpreters. "Give the modernist three words," William Jennings Bryan complained, "allegorical, poetical and symbolical, and he can suck the meaning out of every vital doctrine of the Christian church."[4]

Bryan was not far off. Meanings were interpreted and reinterpreted away, the supernatural message of the Old Testament and the New was rationalized. Thirty years after Friedrich Strauss had turned the Bible into a collection of allegories and myths, Ernest Renan had come to present Jesus as a charming, lovable preacher more suited to the drawing rooms of Paris than the barrens of Gallilee. Even the Belgian painter James Ensor presented a sarcastic 1888 version of the Second Coming in *Christ's Entry into Bruxelles*. And yet, beneath the skeptical surface, apocalyptic thinking soldiered on. Gerhart Hauptmann situated the adventure of his country prophet, *The Fool in Christ: Emanuel Quint*, in the Germany of the 1890s, where expectations of God's second advent on earth "penetrated to the remotest corners of the land." Hauptmann wrote about credulity and delusion, "which, like every delusion, it is difficult for the sober-minded to comprehend."[5] But in those same deluded 1890s, Nietzsche's essay on the Antichrist appeared, and so did Odilon Redon's somber lithographs on the Apocalypse.

In faraway Russia, Vladimir Solovyov, too, was voicing pre-monitions of a speedy end of the world and the coming of An-tichrist. "Something is preparing," Solovyov wrote to a friend, "someone is coming . . . I mean Antichrist." In 1900, "conscious of the not too far distant image of pale death" and world catastro-phe, the philosopher and mystic wrote "A Short Story of An-tichrist," which comes to a head as the Jews, who first followed the deceiver, rebel when they discover he was not circumcised, and rise up like one man, moved "not by calculation and greed for gain but . . . by the hope and wrath of centuries-old messianic faith." So all ends well, and the saints reign with Christ for a thousand years.[6]

More influential than Solovyov's apocalyptic imaginings was the work of a sober-minded theology student at the University of Strasbourg who went off for military service in 1894 carrying a Greek Testament, which he read even on maneuvers. He found little in it to justify current sophistries, and by the time of his exams he felt ready to take issue with the rationalization, spiritu-alization, and ethicization of what he recognized as concrete expectations of a supernatural kingdom about to dawn immedi-ately. Jesus, insisted Albert Schweitzer, showed the messianic expectation of late Judaism, which went back to the old prophets. Knowing himself to be the Son of Man who comes at the end of the world's existence, he continually exhorts his hear-ers to be ready for Judgment at any moment.

By 1906, Schweitzer's *Quest for the Historical Jesus* had es-tablished him as a theologian to reckon with. Caught up in the apocalyptic vision of his time and people, Schweitzer's Jesus ex-pected to usher in the New Age, suddenly and soon. He proved to be wrong. But St. Paul, who also emphasized the expectation of his immediate return, was able to maintain the fervor of ex-pectancy in a New Age still to come. This expectation had lost credit by Schweitzer's time, and Schweitzer knew that well: "Today we don't expect to see a Kingdom of God realizing itself in supernatural events." But he reminded readers that Christ had so expected, and that "we must reconcile ourselves to the fact that Jesus' religion of love made its appearance as part of a system of thought that anticipated a speedy end of the world."[7]

No such exegesis would have been needed a hundred years before. But mentalities—the mentality of the educated, of those who count and of whose doings history gives account—had changed radically. William James spoke true: religion, at least literalist religion, was something that enlightened humanity had outgrown. Schweitzer had to labor points that, to fifty generations of Christians, would have been obvious. They would never be obvious again.

On the other hand, beliefs once based on prophetic revelations tended to shift to other auspices. Schweitzer's contemporaries had settled into scientism: belief in the power of scientific knowledge, which turned out to be as superstitious as other blind beliefs. Wireless was assimilated to telepathy, x-rays to magic, and the astronomer Camille Flammarion joined the French Spiritualist association to advance "a science dedicated to the experimental demonstration of the existence of the soul and its immortality by means of communications with . . . the dead."[8]

The heavens, too, had been disenchanted. Comets had been omens. King James I, patron of the Authorized Version of the Bible, firmly believed that the great comet of 1618 foretold the Thirty Years' War. By 1872, Louis-Auguste Blanqui, the renowned revolutionary, dismissed the wandering stars: "Everyone despises them . . . Complete disgrace!"[9] The passage of Halley's comet in 1910 would demonstrate that Blanqui was premature. Cartooned, postered, illustrated in magazines (*Harper's Weekly* published a drawing, "Waiting for the End of the World") and in sometimes terrifying picture postcards, set to music (there were at least two Comet Rags), and jeweled in pins and brooches, the comet also stirred anxieties that rose to panic levels.

There were still those who feared the comet as an omen of disaster. In London, General William Booth of the Salvation Army, who expected the end of all things, predicted destruction by water and fire. In Paris, the fashionable prophet Madame de Thèbes, who correctly forecast the torrential rains and floods of the year's beginning, foresaw humanity's destiny stained red with blood, a financial crash impending, and terrible changes imminent. German postcards depicted the end of the world: "Der Weltuntergang Am 18 Mai." Worriers were confirmed, and the sensationalist press was sustained by the unusual weather, the apparition of lesser comets, sunspots, meteor showers, spectacular displays of *aurora borealis*, and, on May 6, the sudden death of King Edward VII of England.

Schooling and science had doused superstition, and few lost sleep over prospects of the comet's collision with the earth. Dread now focused on the comet's tail, known to contain cyanogen, which, mixed with hydrogen, produces prussic acid, hence instant death. *L'illustration* quoted Flammarion, ever the optimist, as opining that "cyanogen gas would impregnate the atmosphere and possibly snuff out all life on the planet." Sales soared of masks and comet pills, guaranteed to protect people from the effect of gases. The *New York Times* quoted the pope as ridiculing Romans who had bought up all the oxygen supplies available in the city, to keep themselves alive until the earth passed through the comet's tail.

All over the world, prayer and panic went together: churches filled up, miners refused to go down into the shafts, women stopped up doors and windows to keep the deadly gas out. The *New York Times* reported on May 18, 1910, that "terror occasioned by the near approach of Halley's comet has seized hold of a large part of the population of Chicago." It affected New York as well, where, during the night of May 18 to 19, "some of the more superstitious in the sections largely inhabited by foreigners were on the verge of panic, and the police were called upon at different times to calm them . . . Many prayed on bended knees in the streets and parks, and several religious processions took place in different parts of the city." In France, too, the rainy night between the 18th and the 19th found anxious crowds everywhere; in the morning, when the comet had passed, people embraced and danced in the streets.[10]

As Henri Focillon pointed out when he wrote about the year 1000, periods of dislocation and societies that are deeply troubled tend "to give an apocalyptic interpretation to history, to worship the God of terror, and to live in expectation of Judgment Day."[11] We have seen how this generalization applied to earlier centuries; now we shall see how it applies to our own. Specifics change, but the general lines remain the same. In James Joyce's *Ulysses*, which is set in Dublin in 1904, Molly Bloom grumps about the woman who "had too much old chat in her about politics and earthquakes and the end of the world let us have a bit of fun first God help the world if all women were her sort down on bathingsuits and lownecks." And, indeed, bathing suits and lownecks, beaches full of nakedness, dancing that was lewdly close, and failure to attend church on Sunday were simply more signs of the approaching end.

Within a few years of Molly, Christabel Pankhurst was warning that Antichrist, the Man of Sin, would "have recourse to radio, atomic energy, solar heat, means as yet undreamed of." And the Man of Sin himself was assuming human shape in Mussolini, cast in the role of Antichrist reviving the Roman Empire. The Duce was fascinated when Belgian pre-millenarians told him of the role attributed to him: "Is that really described in the Bible? Where is it found?"[12]

There were those who suggested that the fascist salute was the Mark of the Beast or preliminary to it; others cast Russia as Gog (and Magog), Germany as Gomer, symbol of faithless Israel running after false Baals. As it had in the past, economic depression inspired anticapitalist themes and recollections of James

2:6: "Do not rich men oppress you?" Babylon was the evil empire of bankers and traders, who showed no mercy and despised the poor.

Anti-Semitism had its votaries who looked on the *Protocols* as plausible, but most Christian millennialists found it repellent.[13] The strangest story is that of the Expressionist German painter and printmaker Hans Beckmann, whose service as a medical corpsman during the First World War must account for the violence and distortion of his figures. Beckmann painted Christian themes seared, as most of his mature paintings are, by sadistic torture and repulsive colors. In 1932, the Nazis, declaring his art "degenerate," forced him to resign his art school professorship; in 1937, he left Berlin for Amsterdam, where he began work on a cycle of the Apocalypse. The resulting book was printed privately in Frankfurt in 1943, at the height of Nazi war, with a complete text in German. Which hand did not know what the other was doing?

The strongest testimony against the apparent diseschatologization of religion came from the Marial apparitions which, having marked the nineteenth century, persevered stubbornly through the twentieth century as well. The best known of these took place in Fatima, a small village some 80 miles north of Lisbon. In the spring of 1917, when Portugal, ruled by an anticlerical regime, suffered from food shortages, high prices, and bread riots, the Virgin appeared to a shepherd girl and, warning of war, starvation, and persecution, called for prayers to bring peace to the world.[14] As in 1876, when the Virgin had appeared at Marpingen at a similar time of agricultural depression and religious persecution, the divine apparitions coincided with difficult conditions. The Virgin appeared in 1931 at Ezquiroga in Spain, in 1932 and 1933 at Beauraing and Banneux in Belgium, in 1938 in Brittany. In April 1931, the Spanish king had fled the country, to be replaced by an anticlerical Republic; the early 1930s were times of severe economic depression in Western

Europe, socialist advances, and the rise of Hitler; the Munich Crisis took place in September 1938, when the Breton, Jeanne-Louise Ramonet, had her first vision. The Catholic right in Spain was specially interested in the end of the world, variously predicted for 1930 or 1958, and was persuaded that the ascendancy of the devil (evidenced not only by dancing and bathing suits, but by the number of churches and convents burnt) signaled calamities, judgments, and chastisement. The Belgian apparitions were exploited by Léon Degrelle's Catholic Action movement, which also publicized Ezquiroga. Ramonet's message, like the others, warned of trials, torments, scourges, storms, upheavals, blood, and fire.[15] All were right on target.

The lady who appeared to Ida Peederman in Amsterdam in the fraught weeks of warring 1944, just before the city's liberation from the Germans, also spoke amid famine and fear, but more diplomatically: "All sorts of currents lead to socialism," she said, "which is good, but only under the direction of the Church." Peederman continued to prophesy into the 1960s, and she was not alone. Between 1945 and 1952, some 2000 miracles were investigated in countries behind the Iron Curtain; between 1930 and 1950, the church in Western Europe investigated thirty series of Marial apparitions and some 3000 individual girls and boys who brushed against the sacred. As Karl Rahmer, who chronicled many of these encounters, has commented: "In turbulent times the minds of men are agitated not only by events, but by the search for interpretation and promise for the future." That was in 1963, and to Rahmer it seemed as if "expectation of the revelation of God in history has been superseded by expectation of the revelation of God which will end history."[16]

Apocalypse had come back into its own; and it had done so, as Christabel Pankhurst foresaw in 1924, by liberating the energy of atoms.[17] And just as secular religions borrow apocalyptic imagery, so concerned atomic scientists dipped into Adventist imagery when they produced the Doomsday Clock, supposed to count the minutes until "the heavens shall pass away with a great noise, and the elements shall melt with fervent heat, the earth also and the works that are therein shall be burned up" (2 Peter 3:10). Since 1947, the minute hand of the clock featured by the *Bulletin of Atomic Scientists* had reflected mostly international tensions. After March 1979, when the nuclear reactor at Three Mile Island, near Harrisburg, Pennsylvania, broke down, the minute hand showed nine minutes to midnight. No one died at Three Mile Island, but thirty-one died and tens of thousands suffered when, in April 1986, a unit of the nuclear power plant at Chernobyl, near Kiev, went out of control and the worst nuclear accident in history followed. By that time, nightmares of nuclear holocaust marched hand in hand with nightmares of ecodisaster.

In 1962, Rachel Carson's *Silent Spring* raised dire questions about the future of human life in a world increasingly poisoned by chemicals. Since then, the population explosion has raised doubts about sustainable life; and ozone destruction, the greenhouse effect, rampant pollution, water shortages projected and real, agricultural exhaustion, volcanic eruptions, meteors, asteroids, exploding stars, interstellar clouds, and extraterrestrials have all crawled out of Pandora's box to confirm them. When, in 1975, the International Foundation of Humane Sciences gathered a distinguished group to discuss "The Terrors of the Year 2000," the menu was unsurprising: runaway demography, food shortages, pollution, biological manipulation, electronic oppression, declining liberty, and deteriorating society.

These fears were shared by more sharply focused friends of the earth. In Tucson, Arizona, in the early 1970s, a woman and three men who called themselves Eco-Raiders slowed real estate development and gained local fame by disrupting building projects, sabotaging bulldozers, and setting billboards on fire. Chronicled in Edward Abbey's 1975 novel, *The Monkey-Wrench Gang*, their guerilla activities inspired the foundation of Earth First!, dedicated to saving Nature from rape by industrial civilization. Population growth threatened biodiversity. Anthropocentric humans were sucking Nature dry: oil, gas, and water were running down; wilderness was receding; the accelerated disappearance of plant species would soon extinguish animal species; and the earth stood on the verge of biological meltdown.

Only biocentric millenarian activism could return mankind to a biocentric perspective. *Ecodefense: A Field Guide to Monkeywrenching* (1973) recommended Luddism, or war on machines and tools that destroy life: spiking roads with barbed metal stakes, spiking trees with bars that destroy chainsaws and sawmill equipment, and sabotaging the instruments used to rape natural surroundings. The campaign should continue until collapse or cataclysm ended the ongoing horrors, brought "imminent, ultimate, collective, this-worldly salvation," and persuaded the surviving remnant to abandon man-centered for nature-centered perspectives: "The Goddess Mother . . . is calling for us to Monkeywrench the Millennium."[18] Whether biological meltdown could be avoided or not, the Earth First! elite would operate as the saving remnant whose ecological consciousness allowed it to recreate the world. Then people would function as they had in the Pleistocene era, in small, ecologically sound communities in harmony with nature, at peace with the earth.

It would be unjust to dismiss the holders of such views, when President Ronald Reagan worked in the perspective of imminent Apocalypse and Armageddon, and his secretary of the interior felt little need to worry about environmental protection because the world would end long before its resources were exhausted. As James Watt told a committee of Congress in 1981, "I don't know how many future generations we can count on until the Lord returns."[19] Old-fashioned eschatology had to run hard to keep up with environmental eschatology, but the latter brought grist to the former's mills. Tim La Haye's *Revelation* (1975) envisioned the population explosion, world famine, and water and pollution problems preceding the devastating Armageddon that ushers in the Second Coming. In that perspective, religious survivalists (perhaps dubious about rapture) advised Christians to buy gold and silver coins, basic tools, durable consumer goods, and dehydrated foods that might see them through the tribulation.[20]

Ecological eschatology unfolded against the more urgent background of atomic apocalyptics. When the Korean War broke out in the summer of 1950, the Paris press was not alone in asking whether this was the beginning of the Third World War. Those of the French who could bought gold and hoarded what they could. Some planned to leave Europe for distant continents, and a few actually did.[21] This exodus inspired the plot of a film by André Cayatte, *Before the Deluge*: fear drives two teenagers to run away to the Pacific to escape atomic holocaust at home. Since life imitates art, in 1954, the year of the film's release, a policeman was accidentally killed in a burglary undertaken "to buy a boat and leave France." For frightened fantasies, however, the South Pacific offered no more escape than its northern shores. In Nevil Shute's 1957 novel, *On the Beach*, which Stanley Kramer turned into a film, the northern hemisphere has perished in the wake of atomic conflict. Australians now await the pleasure of the winds spreading the radioactive contamination that will end human life on earth.

This was a mood the West had hardly known for more than a hundred years, and the trickle of apocalyptic predictions was turning to a flood. Prophecy flourished. Published in 1965, Jeane Dixon's *A Gift of Prophecy* sold over 260,000 hardbound copies and nearly 3 million in paperback. Catholics like Father Cyril Marystone predicted a Communist victory and then defeat, followed by the traditional apocalyptic menu. So did Hoosier disciples of the pre-millenialist William Branham (who failed to resurrect in 1965 as predicted),[22] and the UCLA auxiliaries of Hal Lindsey's Campus Crusade for Christ. In 1970, Lindsey found fame when he published *The Late Great Planet Earth*, predicting the literal accomplishment of Bible prophecies before the century ended and Christ's return to set up his millennial kingdom.[23] The book sold 20 million copies worldwide and spawned a family of follow-ups (*Liberation of Planet Earth; Satan Is Alive and Well on Planet Earth*), none as successful as Lindsey, whom the *New York Times* proclaimed the best-selling author of the 1970s.

Confirmation for Lindsey's prophecies was found in the foundation of Israel and in the Jews becoming a nation once more. So, as Israel received almost unanimous fundamentalist support, 1948 became a milestone on the road to rapture—the more so since the birth of Israel was accompanied by other omens. Broached between the wars, the World Council of Churches finally brought together most Protestants and Eastern Orthodox into one fellowship, all of whose members accepted Jesus Christ as God and Savior. But ecumenism, which is about reconciling beliefs and values that differ, also implies the slurring that comes more easily when beliefs falter and values wane. The compromise of denominational differences could be taken as the Great Apostasy that would mark the reign of Antichrist; and European Union looked suspiciously like the evil empire that Antichrist would rule. In 1957, the Treaty of Rome explicitly linked the Common Market with the ancient Roman Empire; in 1981 the admission of Greece brought its membership to the ten required by Revelation 17:12–14 to support the Beast and make war with the Lamb. The European Economic Community's computer complex in Luxembourg was soon identified as the Beast, and the community's secretary general as Antichrist.

When not assimilated to international organizations, Babylon, no longer Roman and pontifical, became a metaphor for big business, global trade, invasive unionism, capitalism, and technology. The League of Nations and, following it, the "Jewnited Nations," had long been denounced as satanic. Socialists inspired by Satan adapted Christian visions to diabolic ends. The paradise they promised would blossom under the auspices of

Antichrist. Trade unions too worked for the abomination of desolation: union-made labels were marks of the Beast without which, as Revelation predicted, none would be able to buy or sell. And Revelation also offered texts to damn commercialism.[24]

In the 1950s, believers in pursuit of devilish conspiracies were reported to have forced the withdrawal of a Canadian banknote where the sworls of Queen Elizabeth's hair revealed a grinning Satan. But new technologies turned up too many snares to cope with: television, computers, credit cards, ATMs, commsatellites, lasers and laser readable price markers, microchips, transponders, and fiber optics all established new levels of social control that Antichrist could use. Revelation 13:16–17 speaks of the beast that "causeth all . . . to receive a mark in their right hand or in their foreheads; and that no man may buy or sell, save he that had the mark, or the name of the beast, or the number of his name." By 1973, Willard Cantelon's *Day the Dollar Dies* predicted the creation of cashless credit systems complete with magnetic ink numbers tattooed under the skin. Published in 1981, Mary Stewart Relfe's *The 666 System Is Here*, which sold 300,000 copies within three months, alerted readers to the ill-omened presence of the beast's number in product codes, computer programs, license plates and telephone prefixes. In 1995, the Internet was associated with the fourth beast of the Apocalypse, and Bill Gates with the Antichrist. Subtle researchers also revealed that when the nine-digit zip codes that the U.S. Post Office used were added to the nine-digit numbers of the Social Security Administration, the ominous total came to eighteen. But eighteen is simply 6 multiplied by 3—in other words, 666: the number of the beast's name.[25]

Not all apocalyptists could be dismissed as cranks, eccentrics, crackpots, or, as Mencken dubbed them, morons. Unquestioning believers in Biblical inerrancy no longer represented the vast majority of Christian societies; and Western societies still calling themselves Christian were more indifferent to religion than they had ever been. But drain religion of plain faith, and superstition rushes in. People need something to reassure them about the uncertainties of life. As William James foresaw, the legitimation of occult phenomena and the peculiar claims advanced under new-found scientistic titles also proceeded apace. Rationalism did not mean rationality; secularism easily adjusted to magic, mysticism, and astrology; and a diet of second-hand, second-rate religion substitutes created more demand for religious revival and revitalization.

In 1952, an Oxford scholar, C.S. Lewis, creator of Narnia and *The Screwtape Letters*, had written an essay on "The World's Last Night" that took issue with the memory hole in which the Apocalypse had lapsed: "The doctrine of the Second Coming is deeply uncongenial to the whole evolutionary and developmental character of modern thought." Yet, once again, the Apocalypse teetered on the brink of oblivion and failed to fall. The sudden, violent end that it foretells fitted the conditions of our time too well. Not the violent end, Lewis argued, but "the idea of the world slowly ripening to perfection" was the myth—"our favorite modern mythology." The doctrine of the Second Coming was "the medicine our condition especially needs."[26]

Lewis was better known for his science fiction and his children's stories, but by the time he died in 1963, holding the chair of medieval and renaissance English at Cambridge, other serious students were taking eschatology seriously. In 1970, the German theologian Klaus Koch published *The Rediscovery of Apocalyptic*, soon translated into English, whose second chapter traced "the sudden turning to apocalyptic" in the past two decades and the recognition of it as "the mother of Christian theology."[27] So much scholarly work confirmed this trend that, by 1981, one outstanding contributor of the apocalyptic renaissance could comment on the "recent fascination" with a subject that had "become extremely popular in modern culture and scholarship."[28] Perhaps the same forces of convention that made the apocalyptic seem irrelevant or just bad form were revealing its relevance and "fascination" when contemporary history looked strikingly apocalyptic. In 1990, George Carey, a charismatic evangelical Christian, became Archbishop of Canterbury. Though the London *Times* quoted fears that he might "make the church look slightly dotty,"[29] his tenure of that eminently respectable office confirmed the timeliness of Lewis's views, and Koch's.

Carey's elevation to the see of Canterbury passed relatively unnoticed, compared with activities taking place on the enthusiastic fringe. In 1973, Saleem Kirban, author of *666* and other best-sellers, founded Second Coming Inc., and a 2000-member church in North Hollywood took legal steps to preserve its property and the continuity of its leadership once the secret rapture removed its officers to heaven. Insurance companies agreed to delay payments for seven years, when Jesus would return in judgment and church officers with him. Enthusiasm did not exclude foresight. As one evangelist explained, though Christ would come within his generation, it would be prudent to arrange finances for some decades ahead. "He won't be upset with us for having planned ahead."[30]

Humanity once again stood on the threshold of a Second Advent; and this time its prophets made use of publicity machines their forerunners had ignored. David Seltzer's films *The Omen* (1976), *Damien Omen II* (1978), and *The Final Conflict* (1981) featured the birth of Antichrist whose reign, the tribulation, would cover the seven years following the rapture. This last (Michael Tolkin's *Rapture*, 1991) featured a heroine, Mimi Rogers, who converts just in time for the end of the world.

As early as 1979, the television income of religious broadcasters was nudging half a billion dollars,[31] and the Reverend Pat Robertson apparently planned to televise the Second Coming. "We even discussed," recorded an acolyte, "how Jesus' radiance might be too bright for the cameras."[32] The media were getting used to end-of-the-world talk: in a feature entitled "The Deluge of Disastermania," *Time* (March 5, 1979) called Armageddon a growth industry. *Paris Match* agreed. In June of that same year, "Les Français et la sinistrose" (The French and Disastermania) found that for 54 percent of those surveyed, especially the young, the year 2000 represented "a fear." At the 1975 Charismatic Congress in Rome, several prophecies had foretold a time of trials, imminent darkness, and desolation. Belief in the imminent millennium was widespread among Catholic Pentecostals, the majority of whom, like their non-Catholic fellows, believed that the Parousia was near and that God's wrath was impending.[33] Nor were Pentecostals far ahead of other observant Catholics, since, in 1981, a Jesuit, Father Vincent Miceli, published *The Antichrist,* with a foreword by Malcolm Muggeridge.

Belief in a second advent, Antichrist, and a millennium was doctrinally sound and unexceptional as long as the qualification was made that "of that day and hour knows no man, no, not the angels of heaven, but my Father only" (Matthew 24:36). But it made sense to heed Christ's simultaneous assurance that these events were on the point of happening, and his warning to be ready for them. Throughout Christian history, authoritative sources had played down imminence, enthusiasts had stressed it, and believers had hovered between the two. Charles Strozier, a serious student of fundamentalist psychology, found that most fundamentalists showed "considerable equivocation about the end, mixing a very human kind of hope that the world will not self-destruct with a conviction that the end is prophetically assured."[34] Death also is certain, but uncertain too. Rationalizing cautions reassured, but dramatic destiny and doomsday signs provided alluring thrills. Apocalyptosophes and apocalyptophiles abounded. That may be why one American in three thought that the Bible was true word for word, two in three had no doubt that Jesus would come to earth again, and four in five were certain they would appear before God on Judgment Day. By 1992, 53 percent of adult Americans expected the imminent return of Jesus Christ and the fulfillment of Biblical prophecies about a cataclysmic destruction of evil.[35]

The question was when. A Millennium Watch Institute kept an eye out for signs of the Coming. The Socialist National Aryan People's Party predicted 1985. Elizabeth Claire Prophet, head of the Church Universal and Triumphant, predicted 1989. In a full-page advertisement in the *New York Times* (March 18, 1991), Jews-for-Jesus linked Saddam Hussein with Antichrist and urged readers to call 900-4-MESSIAH for further information. In 1992, the Mission for the Coming Days forecast the rapture for October that year, and bumper stickers cautioned: "If you hear a trumpet, grab the wheel." More cautiously, in a novel he published in 1995, Pat Robertson mooted the end of the Gentile age for 2007. Endism was everywhere and, to deal with its obsessions, a Wall Street broker and a Wall Street lawyer who was also a graduate of Yale Divinity School, set up Fundamentalists Anonymous, which also offered a hotline: 212-696-0240. Within two years of its foundation in 1985, the organization's membership was 30,000 and growing. In 1987, also, the electronic clock installed in the Pompidou Center in Paris was set up to flash the number of seconds left in the twentieth century. They were ticking by fast. Drugs, AIDS, crime, and illiteracy were all signs, "part of the end time and approaching Armageddon . . . It's God trying to get our attention."[36]

God's efforts to attract attention were to become painfully obvious in the small hours of Monday, January 17, 1994, Martin Luther King Day, when an earthquake, 6.7 on the Richter scale, hit the San Fernando Valley and the Los Angeles basin. Many born-again Christians regarded the worst shaking that southern California had endured since 1769 as the first sign of the next coming.[37] And that, in our context, was unexceptional. Belief in the Parousia is crucial to fundamentalist theology, if not to all fundamentalist thought. But such beliefs are flexible and ready to change in detail. So, in the wake of the Second World War, last days would often feature nuclear holocaust, alien invasion, or destructive and preservative spaceships, none of which were any more extraordinary than the horned beasts, flying chariots, and airborne horses of traditional imagery. What happened in the second half of the twentieth century, however, complicated this scenario by miscegenation with some contemporary creeds. And in this respect the 1960s proved particularly creative.

In Latin America, one kind of apocalypticism or another had thrived for a long time, offering expectations of miraculous deliverance that drew inspiration from Anarchist, Christian, and Marxist sources, but that mostly used what lay ready to hand: the imagery of death and regeneration irrigating the soil with the blood of martyrs before the millennium brought heaven on earth. The theology of liberation that was born in the 1960s reedited all these themes to promise escape from history, or at least transcendence, through the creation of a new humanity.

Further north, the International Society for Krishna Consciousness, founded in 1966 by an incarnation of the god Krishna (hence its better-known name, Hare Krishna), presented the current materialistic age of Kali-Yuga as the last of a four-millennium cycle now drawing to a close and waiting to be replaced by an era of peace, love, and unity. The saffron-robed adepts of Hare Krishna lived in temple communes where gambling, intoxicants, meat, and illegitimate sexual activities were banned pending the world's imminent collapse and the new era's advent. Even more clearly marked by the spirit of the 1960s were the CWLF (Christian World Liberation Front), whose prophets announced Christ's early and literal return in Jesus rallies, songs, and that emphasized the invocation "Maranatha" (supposedly Aramaic for "Our Lord Come"); and the 3HO (Healthy, Happy, Holy Organization), which taught the end of the 2000-year Piscean Age, to be followed by the radically different (and better) Age of Aquarius, when group-and-God-consciousness would replace the individual.

The Age of Aquarius also figured prominently in a movement as diverse as the counter culture of the 1960s in which it plunged its roots: New Age. The transition from the Piscean Age inaugurated by Jesus Christ's first coming to the Aquarian (and Biblical) millennium of love and brotherhood would be fraught with violence and peril for the spiritually unprepared. On the other hand, those attuned to the impending transition would "enter a new age of abundance and spiritual enlightenment . . . in which, guided by advanced beings, perhaps angels . . . perhaps emissaries from an extraterrestrial civilization whose spacecraft were the UFOs, they would help to create a new civilization."[38]

In one version of New Age eschatology, Antichrist was expected to reveal himself around the end of the present century, amid the violent images of annihilation dear to apocalyptists of all kinds, not least the battle between good and evil, and the cataclysmic destruction of nearly all the earth. A new-model rapture, meanwhile, preserved the saints. A major planetary activation permitted 144,000 "Activated Star-Borne" initiates to participate in "mass ascension to new realms of consciousness." Once the sinful planet had been cleansed and preserved, the newness of the age that followed would be assured by the high spiritual development of those who survived, and by the God who had just demonstrated his benevolence by annihilating those who didn't.[39]

The dictionary defines syncretism as "the process of fusing diverse ideas into a general inexact impression." Each of the movements described above attempted to reconcile a diversity of notions, both banal and futuristic, in a hybrid mix. None did this with more zest than the sects and subsects that can be generically described as Black Muslims. The various communities so labeled differ among themselves, but all use religious vocabulary to assert black nationalism. They all appear to have evolved out of religious black nationalist organizations of the early twentieth century which sought redemption from racial oppression by stimulating black pride and black community within what Wallace Fard (Farrad Mohammed) described as "the Lost-Found Nation of Islam in the West."[40]

Believed by his followers to be an incarnation of Allah, Fard immigrated to the United States from Mecca in the 1920s, established the temple of Islam in Detroit in 1930, and echoed the pent-up frustrations of his congregation when he preached that the reign of white devils was coming to an end. However, before the slave masters could be overcome, blacks had to give up Christianity, which was simply a white contrivance to enslave and manipulate nonwhites, assert their historical and economic independence, reclaim themselves, and prepare for Armageddon—the final struggle between good and evil. In 1934, Fard disappeared without a trace (his birthday, February 26, is still celebrated as Savior's Day) and was succeeded by Elijah Poole, who, as Elijah Muhammad, had become Fard's assistant a few years before. It was Elijah Muhammad who founded the Nation of Islam, a separate nation for Black Americans based on the worship of Allah and the belief that blacks were his chosen people; and it was Elijah Muhammad's rigorous asceticism that turned social rejects into productive, self-respecting people.

Black nationalism, race pride, and hatred of the white oppressors, whose Ku Klux Klan burned down his family home, soared in the brilliant, bitter eloquence of one of Elijah Muhammad's converts, Malcolm Little, later Malcolm X. In 1963, reasonably enough from his point of view, Malcolm X described President Kennedy's murder as a case of chickens coming home to roost when white violence, so often directed against blacks, affected the very leader of "the blue-eyed devils." In 1964, Malcolm X went on a pilgrimage to Mecca, converted to orthodox Islam, and abandoned his counter-separatism and racism for dreams of world brotherhood. Too late. In February 1965, his own chicken came home to roost when he was shot to death in a Harlem ballroom.

His moral and cultist successor in the public eye would be a man who briefly followed both Elijah Muhammad and Malcolm X—Louis Eugene Wolcott, later Louis X—and most recently Minister Farrakhan, founder of the reorganized Nation of Islam, prophet of the Lord of Retribution, avenging voice "of generation upon generations of black people whose blood cried out for justice, and not only justice—but for revenge."[41]

The literature of the Nation of Islam reads either like a farrago of nonsense or an updated mirror image of Biblical prophecies, which also sometimes sound like ravings and sometimes radiate the compelling logic of a deep-held faith. In brief, the Nation of Islam lives at the end of time. The 6000-year-long rule of the white devils is about to close, the era of the devil expired in 1914, and the Second World War and all subsequent conflicts have been identified as Armageddon. Islamic numerologist Tynetta Muhammad has calculated that the end will come in 2001.

God and the divine scientists dwell in a gigantic wheel-shaped manmade planet known as the Mother Plane or the Mother Ship. In this magnificent New Jerusalem, they and the saved black remnant will survive the final battle and form the nucleus of a new civilization. Shortly before the scheduled end, a trumpet of doom will sound the final call, and spacecraft will scatter leaflets in Arabic and English urging the faithful to gather for rescue in this new-version rapture. Baby planes will ferry them to the Mother Ship before the white devils and their world are wiped out by more planes (or "wheels," see Ezekiel 10:2) dropping coals of fire (bombs). As Farrakhan declares: "When you see him coming in the clouds of heaven," Jesus "has got a sword, and it's dripping with blood. No come back to teach nobody. He comes back to judge the wicked."[42]

Here, as it so often does, exasperated protest shades into revenge. James the apostle had seen this well enough when he promised judgment without mercy to those who show no mercy (2:13); and Gerhart Hauptmann too, whose *fin de siècle* weavers

dreamed "not pardon but revenge . . . the reward for suffering."
To the extent that Mencken had been right when he insisted that
"evangelicals are about hate"—and he was only partly right in
finding hatred the "basic religion of the American clodhopper
today"[43]—black Americans were as American as their fellows.

Sometimes such hatred turned outward in mythologies of
revenge; sometimes it turned inward in self-destructive paroxysms. In November 1978, 913 followers of a charismatic preacher,
James Warren Jones, committed suicide by drinking cyanide-
laced punch at Jonestown in Guyana. A Pentecostal in his youth,
Jones had visions of the nuclear holocaust that was to happen,
but didn't, in 1967. He fled for refuge to Brazil, then to Ukiah in
northern California (the furthest he could get from his native
Indiana without falling into the ocean), and finally to San Fran-
cisco, where his People's Temple made him popular and
famous. After being appointed to the city's housing authority, he
became its chairman and went on to win the Martin Luther King
Humanitarian Award and several others. He offered salvation
and liberation to the disenfranchised, dehumanized victims of
American society: blacks to begin with (blacks made up 80 percent of the membership of the People's Temple and 75 percent of
Jonestown), but also other "niggers"—women, the poor, the old,
Indians, Chicanos, Jews. He rejected the Christian Sky God,
selfish and wicked or else indifferent, and presented himself as
the living manifestation of the real God of Apostolic Socialism.
Savior, liberator, and redeemer, he claimed the power to heal and
to resurrect. Had he not walked on water, turned water into
wine, and caused rain to fall and smog to disappear?

But the temple, its properties, and its accounts were not kept
up properly—presumably because end times were coming—and
the accusations of defectors, who denounced him as Antichrist,
and of more mundane critics drove him away from the Bay Area
to found Jonestown, an isolated agricultural colony where believers could prepare for Parousia. "We've got to get ourselves

ready for a great day. We've got no time." When a U.S. congress-
man accompanied by newspeople pursued James Jones to
Guyana, they were ambushed and several were murdered. The
time of which there was so little ran out, and the mass suicide
that had been rehearsed on previous occasions brought final
healing.[44]

No artisanal apocalyptic entrepreneur has in our time surpassed Jones's murderous and self-murderous consummation.
But that was not for want of trying. Thus, Cyrus Reed Teed, one
of the nineteenth century's many divines, would provide one
piece of inspiration for successors who surpassed him. Teed was
to his followers *Koresh*, that King Cyrus whom God once "charged
to build him an house at Jerusalem" (Ezra 1:2), the prophet of a
divine message destined to redeem the human race. Teed called
himself the second Christ, warned against the forces of Gog and
Magog—big business and big labor—mobilizing for the final battle that would decide the fate of earth, and sought 144,000 elect
who might be saved from this world. Those who harkened to
him turned over all property to the collective, but they were few
in number and, after Teed's death in 1908, their Holy City in
Florida dissolved. Koresh, the name that Teed adopted, would
be picked up some four score years after him by a more thor-
oughgoing prophet: a journeyman carpenter like Jesus.

Born as the 1950s ended, Vernon Howell never could spell,
not even the word *angel*. But he was raised in the Adventist
church and, by the age of twelve, had memorized long passages
from the Bible. By the time he came to Mt. Carmel, near Waco,
Texas, he had been talking to God for years and expected the millennium to come in his generation. The community he joined
called itself Branch Davidians. They had split off in 1959 from
the Davidian Seventh-day Adventists, who had themselves split
off from the Seventh-day Adventists in the late 1920s. Davidians,
who believed they lived in the last days, also believed that
William Miller had preached the message of the first two angels

of Revelation, while successive prophets represented the remaining five. They regarded themselves as the righteous remnant destined to play its part in the grand scenario of Armageddon.

Howell, who soon changed his name to David Koresh, was recognized as the prophetic seventh angel as well as the eschatological Lamb destined to open the seven seals of Revelation 6 and to explain their hidden meaning. Before they shared in Christ's victory at Armageddon, his Branch Davidians had to survive the coming tribulation and reign of Antichrist. That was why their settlement was named Mt. Carmel, after the site where Elijah once confounded the prophets of Baal, and where God's armies could wait out Armageddon on the Megiddo plain below; and that was why David Koresh stocked provisions and weapons, with which to ride out the great days of wrath that followed the opening of the sixth seal, scheduled to come soon after March 1993.

Like the people of Jonestown, the Branch Davidians of Mt. Carmel were not outwardly aggressive, but separatists from a corrupt and dying world who hoped to find escape in heavenly flying saucers—God's chariots of fire of Psalm 68:17. In April 1993, after a fifty-one-day siege, Koresh, along with seventy-three men, women, and children, and several federal agents, was to die in a radiant holocaust, much as seventeen centuries earlier the Montanists prescribed by Roman authorities died in their burning churches.[45]

Strategies for negotiating deliverance and salvation differed, but small savior-led theocracies continued to spring up, to offer refuge from a sinful world and staging areas for expected transportation to heaven. Under pressure from the authorities or media, from defectors and "concerned relatives," such isolated sanctuaries would implode in mass suicide designed to escape persecution characteristic of end times, or explode into aggression against other humans under Satan's sway.

Thus, in the fall of 1994, forty-eight believers died in Switzerland and five more in Quebec, some brutally murdered, others suicides, including their Messiah, the forty-six-year-old Luc Jouret, a Belgian obstetrician and founder of the *Temple Solaire*, or Order of the Solar Temple. Jouret had graduated from radical politics in the 1970s to evangelism in the 1980s, peddling a heady mix of revolution, occultism, healing, and communal living in a former monastery at Ste-Anne-de-la-Pérade in Quebec, where the Solarians raised organic vegetables and operated a bakery. Jouret's message was New Age apocalypticism: environmental ruin, economic collapse, ensuing violence, which only the chosen (and armed) few would survive. The chosen few were neither marginal nor oppressed: professionals, a small-town mayor and his wife, and business people—members of the middle class no less ready to follow a warrior Messiah into the New Age.

Internal quarrels, mostly over Jouret's financial dealings, as well as Canadian and Swiss government investigations activated the leader's suspicions of evil conspiracies against him and his sect. The world had been offered salvation and had rejected it; now it pursued the faithful. Jouret's predictions about the end of the world became increasingly specific. A three-month-old boy identified as the Antichrist was slain and had a stake driven through his heart. Managed catastrophe seemed preferable to doom and discredit. "We are leaving this earth," declared a document left behind by the outward bound, "to found . . .a new dimension of truth and absolution, far from the hypocrisy and oppression of this world, in order to achieve the seeds of our future generation."[46] One hopes that the Belgian Messiah was a better master of the forceps than he was of the English language.

Then, in March 1997, at Rancho Santa Fe near San Diego, thirty-nine members of a "computer related cult" that believed spacecraft would ferry them to heaven died in a mass suicide after leaving a farewell message on the group's Web site. Led by "two members of the Kingdom of Heaven (or what some would call aliens from space) incarnated in two unsuspecting humans," the group had long prepared to leave earth for a

Higher Level. Its leaders described themselves as "pillars" in the temple of God (Revelation 3:12), come to unfold the mystery of "the new Jerusalem which cometh down out of heaven," to which the faithful could accede through Heaven's Gate or Heaven's Door "now briefly open," and thus escape the "spading under" of humanity.

Forthcoming faithful unfortunately were few, and Heaven's Door was closing. By the 1990s, the present age had almost petered out, Lucifer controlled the earth, and humans were about to perish in apocalyptic flames. In 1995, the approach of Comet Hale-Bopp provided the expected sign that a rescue mission, probably in a spaceship traveling in the comet's wake, was approaching to remove the expectant remnant. On March 23 and 24, 1997, just when Hale-Bopp passed closest to earth, barbiturates and vodka sped them on their way. One may regret that less discreet and more destructive humans do not remove themselves from earth with as little fuss as the inhabitants of Heaven's Gate.[47]

On the far shores of the Pacific, meanwhile, a particularly vehement apocalyptic enterprise confirmed such wishes. Japan's spiritual rush hour, as David Kaplan called it,[48] began in the 1970s—perhaps because the country's stiff obstacle course to success left many maladjusted and frustrated, seeking escape from or revenge against the society in which they failed. There were old, established sects like Tenrikyo, which counted several million members and hoped to found an earthly paradise free from suffering, sickness or need; and Soka Gakkai, a dispensationalist pre-millenarian form of Buddhism, for which the world was blundering through a last-days' situation: "the end of Dharma." There were newer and lesser sects like the Institute for Human Happiness, founded by a former Tokyo stockbroker in whom Socrates, Henry Ford, and other worthies had found reincarnation, pending the apocalypse that would be survived by Japan alone. The archipelago as a whole boasted more than

200,000 registered religious sects, claiming membership greater than the country's population.[49]

In 1984, a failed herbalist, Chizuo Matsumoto, who had found enlightenment in the Himalayas, founded the New Society of Aum, or the Aum Association of Mountain Wizards, or Aum Shinrikyo (the true teaching of Aum)—Aum or Om being the Sanskrit mantra representing the Hindu trinity of Brahma, Vishnu, and Shiva. Especially inspired by Shiva the Destroyer, by Nostradamus, whose Japanese translation in the 1970s proved a best-seller, by Isaac Asimov and Jonathan Livingston Seagull, Matsumoto became Shoko Asahara, the reincarnation of Imhotep who had built the pyramids of Egypt. His enterprise was recognized as a religious corporation, with all the tax advantages this status implied. By the mid-1990s, Aum Shinrikyo's worldwide following was estimated at 50,000, and its global assets at over one billion dollars.

Meditating on a beach, Asahara had learned that Armageddon would come around the end of the century. Books and pamphlets with titles like *The Day of Annihilation* announced the coming crisis; predicted the end of the world beginning in 1997, or 1999, or 2001; and invited believers to seek shelter in communities where Aum members could hope to ride out the devastation. The sect would not only pile up provisions, but would prepare fantastic weapons: lasers, particle beams, heavy artillery, chemical and biological agents, even new generations of nuclear bombs. If Aum tried hard, reflected Asahara, it might reduce the victims of Armageddon to one-quarter of the world's population. But they could expect salvation only if they believed in Asahara.

Aum USA, founded in 1987 and registered as a nonprofit organization in New York State, recruited only a handful of members. But we can learn what they and other Aumnipotents apprehended from a nineteen-year-old Columbia religious studies major whom Nippon Television interviewed in 1995:

"I believe in Armageddon, in the sense that there will be a catastrophic war between the US and Japan, that the US will attack Japan, and the world will go into chaos."[50]

The pressure to cope with the imminent chaos began to increase when twenty-five Aum candidates, led by Asahara himself, ran for election to Japan's Parliament in 1990, and all failed miserably. Asahara's attempts to take refuge from the humiliation of public failure and from its cosmic fallout were foiled by media attention and by nagging questions about possible mass suicide. That was when the Guru went ballistic. He declared himself to be Jesus Christ, the last messiah of the century, but specifically the combatant Christ of Armageddon and of the Last Judgment. Asahara's Buddhism, never overly gentle, was henceforth liberally laced with the violence of Revelation, the more apocalyptic prophecies of Nostradamus, and the *Protocols of the Elders of Zion*. Jews, already responsible for mass murder in Cambodia, Bosnia, and Rwanda, now planned to kill off the world's entire population by the year 2000. And Jews included the Japanese emperor, President Clinton, Madonna, as well as rival sects like Soka Gakkai and Sun-Myung Moon's Unification Church. But the satanic Antichrist was also identified with the British royal family, and, much more likely, with Asahara's beast of choice: the United States.[51]

Defectors, investigators, and accusers were closing in on Aum's arms warehouses and laboratories, forcing the cult to "strike back" with kidnappings and murders. In 1980, Hal Lindsey had predicted that the so-called Jupiter effect would set off "history's greatest outbreak of earthquakes." Now Asahara prophesied that in January 1995, Pluto's entry into the sign of Sagittarius would bring catastrophe; and Asahara was right. On January 17, 1995, one year to the day after the Los Angeles groundwave, an earthquake devastated the city of Kobe. Six thousand perished in the worst disaster to strike a Japanese city since the Second World War, and several more thousands lost everything in fires and ruins. Asahara attributed the disaster to American secret weapons, first tested in the Gulf War of January 1991, then in the Los Angeles earthquake of January 1994. Armageddon had clearly begun; and just to make sure that all took notice, Aum's scientists worked overtime to bring Asahara's prophecies to the attention of the public. First they sprayed Tokyo and its surrounding areas with toxins containing germs of anthrax, botulism, and Q fever (an incapacitating disease whose microbes they corralled on their large Australian sheep ranch). When this infection did not work, they attacked the Tokyo subway system with sarin gas, a deadly nerve agent. Eleven dead and thousands affected finally attracted the attention Asahara sought, and suggested the possibilities of bioterrorism.

Christianity too began as an apocalyptic sect. Christians too, when given the opportunity, had sought to destroy unbelievers and misbelievers, including fellow Christians clinging to false versions of their faith. Deuteronomy 13, which commands the killing of all, including family and friends, who pursue other gods, has been much invoked by true believers; and its spirit presides over all totalitarian mentalities. Like Aum, Christianity was not necessarily about making the world a better place to live, but about awaiting the end and doing what one could to hasten its coming. At Jonestown and at Waco, assault by (evil) outside forces precipitated the immolation of the saints. One year after Waco, a similar sense of apocalypse impending sent Asahara's murderers on to the attack. Davidians destroyed themselves, Aum destroyed others; but expectation of the millennium, hope of accelerating its advent, inspired both sects. As a Japanese scholar put it, "they wanted to destroy everything in preparation for a rebirth."[52]

God's expected doom was getting plenty of attention, even from academics. *The Chronicle of Higher Education* (October 24, 1997) featured "a host" of books and college courses about "Apocalyptic Predictions and Millennial Fervor." It quoted Professor

Richard Landes of Boston University, who foresaw "a wave of millennial activity"—a safe prediction almost at once confirmed by singer Marilyn Manson's newest album, "Antichrist Superstar." Like every popular product, apocalyptism was being gobbled up by the market. Babylon had replaced Jerusalem, and believers could only await the decisive moment when Babylon, that great emporium, fell "because she made all nations drink of the wine of the wrath of her fornication" (Revelation 14:8). That moment, it seemed, was not far off.

In 1997, Michael Drosnin's *Bible Code* became an international best-seller. If the 304,805 Hebrew letters of the Torah (the first five books of the Bible) are arranged in rows, names apparently appear that can be read straightforwardly, diagonally, upside down, or backwards, and these foretell the future, especially if it is past. Drosnin believes that the code helped avert nuclear war in 1996, and may prevent Armageddon in the near future. But if Armageddon may still be averted or delayed, what a book of the same year called *The Millennium Bomb* still hovers in the offing.[53] The world economy, from banks to weapons systems, is now based on computers; and computers, until the other day, were programmed to use only two digits to denote a year. When, before long, computers tick over from 99 to 00, they will be lost, stumped, baffled. So will whatever contains microchips driven by clock mechanisms, including traffic lights, air traffic and other control systems, power stations, chemical works, communications, libraries, savings accounts, and electronic data banks of every sort. Companies and governments the world over are scurrying to right the problem, with no certainty of success and the certain expectation of a cost of billions of dollars. As Ezekiel once warned (7:25), "Destruction cometh; and they shall seek peace, and there shall be none."

CONCLUSION

Begin at the beginning, said the King of Hearts
to the White Rabbit, and go on till you come
to the end: then stop.

– LEWIS CARROLL

A T FIRST there was nothing. But God was: "I am
the first and I am the last; and beside me there
is no God." History begins with Genesis, and
Genesis begins with the Word—an arbitrary act of creation. The
Word is God's will, history is God's will being worked out on
earth, and wisdom is the fear of God, which, says Proverbs 1:7,
is the beginning of wisdom. "Let [the Lord] be your fear, and
let him be your dread" (Isaiah 8:13). The world without God
and without fear of God made no sense. It did not lend itself to
rational understanding, but neither did God: awful, incomprehensible in his ways, and manifesting himself mainly in fits of
ill-temper.

God created the world, and men and women in it. What God
did was good, but it became bad—the men and women, too. Led
by Satan, evil spirits opposed God and ruled the world of men.
Darkness made war on light, evil outbid and outdid good. The
struggle between good and evil would be pursued with mixed
results until the end, but then its resolution would be absolute.

One day soon God would put an end to the world. His kingdom would appear throughout all creation, Satan would be no more, nor would evil and sorrow subsist. Before that came to pass, however, God would send signs of the end: there would be woes and terrors, unnatural happenings, and a rising tide of evil until God's anointed son, the Messiah, was revealed and began to rule the survivors of terminal trials and torments.

Thus the Jewish Apocalypse. Their God was omnipotent and unfathomable, and the only way of following his will (or caprice) was through obedience, submission, and resignation. Laws were laws not because they were just, but because they were laws. Sin was equivalent to disobedience, transgression to rebellion against authority, reverence to terror. The rules of the good life were not spiritual, but practical and material. Ethics were communal, legalistic, particularist, and commonsensical. (It was Jesus himself who would first point out the virtue of gratuitous charity.) Ideally, righteousness, justice, legalism, and ritualism dominated moral life. A good man was honest, reliable, modest, and kept the faith; special religious zeal manifested itself in scrupulous observance of particular maxims affecting daily life.

Defeated, their territory occupied—most lately by the Romans—Jews looked for the restoration of David's glorious kingdom under an anointed king of the line of David. This Messiah (rendered in Greek as *Christos*) would set up his throne in Jerusalem, reassemble the dispersed tribes of Israel, and, after AD 70, rebuild the temple. The Messiah, like David, would be a warrior hero, but of a special kind. He would not "put his trust in horse and rider and bow, nor multiply for himself gold and silver for war, nor gather confidence" from numbers, but would destroy his enemies "with the word of his mouth."

When Jesus preached that the kingdom of God was at hand, he was voicing an opinion commonly held by Jews of his time; and, of course, he was himself a Jew. What was new and different about his message was its criticism of traditional outward piety, concerned with rules, with forms, and with that law which the incoming millennium would abolish. Jesus came, he said, not to destroy but to fulfill God's Word, and God's Law, in expectation of the imminent end; and in that perspective to warn his people of the wrath at hand and tell them how they might escape it. Relation to God, taught Jesus, is not about behavior, but about the spirit in which life was led and God addressed. The notion of a covenant between God and Jews was misleading, first because his Father was the God of all, not only Jews, and then because He demanded not obedience, but love, in exchange for the love he offered. God's love for His creatures was no contract, but a gift freely given; and it was individual, not collective. God's grace was about gratuitousness, not accounting for price, to be returned not only to God but to fellow men. None need go through motions of worship to secure salvation that was offered free. Yet judgment was nigh, repentance or self-judgment indispensable to survive it, and mercy would follow.

The essential component was love—"fulfillment of the law"— and assurance that the time is fulfilled and the reign of God has drawn nigh. The love that Jesus preached would confuse issues for those to whom a god of love meshed ill with a god of fear. The problem was solved, at least in theory, by arguing that God—the god of love—had set a term to vengeance and punishment. A catastrophic end of the soiled, suffering world would usher in perfection, and the rule of a lord not vengeful but benign. The most unnerving book of the New Testament would sublimate the terrors of the Old and replace fear with hope.

Christ's hearers expected "signs" that this was the case. He told them not to look for signs, yet provided them. He cast out demons, healed the sick, resurrected the dead: "No doubt the kingdom of God is come upon you." It was here because Jesus was. The last hour was now, yet it was not. Had Christ been speaking figuratively, or was he simply wrong?

Neither, said the apostles. Paul stubbornly repeats: "Now is the accepted time; behold, now is the day of salvation." The kingdom is right here for those who have eyes to see, ears to hear, the will to accept and enter. The hour of decision was there in Palestine, not long ago; but it continues open to those who place their destiny in the hands of the Christ whose appearance on earth inaugurated the eschatological process, and whose reappearance will bring it to an end. And the kingdom remains open through the church which, after His resurrection, acted as *locum tenens:* the temporary representative of Christ's body on earth.

When prophecy fails, Frank Kermode has suggested, sects are either forgotten or become institutions. The sect of those who followed the Gallilean became an institution; and institutions don't much like enthusiasm, or the perspective of an imminent end. Gradually, eschatological expectations seeped out, ritual and ceremony seeped back in, and so did the law that was supposed to end with the millennium that Jesus opened. The imminent end of the world was still expected by most—the Second Coming, the resurrection of the dead, the Last Judgment. But fewer, especially among the educated, retained the sense of living in last days; and Christ, no longer understood as the Greek translation of Messiah, Lord of Redemption, became a proper name: first for the son of God, then for those of His followers whose parents chose to use it.

"Jewish" eschatological expectations ill-fitted a Roman church; and that eminent fourth- (and fifth-) century scholar, Augustine, put them in their place. The classic signs of imminent judgment are there at all times, Augustine told one of his correspondents; hence, they are hardly worth eschatological notice. Better, thought the bishop of Hippo, to lift Jewish fantasies of retribution and compensation from their local context to a cosmic plane, from a temporal context to a timeless one, from a literal reading to a spiritual one. Christ's eschatology had been a short story with an early ending. That of Augustine and of the institutions following his lead became an open-ended serial that we follow, not knowing quite when or how it will come to end.

Like the Old Testament but more so, Christianity was an accretion of different, sometimes discordant tenets—some Jewish, some apostolic, some Greek, and some contradictory. The world is the creation of God, yet also the realm of Satan; the earth is the Lord's, yet subject to Old Testament corruption and sin; it is the end time, but the Parousia is on the back burner. It was best not to talk about Advent, yet annually Advent sermons reminded the faithful of the promised Coming, just as Easter sermons reminded them of Christ's Passion.

The dialectic between now (suffering, travail, oppression) and not yet (redemption, emancipation, triumph) went inescapably on. Times of trouble, danger, or suspense never lacked to spur temporal urgency: moments when the perspective was blocked, the future inconceivable, the problems insoluble. That was when hope alone could help, and Revelation suggested an issue: escape from fear to a happy end. The millennial carrot dangled enticingly before a Christendom admonished in the same breath to ignore it and adore it. And the Scriptures were there, adorable too, their coded messages waiting to be decyphered by those with ears to hear and eyes to see.

Augustine and company counseled apocalyptic moderation, but apocalyptic times fueled apocalyptic fervor. Legends of Antichrist (Paul 2, Thessalonians 2), of angelic popes, of the two witnesses, of emperors of last days, anointed of the Lord like Cyrus (Isaiah 45), sprang up not to compete but to accrete; a treasury of possibilities for different occasions, just like the signs and wonders against which Augustine warned.

Biblical motifs were rearranged but not abandoned; apocalypticism thrived and went on thriving into the seventeenth century. Permeated by analogy and anagogy—by correspondences and correlations, by spiritual and mystical interpretations—medieval and early modern imagination never ceased to relate current experience to Biblical doings and Biblical prophecies. For twelve hundred years, from Augustine to Newton, learned men and less learned ones compared, assimilated, and reasoned from similar cases, circumstances, and illuminations, not least the Revelation of John. The Crusades were about preparing Jerusalem for the return of Christ; Columbus sailed in part to make Christ's Word heard, so that eschatological redemption could advance; Luther, like Paul, was fascinated by Antichrist, and died believing "that we are the last trumpet which prepares for and precedes the advent of Christ."[1]

Rulers, princes, and prelates were assimilated to Biblical or similar Sibylline figures, and events to apocalyptic signs; undertakings were justified in apocalyptic terms. Frederic II, Hohenstaufen, was one last emperor, and perhaps the best known. But there were other Frederics and other apocalyptic figures down to Napoleon and Tsar Alexander, forerunners for good or ill of an eventuality that seldom loosed its grip on the visions of the West.

True, as the seventeenth century wore on, the public language changed as the educated emancipated themselves from long-lasting obsessions with the final term. But the linguistic and referential imprint was scarcely shaken. Andrew Marvell, Cromwell's laureate, beseeches his coy mistress not to continue to refuse "till the conversion of the Jews"—a convenient rhyme, but also a trope for the end of time. Two hundred years after Marvell, Cardinal John Henry Newman devotes his Advent sermons to Antichrist, and finds in "Mahometan decline" another sign that the sands of time are running out and Christ's coming is not far off. Two years after Newman's sermons, in 1837, the year of Victoria's accession, *Moore's Almanac* suggests that the millennium might be near.[2]

The 1830s were anxious years in Western Europe, but Augustine would have asked what years were not. They also coincided with long-held Jewish belief that the Messiah would come in 1839–40 (5600 in the Hebrew calendar) to deliver and restore

Israel. Jewish millennialism has not concerned us here, but it hovered behind Christian millennialism, which it inspired to begin with, and which it continued to affect by its scholarship, its calculations, and by the messiahs it threw up—not least in the ominous year 1666. Jews also play a crucial role in scenarios of the Second Coming, whether as last-day converts or as auxiliaries of Antichrist, or both.[3] Another millenarianism, however, looms much larger.

Millennialism, millenarianism, and chiliasm all look to a supernaturally inaugurated, marvelously better time before the end; and sociologists relate all these beliefs to times of crisis and tension, danger, distress, and discrepancy between reality and expectation, moments when suffering, injustice, and the general ill-ordering of the world stridently call for catastrophic resolution. Fundamentalists have been described as evangelicals who are angry about something.[4] It looks as if millenarians are angry about many things: material deprivation, social dislocation, political persecution, and often, quite simply, change. Change discomforted so much that it could be a sign of the end; or change did not come fast enough, and the upheaval that might usher in a radically different life had to be hastened.

De Profundis Clamavi—"Out of the depths have I cried unto thee, O Lord," begins Psalm 130: "I wait for the Lord, my soul doth wait and in his word I hope." The deeper the depths, the longer the wait, the more fervent the hope ready to explode. The greater the suffering, the more passionately awaited the deliverance, the more powerful the impulse to violence. As Norman Cohn put it when writing about those early Christian millenarians, Montanists and Donatists, "in the very afflictions descending upon them, the millenarians recognized the long-awaited messianic woes; and the conviction gave them militancy."[5]

We have returned to the original tension between fear and love, between dread and hope, between punishment and forgiveness. The trouble with Christianity was its Jewish God: the discrepancy between the terrifying father and his tender son. It had been obscured, overlaid, ignored, and rationalized for centuries, until agnostics and atheists shook themselves free of a deity that appeared too cruel, too capricious, too indifferent. The God of the churches, meanwhile, became more rational, more liberal, more indulgent. Yet worshippers (and there were many left) did not desert the old god of fear, appropriately compatible with what they saw in the world around. Apprehension of God places lesser apprehensions in perspective, and dread of his judgment saves us from fearing the judgment of fellow men. Besides, the Christian message too often contradicted everyday experience, while the Jewish model fitted it compellingly. Ninety-eight verses (of over four hundred) in the Apocalypse of John speak of catastrophe, and 150 refer to joy, consolation, brightness, and hope. That Christian culture retained the former perspective and placed its hopes in terror, not in joy, should tell us something about human nature—or human experience.

Terror and hope went together. Christ's reign of a thousand years provided the most attractive aspect of eschatological scripts, even for those who did not share the Christians' faith. And just as disasters filling end-time scenarios fitted everyday experiences in a corrupt world, so expectations placed in the millennium fitted longings, yearnings, but, most of all, resentment, rancor, and rage.

Christ was a millenarian, and there were others not unlike him in whose preaching revelation turned to revolution. Only decades after the Gallilean's passage, Josephus reported "such men as deceived and deluded the people under pretense of divine inspiration, but were for procuring innovations and changes of the government; and these prevailed with the multitude to act like madmen, and went before them into the wilderness, as pretending that God would there show them the signals of liberty."[6] Signals of salvation inspired people to act like madmen. The will to liberty, to the elimination of conflict and violence, could spur the conflict and violence without which liberty and peace would not come; and a determination to blot out oppression might generate despotism and destruction. The struggle to change the world, to usher in a new heaven and a new earth, turned Christians and post-Christians into antinomians and legitimized excess in second-century Phrygia, in sixteenth-century Münster, in seventeenth-century England, eighteenth-century France, twentieth-century Russia. As Saint-Just declared, when he helped to rule France during the Revolutionary Terror, "What constitutes a Republic is the total destruction of that which is opposed to it."[7] For Republic read millennium: the principle is the same.

This was the fairy coinage of the mind inspiring the socialists of the nineteenth century, some Christian, some not. Historical change was changing, responses to change changed too, but Biblical references remained constant. Jesus had been hailed as a *sans-culotte* in the 1790s, and he would be hailed as a prophet of love and freedom in the 1840s; pre-Marxian communism would be recognized as an avatar of Christianity, or perhaps an improvement on it. Dreams of millennial perfection provided inspiration or compensation not only to the insulted and the injured but to reformers too. Evangelical reformers in England, Social Catholics on the Continent, and post-millenarians in the United States, preferred a millennial transition that was less catastrophic and more incremental. Society had to be Christianized and purged of evils like slavery and alcohol. Men would bring about their own millennium. But the long, slow redemption they envisioned was also a preparation for Christ's return.

One more component of endism—the hope of a rebirth, regeneration, and revival of the world—had been familiar to the ancient world, but had played a less prominent part in the eschatology of the centuries in between, when expectation of a shortish road to the Second Coming overshadowed it. In his *Myth of the Eternal Return*, Mircea Eliade described palingenesis—the formation of something new from something that exists. He discerned a universal need for periodic regeneration of life and time, and for "a new Creation, that is a repetition of the cosmogonic act . . . [a] cyclical regeneration of time."[8] Every new year, a new beginning: repetition of the mystical passage from chaos to cosmos. And every century, too.

Apocalypse is about the world's progress to an appointed end. The expected consummation implies a new beginning ("The king is dead: long live the king!"), but only to a term outlined in Revelation, which marks the end of mankind's history. Eliade speculates about a periodic recycling—"salvation"—of man, a cosmogonic victory over foes and evil so grand that it justifies messianism and apocalypticism, and "lays the foundations for a philosophy of history."[9] And Eliade is right to do so because, given centuries of Christian conditioning, the Western world was going to meld apocalypse and palingenesis in the imagery of decadence.

Before it did that, it tried to avoid the issue. Indeed, part of this book has been about our contemporaries and our forefathers—some since Augustine, more since the eighteenth century—trying and failing to avoid the issue. For the last three centuries, educated opinion has dismissed Revelation, subjected it to textual criticism, or savored it only as a catherine wheel to spark poetic imaginations. Its enthusiasm was too emotional, too devout, too radically excessive. Discomforted, disconcerted by the lurid violence of its religious message, nineteenth- and twentieth-century scholars swept the Apocalypse out of Christianity, and out of Judaism too, ignoring historical experience for the sake of intellectual comfort.

Bizarre, fantastic prophets and other apocalyptists seemed unfit for the attention of sensible people. In an excellent book published twenty years ago, W.H. Oliver was not alone in dismissing Joanna Southcott and "others of the weak-minded fanatics who populated the religious underworld of the period."[10] In

1910, the eleventh edition of the *Encyclopedia Britannica* devoted nearly three pages to Antichrist; in 1972, the fifteenth edition offered nothing on the subject. And a recent study entitled *The Second Coming: The New Christian Right in Virginia Politics* (Baltimore, 1996) has nothing to say about apocalypse, millennium, the book of Revelation, or even the Second Coming. Who was it that referred to the enormous condescension of posterity? We would do better to bear in mind Montaigne's admonition: "It is a dangerous and consequential rashness, beside the absurd temerity that it entails, to despise that which we cannot conceive."

Rationalists who dismissed apocalyptic ideas as superstitious survivals forgot that even calculated activities may stem from irrational motives, or else from very conscious "prophetic" or "superstitious" persuasions. Arguments based on Scripture have proved as historically significant as arguments based on race, class, or economic interest, to which we listen more readily. And, after all, even historical fantasies are part of history. "Superstition" is the sort of word we bandy about *their* views, not *ours*. The dictionary defines it as irrational belief founded on ignorance, fear, or simply false assumptions. But many assumptions provide a base for action before they are pronounced false; and many beliefs seem rational to believers—enough to influence politics, diplomacy, legislation, and economic activities. Denying aspects of the past that no longer fit our thought frame suppresses vital elements of history.

Circumscribing these aspects can also be misleading. Norman Cohn's admirable *Pursuit of the Millennium*, which did so much to revive interest in the subject, also linked it with the chiliastic fantasies of the poor and the oppressed. The title of the book's French translation, *Les fanatiques de l'Apocalypse*, with its implications of zealotry, bigotry, and crackpottiness, fitted dominant preconceptions even better. Apocalypse and millenarianism *were* historically significant after all, but chiefly or only in certain contexts and for certain groups. In fact, we have now seen that apocalyptic and millenarian beliefs need not and should not be attributed to the oppressed and disinherited only. Chiliasm may reflect despair, but it does not necessarily do so. Perfectly respectable members of the middle and upper classes shared eschatological notions that we tend to attribute to the insulted and the injured, or to crackpots only. Irrespective of social status, many generations took apocalypse for granted. Able and well-situated men and women have held apocalyptic views, from Columbus and Kepler to Pat Robertson, the televangelist offspring of a senator, himself a Yale graduate and chairman of his Christian Broadcasting Network. Many contemporary fundamentalists have had access to higher education, especially in the technological and applied sciences; many eighteenth-century millenarians did too.

To the extent that traditional eschatology no longer fits world views we now consider rational, it has been marginalized or swept under the carpet. Newton's apocalypticism is best ignored; George Eliot's views on class relations are relevant, but her views on relations with God less so. Habits of mind that don't contribute to our end-directed view of the past get lost on the way. To the extent that our crystal balls function like rearview mirrors (to quote Northrop Frye), clouded or fogged images of the past will suggest false perspectives in the present. The preceding pages may have helped to clear the fog a little, or at least to suggest a less teleologically skewed image of times gone by, emphasizing not just the otherness of the past but also the otherness of some presents.

To the extent that I have succeeded, the new perspectives about the certainties of others will undermine some of our own. But then, if apocalyptism and millenialism are not exceptional and cranky, why were they so commonplace? And what accounts for their stubborn survival?

Apocalyptic discourse is about the final conflictual aspects of life. When troubles are dominant, apocalypse is in the ascendant; should it be missing, people would begin to worry. But (Augustine again) conflict and its fallout are always and everywhere. From Zoroaster through the Old Testament and the New, the struggle between light and darkness, between the saints and the minions of sin, is a familiar theme. Belial and the hosts of evil dominate present times as a prelude to the inevitable end, when Michael, prince of angels, or Christ, or even God himself will resolve the issue. Why the recurrent motif of the Apocalypse, especially when happy ends that we might wish or seek are only reached by way of traumatically calamitous events? One is inclined to offer a banal answer: death is the beginning of religion, reflection about death leads to reflection about life, and life calls for some understanding of its issue, which is the passage through trauma, death, and (wishfully) resurrection. That is the apocalyptic order[ing] that reflects both everyday experience and its dignifying within religious explanation.

Religion provides keys to the social order, and to disorder, too. Unbelievable events provide occasion for belief; so does routine. Security in this life calls for a balance of security in the next, while insecurity down here sharpens the search for supernatural reassurance. We suffer, and suffering is catastrophic, sometimes unbearable, sometimes final. Articulate the unspeakable and you begin to exorcise it. Even as we suffer, everyday reality is commonplace and trite. We yearn for some explosive, extraordinary escape from the inescapable and, none forthcoming, we put our faith in an apocalyptic rupture whereby the inevitable is solved by the unbelievable: grasshoppers, plagues, composite monsters, angels, blood in industrial quantities, and, in the end, salvation from sin and evil—meaning anxiety, travail, and pain. By defining human suffering in cosmic terms, as part of a cosmic order that contains an issue, catastrophe is dignified, endowed with meaning, and hence made bearable.

The darkness of men, displaced, becomes the darkness of the world; explained, it is recognized as the rule of sin in the world; better still, it becomes the invasion of the world by sin, evil, and darkness from without. From these evils, the world will be miraculously, violently, and vividly delivered by a triumph of the powers of light more easily imagined as being brought about by outside intervention. "We are at the beginning of the Christian era. In our time the West (and probably the whole world) has become such an enigma to itself, is faced by such fearfully unprecedented problems and such terrifying ordeals, that it must at long last consider the possibility that only the coming of Christ will give it the arguments and the strength to assume its destiny." Thus Jean-Marie, Cardinal Lustiger and archbishop of Paris, writing in 1990.[11] Some things have not changed since the beginning of the Christian era.

With the world foundering in iniquity, even if God did not intervene, wear and tear, dilapidation, decline, and decay would ensure its finitude. Adversity is good for faith, and adversity is ever present. Ages of decadence always suggest an end; few ages have not struck contemporaries by their decadence, and recent centuries' switchback ride from hope to fear was no exception. Eustache Deschamps in the fourteenth century, wailing about the decadence of present times, every year worse than the last, echoed Ezra, the second-century scribe, and anteceded the numerous company of self-styled decadents and denouncers of decadence associated with the nineteenth-century and its tag end.

Ends and beginnings, round numbers and sacred numbers, anniversaries and jubilees entrap the mind, arouse attention, and suggest figures of speech and thought that turn metaphor into reality. The image of *fin de siècle* was a case in point, and the marriage of decadence and end followed naturally. Its offspring were all around: a flood of novels, poems, plays, articles, and sermons about twilight, endings, deterioration, degeneracy, and decay. That was when the French word *ennui*, "mental weariness or dissatisfaction arising from lack of occupation or interest," as the *Oxford English Dictionary* explains it, entered the English language, and several others too. Too many fat, idle children had too much time to stare at themselves and find the world wanting. Life, declared Huysmans's Des Esseintes, was a great disappointment. Art was better and, if not art, artificiality.

As in our day, decadence was self-confirming: artificiality inspired perversity, obscurity, and promiscuity. Decadence was self-generating: Wagner's *Ring* inspired Elemir Bourges's *Twilight of the Gods* (1884); Huysmans's *Des Esseintes* (1884) became Oscar Wilde's *Dorian Gray* (1888). But decadence and its celebrants reflected a world of plenty in which dissatisfaction had to be manufactured, not escaped. The decadents perhaps were dying, but otherwise were quite well. It took a competitive accumulation of apocalyptic horrors to confirm their claims. The Thirty Years' War that began in 1914, whose fallout seared most of the century, anachronized the decadent association of a *fin de siècle* fated, at least semantically, to be the first and last. Apocalypses, millennialisms, prophets, witnesses, tribulations, and doomsdays came back into their own. It is not the *siècle*, but the *fin* that matters.

It stands to reason that, if history begins with arbitrary creation, it is bound to end with arbitrary destruction. In the twentieth century, that idea seems less than surprising. Movie and television screens, which hold the mirror to our times, testify to the popularity of disaster films: ecodisaster, biodisaster, meteodisaster, astrodisaster, tidal or thermo- or seismodisaster, comets, asteroids, or mere monsters and space alien invasions inspire epics of global destruction that threaten the end of civilization, the extinction of the human species, the obliteration of the fragile platform on which we stir. Endism is in fashion once more because it provides a context: an ideology of catastrophe.

As we approach another century's ending, now dwarfed by the billennium, preoccupation with end times rises to new heights in a world saturated with them.[12] Much of this is simply mimicry and affectation. But even that reflects a widespread, demotic sense that the end of a calendric term somehow coincides with the end of an era, a culture, a civilization, an ecology, a history, an end of progress and of "man," hollowed of past attributes. We live this apocalypse in greater comfort than mankind has ever known, but our moral discomfort makes it apocalyptic nevertheless. We recognize the many false prophets and the many deceivers about whom John the Apostle warned his hearers; we suspect that monsters of Revelation roam around, no more bizarre than those of the cinema or television; we wonder what rough beast, its hour come round at last, slouches toward Bethlehem to be born.

The basic themes have been restyled. Diffuse anxiety now partners focused fear. Century-old *fin de siècle* sighs and yearnings have been replaced by uncertainties, multiplicities, confusions, credulousness, and denial. "The best lack all conviction, while the worst are full of passionate intensity." Like so many of our ancestors for so long, we acknowledge that "we are not in control . . . we are *not* in fact in control."[13]

We have experienced chaos, have theorized but scarcely mastered it. Our mental and physical environment is like a street, ever dug up for works that are never finished; like a garden where we remember flowers but see only holes. Processing, clicking, we continue clueless in worlds marked less by purpose than by accident. We have become used to apocalypses as violent and climactic as John's, to eschatologies as intimidating or haunting as those that obtained so long. It becomes hard to discriminate between religious visions, mystical raptures, appearances of supernatural creatures, extraterrestrials, flying saucers and other unidentified flying objects, all grist to the mill of the media, sociologists, psychiatrists, and enthusiasts, and to the glutted indifference of a jaded public. It all depends, as a recent commentator put it, "on the predominant belief structure of a given culture." Except that cultures now, like apocalypses, are not *given* but made; and that literal end-of-the-world predictions suggest "a disquieting border area of theology and psychopathology."[14] Some would say that the borderland between theology and psychopathology has always been indistinct; others, that when we know so little about things that we are supposed to know, it is presumptuous to advance judgments about things we don't know at all.

The history of apocalyptics and millenarianisms is littered with prophecies made and missed; but so is the history of all inexact sciences. Seymour Martin Lipset calculated that two-thirds or more of the forecasts made by American social scientists between 1945 and 1980 proved mistaken.[15] So, when the nth (1986) edition of C.I. Scofield's *First Reference Bible* tells us that five dispensations since the creation of Adam have been fulfilled, that we live toward the close of the sixth "and have before us the millennium," we should think twice before we scoff. Peter forewarned believers that they might expect just this reaction: "Scoffers will come in the last days with scoffing, following their own passions and saying 'Where is the promise of his coming? For ever since the fathers fell asleep, all things have continued as they were since the beginning of creation'" (2 Peter 3:3–4).

Lord Acton once described Catholics as people who believe facts to be matters of opinion, and opinions to be facts. Acton was a Catholic, but we have encountered many who behaved this way, Catholic and non-Catholic, Christian and non-Christian. Scottish courts sometimes hand down a verdict of "Not Proven"; but absence of proof is not evidence of the contrary. If scores of eschatologists have proved mistaken, the answer is not that one of them will prove right one day, but that too many of them have proved too influential—destructive, constructive, inspiring, consoling—and that it is foolish for historians to dismiss or, worse, to ignore them.

After a life spent studying mainly the economic aspects of the history of mankind, Fernand Braudel concluded that, in its depths, the destiny of a civilization is a religious destiny. The Christian Middle Ages, which lasted a very long time, opposed the reality of the world to the truth of God. We tend to confuse the two words, and hence the concepts. But reality, even encompassed, is not truth; the true is not necessarily apparent in perceived reality; and religions, including the Christian religion, claim to take one nearer to what is true. An agnostic can only report that, in an apocalypse, reality provides means and images for expression, while truth alleged, and believed, transfigures what is real.

Since Eve, Adam, and Prometheus, curiosity has been a defining characteristic of humanity; and love itself a superior form of curiosity, a driving appetite to delve into the unknown and grasp it. Religion knew this, and it knows that error is less noxious than curiosity about things we cannot know. Apocalypse, Revelation, offers to lift the veil between us and such matters. Inspired or imagined, it carries, as Joachim of Fiore said, "the key to things past, the knowledge of things to come": it organizes time, provides versatile benchmarks, and endows the future with a future.

Need there be conclusions that are final? Are there ends that justify finality? Do we find ends that really end in Dante's *Divine Comedy,* Balzac's *Human Comedy,* or Shakespeare's *All's Well That Ends Well?* A *roman fleuve* runs on until a day and hour that "knoweth no man, no, not the angels of heaven, but my Father only."

NOTES

CHAPTER 1: Introduction

1 Christopher Hill, *Antichrist in England* (London, 1971), 1.
2 Wilhelm Bousset in James Hastings, ed., *Encyclopedia of Religion and Ethics* (London, 1925), 581.
3 Norman Cohn, *The Pursuit of the Millennium* (London, 1957), 14–15.
4 Tillich, quoted in Saul Friedlander et al., eds., *Visions of Apocalypse* (New York, 1985), 163.

CHAPTER 2: Chronologies and *Fins de Siècle*

1 Auguste Poulet-Malassis, the publisher of Baudelaire's *Fleurs du mal*, was a republican and an atheist. In 1857, he printed thirty-six copies of Prosper Mérimée's essay on Stendhal "from the printing shop of Julian the Apostate, first year of the 658th Olympiad." In 1874, he printed another edition with a frontispiece by Félicien Rops, dated in the 1874th year "of the imposture of the Nazarean."
2 Thucydides, *The Peloponnesian War* (New York, 1934), Book 2, chapter 6, 84. An early contemporary account of the martyrdom of St. Polycarp, the *Martyrium Polycarpi*, has this second-century bishop of Smyrna burnt at the stake "on the second day in the beginning of

the month of Xanticus, the day before the seventh kalends of March, on a great Sabbath, at the eighth hour. He was arrested by Herod when Philip of Thralles was High Priest and Statius Quadratus Proconsul, during the unending reign of our Lord Jesus Christ." Once again, time has many aspects, all valid in their own terms.

3 Clary, quoted in Donald Wilson, *The Measure of Times Past* (Chicago, 1987), 144.

4 Ezra, quoted by Amos Funkenstein in Friedlander et al., eds., *Visions of Apocalypse*, 44.

5 Christopher Hibbert, *Rome* (New York, 1985), 95.

6 Dennis also started the Christian Era not with the year zero, but with *Anno Domini* (AD) 1; hence our confusion about just when centuries and millennia begin.

7 Dante's *Vita* mentions his death in September 1321, "on the day whereon the exaltation of the Holy Cross is celebrated by the Church," meaning September 14. For Luther, see Lucien Febvre, *Un destin. Martin Luther* (Paris, 1951), 11.

8 E. Le Roy Ladurie, *The Beggar and the Professor* (Chicago, 1997), 63.

9 A. Verjus, *La vie de Monsieur le Nobletz, prestre et missionaire* (Paris, 1666) quoted in Francesco Maiello, *Histoire du calendrier* (Paris, 1996), 140: "le temps . . . qui echappe mesme aux plus curieux . . . ne leur paroist d'aucun[e] considération." Much of the information concerning calendars and dating is drawn from Maiello; Donald Wilcox, *The Measure of Times Past* (Chicago, 1987), and Alfred Crosby, *The Measure of Reality* (Cambridge, 1997).

10 Henry Mayhew, *London Labour and the London Poor* (London, 1851), 1:46.

11 Augustine, quoted by Robert Lerner in Richard Emmerson and Bernard McGinn, eds., *The Apocalypse in the Middle Ages* (Ithaca, 1992), 52. There are other translations of Augustine, who made this point in *The City of God*, Book xviii, chapter 53.

12 Daniel Milo, *Trahir le temps (histoire)* (Paris, 1991).

13 Ernest Lee Tuveson, *Millennium and Utopia* (New York, 1964), 42.

14 For example, in January 1700 Samuel Pepys wished his nephew a

prosperous new century, while Bernard de Fontenelle waited another year to write two poems welcoming the new century in 1701.

15 R.H. Charles, ed., *Pseudepigrapha of the Old Testament* (Oxford, 1913), 2 Baruch 85:10: "For the youth of the world is past . . . And the pitcher is near to the cistern, And the ship to the port, And the course of the journey to the city, And life to [its] consummation."

16 Wendelin Baar, "Vues et conjectures sur l'Apocalypse" (1800), quoted in Alfred-Félix Vaucher, *Lacunziana* (Collonges, 1949), 82. Baar thought papal Rome one with Biblical Babylon, and the future kingdom of Christ to be terrestrial, corporeal, and visible. The earth would be renewed, not annihilated.

17 Phillipe Besnard, *Moeurs et humeurs des Français* (Paris, 1989), 91, 251–54; Norman Cohn, *Cosmos, Chaos and the World to Come* (New Haven, 1993), 25.

18 To quote a few among many, Melchior Hofmann, the Anabaptist, announced the Second Coming for 1533; Nicolas of Cusa thought that it would be in 1734; Arthur E. Ware, interviewed in London's *Daily Express* of May 4, 1933, expected the tribulation on June 12, 1933, to be followed by the millennium in due course.

19 Quoted in George Bernard Shaw, *The Perfect Wagnerite* (London, 1948), 234.

20 George Gissing to Miss E. Collet, Paris, December 29, 1899.

21 Pierre Chaunu, *Histoire et décadence* (Paris, 1981), 71, 282.

22 Ezra in Charles, ed., *Pseudepigrapha of the Old Testament*, 573; Lionel Rothkrug, *Opposition to Louis XIV* (Princeton, 1965), 251; Chaunu, *Histoire et décadence*; François Guizot, *History of Civilization in Europe* (London, 1997), 67; Cardinal Newman, *Discussions and Arguments* (London, 1891), 102.

23 Émile Zola, Correspondence, 1872–1902, in *Oeuvres complètes* (1929), 825, 827.

24 Émile Zola, *Paris*, in *Oeuvres complètes*, 8:566, 651, 1181.

25 Anatole France, *Le jardin d'épicure* (1904; Paris, 1923), 19ff.

26 *The Education of Henry Adams* (1907; 1931), 451, 331.

27 Robert Bessède, *La crise de la conscience catholique* (Paris, 1975), 529 and passim. Also consumed by eschatological fever, another Catholic mystic and friend of Léon Bloy, Ernest Hello, prayed for

signs and begged his ally to pray for one, too, "for it is the waters, the blood, and the fires that bear witness on earth."

28 Ecological disaster in Richard Jefferies, *After London* (London, 1885); astrodisaster in Gabriel Tarde's *Underground Man*, published just before that distinguished intellectual's death in 1904, translated and published in English in 1905 with a preface by H.G. Wells; Armageddon and the rest in Robert Hugh Benson, *The Lord of the World* (London, 1907). Son of an Archbishop of Canterbury, Benson, who had been ordained in the Anglican Church in 1895, converted to Catholicism in 1903.

29 *The Portable Nietzsche*, ed. Walter Kaufmann (New York, 1976), 547.

30 George Bernard Shaw, "The Sanity of Art," in *Major Critical Essays* (London, 1948), 284, 291, 313, and passim.

31 Ernest Renan, *Souvenirs d'enfance et de jeunesse* (Paris, 1883); Holbrook Jackson, *The Eighteen Nineties* (London, 1913); André Billy, *L'époque 1900* (Paris, 1951).

32 Billy, *L'époque 1900*, 481; Jackson, *The Eighteen Nineties*, 65, 70.

33 Raffaelli, in Goncourt, *Journal*, January 5, 1896; Huysmans, ibid., January 11, 1996; Thomas Hardy, "1967."

34 In 1891, answering a survey on contemporary literature, Verlaine described the origins of "decadence" and "decadents": "[The epithet] was thrown at us as an insult. I picked it up as a war cry; but as far as I know it meant nothing in particular. Decadent! Is not a fine day's sunset worth as much as all the dawns! And then, will not the sun that seems to set arise again tomorrow? *Au fond*, decadent meant nothing at all." *Oeuvres en prose complètes* (Paris, 1972), 1136.

CHAPTER 3: Apocalypses and Millenarianisms

1 Yeats's Celtic Armageddon may be found in "The Secret Rose"; Tim La Haye and Harry Jenkins's novels *Left Behind* and *Tribulation Force* (Wheaton, Ill., 1995, 1996) sold about half a million copies. A final book in the novel series is planned for the year 2000, when it

will feature Christ's return (*New York Times*, May 19, 1997). Robert Fleming, pastor of the English church in Rotterdam, published *Apocalyptical Key* in 1701, predicting the coming of Christ, the kingdom of the saints, and the millennium in the year 2000. The book was reedited in 1793, perhaps because the chain of events, according to Fleming, was to begin in 1794. In 1834, the Wesleyan Baptist minister Robert Scott (1760–1834), who had written his own funeral sermon in 1832, predicted the Second Coming and the millennium in 1999. Rodriguez Cristino Morondo's *Proximity of World Catastrophe and Coming of Universal Regeneration* (1922) expects the coming of Antichrist, and the reconstruction of Jerusalem and the temple, in the year 2000. Nostradamus's *Century X, 72*: "L'an mil neuf cent nonante neuf, sept mois, du ciel viendra un grand roi d'effrayeur." Numerological interpretations of the great pyramid suggest the end of the world in 2001: Tynetta Muhammad, cited in Mattias Gardell, *Countdown to Armageddon* (New York, 1995), 149. José Arguelles, *The Mayan Factor* (New York, 1987), expects Quetzalcoatl to reappear in 1999 and Mayan intergalactic people to return early in the twenty-first century to restore intergalactic harmony.

2 Paul Boyer, *When Time Shall Be No More* (Cambridge, Mass., 1992), x, 7, 8.

3 Bernard McGinn, *Visions of the End: Apocalyptic Traditions in the Middle Ages* (New York, 1979), xiv.

4 Cohn, *The Pursuit of the Millennium*, 11.

5 Ibid., 12.

6 Paula Fredriksen, in Emmerson and McGinn, eds., *The Apocalypse in the Middle Ages*, 36.

7 Léon Gry, *Le millenarisme dans ses origines et son développement* (Paris, 1904), 92.

8 D.H. Lawrence, *Apocalypse and the Writings on Revelation*, Mara Kalkins ed., (Cambridge, 1980), 48.

9 Mircea Eliade, *The Myth of the Eternal Return* (New York, 1954), 87–88.

10 Virgil, *Eclogues*, iv, 5.

11 A French Protestant who traveled and traded in seventeenth-century Persia noted the Zoroastrian Apocalypse, when all mountains

and minerals would be melted, "this world shall be leveled," and resurrected souls would behold and praise God. See *Les Six Voyages de Jean-Baptiste Tavernier* (Paris, 1676). Mithraism echoed that eschatology. At the end of time, Ahriman, the spirit of evil, destroys the world; Mithra descends to earth, resurrects the dead, and immolates the primeval Bull; Ormuzd lets fire descend on Ahriman, his demons, and wicked men; the world is renovated, and the good enjoy everlasting happiness.

12   Eliade, *The Myth of the Eternal Return*, 73, 88.

13   Ibid., 125.

CHAPTER 4: In Dark and Bloody Times

1   Gry, *Le millénarisme*, 118.

2   Ernest Renan, *L'Antéchrist* (Paris, 1924), xxiv–xxv, 462. See D.H. Lawrence, writing to a friend on October 10, 1929: "I do hate John's Jewish nasal sort of style"; Lawrence, *Apocalypse*, ed. Kalkins.

3   Frank Kermode, *The Sense of an Ending* (Oxford, 1967), 25.

4   Charles Péguy, "Louis de Gonzague," *Oeuvres en prose, 1898–1908* (Paris, 1965), 940–43.

5   Alfred Maury, *Croyances et légendes du Moyen Age* (Paris, 1896), 18. Every year on Ascension eve the parish priest of Domrémy would recite St. John's gospel by the fairy or ladies' tree (35).

6   Richard Landes, "Apocalyptic Expectations," in Werner Verbeke, Daniel Verhelst, and Andries Welkenhuysen, eds., *The Use and Abuse of Eschatology in the Middle Ages* (Leuven, 1988), 166–68.

7   McGinn, *Visions of the End*, 62–64.

8   See Heinrich Fichtenau, *Living in the Tenth Century* (Chicago, 1991), 384 and passim.

9   See Henri Focillon, *L'an mil* (Paris, 1952), 57–58 and passim. Also Richard Landes, *Relics, Apocalypse, and the Deceits of History* (Harvard, 1995), especially 295.

10   John Williams, *The Illustrated Beatus* (London, 1994), 1:117. In

fact, Beatus seems to have expected the New Age in the year 800.

11 See Rodulfus Glaber, *The Five Books of the Histories*, ed. and trans. John France (Oxford, 1989), especially 95, 111, 185ff, 195; and Focillon, *L'an mil*, 73.

12 See Penn Szittya, "Domesday Bokes," in Emmerson and McGinn, eds., *The Apocalypse*, 374ff.

13 See Robert Fuller, *Naming the Antichrist* (New York, 1995), 33. Crusaders were armed parousic pilgrims. As Paul Alphandéry's *La Chrétienté et l'idée de croisade* (Paris, 1959) 1, 25, 178, 180–81, makes clear, eschatological expectations inspired them, as St. Bernard's preaching to Conrad III inspired the German emperor to take the cross in 1146.

14 See Régine Pernoud, *Hildegarde de Bingen* (Paris, 1995), 44 and passim.

15 E. Randolph Daniel, "Joachim of Fiore," in Emmerson and McGinn, eds., *The Apocalypse*, 78.

16 M. Reeve, in C.A. Patrides and J. Wittreich, eds., *The Apocalypse in English Renaissance Thought and Literature* (Ithaca, 1984), 49.

17 Ronald Knox, *Enthusiasm* (New York, 1961), 110; McGinn, *Visions of the End*, 197.

18 For flagellants, see Cohn, *The Pursuit of the Millennium*, 139ff, 146; but also Laura A. Smoller, *History, Prophecy and the Stars* (Princeton, 1994), 117, who tells us about a Thuringian sect that combined apocalyptism, flagellation, and anticlericalism. Their prophet, Carl Schmid, had prophesied the end of the world for 1369 and had probably been burnt at the stake that same year. But his followers who believed Schmid to be Enoch, the Witness, persevered and some four hundred of them were burned between 1414 and 1416 alone.

19 See "La fin du monde est proche," in *Oeuvres complètes d'Eustache Deschamps* (Paris, 1878–93), 3:185, and ballads 52, 371, 400, 1046, 1446; and Richard Emmerson, *Antichrist in the Middle Ages* (Seattle, 1981), 52.

20 Guy Fourquin, *Anatomy of Popular Rebellion in the Middle Ages* (Amsterdam, 1978), 88; Donald Weinstein, *Savonarola and Florence* (Princeton, 1970), 41.

21 Wycliffe regarded the Bible as the sole criterion of doctrine and translated it into the vernacular. He was disheartened by the Great Schism, and called Clement VII and Urban VI "two halves of Antichrist, together a full Man of Sin." He expected the end of the world from one day to another, recognized the signs of its coming, and persuaded his admirer John Huss that the Last Judgment was at hand. H.B. Workman, *John Wyclif* (Oxford, 1926).

22 See H. Kaminsky, *A History of the Hussite Revolution* (Berkeley, 1967), 311, 312. The parousic prestige of Mt. Tabor had also inspired Pope Innocent III to urge its capture upon the warriors of the fifth crusade. But Innocent died in 1216, before that last crusade floundered to an inglorious end, as Taborites were to do two centuries later.

23 Canon Etienne Delaruelle, *La piété populaire au Moyen Age* (Torino, 1980), 348–49 and passim. For St. Michael, ibid., 345, and Alcuin's poem in Helen Waddell, *Medieval Latin Lyrics* (London, 1947), 91. Contemporaries and later commentators would regard Joan, who saw her king as "king of the last times" destined to fight the Turks, recover Jerusalem, and accomplish apocalyptic predictions, as an heiress of the *pastoureaux*: shepherd- and children-crusaders of 1257 and 1320.

24 Weinstein, *Savonarola*, 88, 129, and passim.

25 Ibid., 334–35. One finds more apocalyptic allusions to signs of the end in late 1499, while Luca Signorelli painted his fresco of the Antichrist at Orvieto. See Jonathan Riess, *The Renaissance Antichrist* (Princeton, 1995).

CHAPTER 5: Revivalists and Antichrists

1 Emanuel Le Roy Ladurie, *The Beggar*, 167.

2 Henri Grégoire, *Histoire des sectes réligieuses* (Paris, 1845), 6:283.

3 Anabaptists had a way of doing that. Belfort Bax presents them as running through Zurich and the surrounding countryside crying "Woe!", denouncing Zwingli as the dragon of the Apocalypse, and

foretelling for the city the fate of Niniveh, which paid no heed to Jonah's warnings. In Heinrich Bullinger's 1531 attack on Anabaptists as enthusiasts and ecstatics who saw visions and dreamt dreams, we recognize the ilk unto our own days: "When under the influence of the Spirit, their countenances were contorted, they gestured wildly, fell on the ground in fits, lay stretched out as dead." *Rise and Fall of the Anabaptists* (1903; reprinted New York, 1970), 19, 36.

4 Peter Stearns, *Millennium III, Century XXI* (Boulder, 1996), 42, 48.

5 Denis Crouzet, *Les guerriers de Dieu* (Paris, 1990), 1:182.

6 Ibid., 108–9, 111, 113, 103.

7 Reeve, in Patrides and Wittreich, eds., *The Apocalypse*, 65.

8 Crouzet, *Les guerriers de Dieu*, 150–52.

9 Le Roy Ladurie, *The Beggar*, 201, quoting Felix Platter.

10 Paul Harvey and J.E. Heseltine, *Oxford Companion to French Literature* (New York, 1984), 75.

11 Quoted in Julien Freund, *La Décadence* (Paris, 1984), 77. In 1950, Fernand Braudel felt that "the sad men of 1560 and after" "nous ressemblent comme des frères" (*Ecrits sur l'histoire*, Paris, 1969, 37).

12 J. Serlier, *Le grand tombeau du monde* (Lyon, 1606), 177.

13 Foxe's *Martyrs* went through several editions in his lifetime. To the last, published in 1583, he added a passage on the "Mystical Numbers in the Apocalypse Opened," and, when he died in 1586, he was working on a commentary to the Apocalypse.

14 Keith Thomas, *Religion and the Decline of Magic* (Harmondsworth, 1973), 157. The paragraphs that follow owe much to his pages 157–63.

15 Hill, *Antichrist*, 104. Sedgwick may have written the anonymous *Doomes-Day* (London, 1647) that foretold "the long-looked-for year that Antichrist shall fall" for the current year.

16 Thomas Goodwin, *Sermon on the Fifth Monarchy* (London, 1654).

17 Emmerson, *Antichrist in the Middle Ages*, 21, 25, 65.

18 Renan, *Antéchrist*, 478.

19 For Calvin, see Joshua Trachtenberg, *The Devil and the Jews* (New Haven, 1943), 39. For Knox, *Autobiography of Mr. James Melville* (Edinburgh, 1842), 26.

20 Hill, *Antichrist*, 39.

21 Emmerson, *Antichrist in the Middle Ages*, 218.

22 Grégoire, *Histoire des sectes religieuses*, 1:373.

23 Hillel Schwartz, *Knaves, Fools, Madmen and That Subtle Effluvium* (Gainesville, 1978), 22–24.

24 Knox, *Enthusiasm*, 356.

CHAPTER 6: Apocalypse and Science

1 Frances A. Yates, in Charles Singleton, *Art, Science and History in the Renaissance* (Baltimore, 1967), 270. Yates points out that Renaissance Neo-Platonism viewed the cosmos as a network of magical forces that men can operate and manipulate: "The necessary preliminary to the rise of science" (255).

2 At the mid-seventeenth century, Cardinal de Retz and the Vicomte de Turenne ran into devils or dark spirits in the Bois de Boulogne, drew their swords, and charged them, only to find that they were a band of Carmelite monks. But it never occurred to them to dismiss the possibility of truly diabolic apparitions. See Cardinal de Retz, *Oeuvres* (Paris, 1984), 161–64, 1279, and Tallemant des Réaux, *Historiettes* (Paris, 1967), 1:499.

3 Yates, in Singleton, *Art, Science and History*, 259, remarks that magic and mechanics were hard to tell apart while mechanics continued as a branch of mathematical magic, the operative use of number as in Campanella's "real artificial magic."

4 Thomas, *Religion and the Decline of Magic*, 269, 271, quoting a Cornish physician writing in 1794.

5 Robert Boyle, *The Excellency of Theology* (London, 1674).

6 *Carion's Chronicle*, quoted in Katharine Firth, *The Apocalyptic Tradition in Reformation Britain* (Oxford, 1979), 18.

7 Newton, *Observations upon the Prophesies of Daniel and the Apocalypse of St. John* (London, 1733).

8 For Leonardo, see E.H. Gombrich, *New Light on Old Masters* (Oxford, 1986), 66, 67.

9 Quoted in Thomas, *Religion and the Decline of Magic*, 320.

10 Paola Zambelli, *Astrologi Hallucinati: Stars and the End of the World in Luther's Time* (New York, 1986), 273. Kepler also believed that the "new stars" discovered in familiar constellations heralded great religious and political changes.

11 King Frederic of Denmark gave Tycho Brahe the Baltic island of Hveen. The towers of the castle of Uraniborg that the astronomer built on Hveen sheltered not only his instruments but also his alchemist's laboratory as well. Mark Graubard, *Astrology and Alchemy* (New York, 1953), 312–14, suggests that, two centuries later, the process of making Dresden china was found as a result of alchemical experiments pursued at the early-eighteenth century court of the Elector of Saxony, Augustus II.

12 Robert Recorde, *The Castle of Knowledge* (London, 1556), quoted in Thomas, *Religion and the Decline of Magic*, 298.

13 Thomas, *Religion and the Decline of Magic*, 363.

14 Graubard, *Astrology and Alchemy*, 191.

15 In 1663, the historian Pierre Petit, following the orders of Louis XIV, published a charge against the political fears that comets caused: *de ignis et lucis naturae*.

16 An English translation of Gassendi's denunciation of *Divination by the Stars* was published in 1655, a year unhappily star-crossed by furious plague. Then came 1666, when wooden London burnt for four days.

17 Quoted by Lucien Febvre, *Le problème de l'incroyance au XVIe siècle* (Paris, 1947), 444 n.1.

18 Bernard Capp, *Astrology and the Popular Press* (London, 1979), 184 and passim. *Diary of R. T.* (London, 1830), 1:132.

19 Graubard, *Astrology and Alchemy*, 92.

20 Frank Manuel, *Isaac Newton, Historian* (Cambridge, Mass., 1963), 165.

21 Thenchard and Shaftesbury, in Manuel, *Newton*, 81, 80.

CHAPTER 7: Enlightenment?

1   Eamon Duffy, *Saints and Sinners: A History of the Popes* (New Haven, 1997), 191.

2   Clarke Garrett, *Respectable Folly* (Baltimore, 1975), 153–54.

3   Thomas Prince, *An Improvement of the Doctrine of Earthquakes* (Boston, 1755), 14, 16.

4   Knox, *Enthusiasm*, 546.

5   Robert Southey, *Letters from England* (London, 1808), 3:232.

6   George Eliot, *Adam Bede* (1859; New York, 1952), 72.

7   Ibid., 90.

8   Clowes, quoted by Deborah Valenze, *Prophetic Sons and Daughters* (Princeton, 1985), 91.

9   Eliot, *Adam Bede*, 46, 28.

10 Grégoire, *Histoire des sectes*, 1:215. "Si non e vero, e ben trovato."

11 Even Gibbon's *Decline and Fall* suggested apocalyptic premonitions. See East Apthorp, *Letters on the Prevalence of Christianity before Its Civil Establishment, with Observations on a Late History of the Decline of the Roman Empire* (London, 1778), 36–37.

12 See Garrett, *Respectable Folly*, 131, 164, 168, 211.

13 Quoted by M.H. Abrams, "English Romanticism," in Northrop Frye, ed., *Romanticism Reconsidered* (New York, 1963), 36.

14 Quoted in Camille Flammarion, *La fin du monde* (Paris, 1894), 183.

15 Ibid., 184.

16 J. Christopher Herold, *Mistress to an Age* (London, 1959), 95.

17 Germaine de Staël, *De l'Allemagne*, v, 49.

18 Daniel Vidal, *Miracles et convulsions jansénistes au XVIIIe siècle* (Paris, 1987), 277, 281, 397, 398. Catherine-Laurence Maire, *Les convulsionnaires de Saint-Médard* (Paris, 1985), 228 and passim; Garrett, *Respectable Folly*, 107–8.

19 See Benoît Laurent, *Les Béguins* (St. Étienne, 1980).

20 Garrett, *Respectable Folly*, 26, 37. Also Albert Mathiez, *Contribu-*

tions à l'histoire religieuse de la révolution française (Paris, 1907), 398.

21 See Alfred-Félix Vaucher, *Une celebrité oubliée. Le Père Manuel de Lacunza y Diaz (1731–1801)* (Collonges, 1941). *The Coming of the Messiah* also concluded that the Catholic hierarchy and priesthood represented the Antichrist. No wonder it was placed on the *Index*, and that an English translation appeared in 1826.

22 Paul Vulliaud, *La fin du monde* (Paris, 1952), 120–21; Grégoire, *Histoire des sectes*, 6:285; Garrett, *Respectable Folly*, 45–47.

23 Mathiez, *Contributions*, 32; ibid. In 1790, Restif de la Bretonne wrote an edifying political fiction play, *L'an deux-mille ou la régénération*. Curiously, but perhaps significantly, the *Théâtre de N.E. Restif-de-la-Bretonne* (Neufchâtel, 1790) gives the title as "L'an deux-mille ou la dégénération."

24 For Blake, see Abrams in Patrides and Wittreich, eds., *The Apocalypse*, 40; and note that Blake, who had been a Swedenborgian, used his *Marriage of Heaven and Hell* (1790–93) to attack Swedenborg's *Divine Providence* and to present his own apocalyptic visions. For Wordsworth, see *The Prelude, Crossing the Simplon Pass*; for Coleridge, see Abrams, "English Romanticism," 359, quoting his "Religious Musings" written in 1794; for Southey, see Abrams in Patrides and Wittreich, eds., *The Apocalypse*, 31.

25 See Ruth Necheles, *The Abbé Grégoire, 1787–1831* (Westport, Conn., 1971), xii, 10, 13, 172.

26 Henri-Michel Gasnier, *Varades* (Maulévrier, 1985), 142; Boissy d'Anglas, quoted by Milo, *Trahir le temps*, 219.

27 Valenze, *Prophetic Sons*, 87.

28 *Times*, March 4, 1795, "The Great Prophet of Paddington Street: Nephew of God."

29 Garrett, *Respectable Folly*, 194, 203–6.

30 Ibid., 118–19. Subsequent study confirmed that the imminent Second Coming would occur in Ireland.

31 Christopher Hill, *Antichrist*, 164–65; Jean Tulard, *L'Anti-Napoleon* (Paris, 1965), passim; Garrett, *Respectable Folly*, 211. See also Lewis Mayer, *Bonaparte, the Emperor of the French, Considered as Lucifer and Gog of Isaiah and Ezekiel* (London, 1806), and J. J. Holmes,

The Fulfillment of the Revelation of St. John Displayed, from the Commencement of the Prophecy, AD 96, to the Battle of Waterloo, AD 1815 (London, 1819).

32 See "The Saint Petersburg Dialogues" in *The Works of Joseph de Maistre*, Jack Lively, ed. (New York, 1965), 288.

33 Geoffrey Hosking, *Russia* (Cambridge, Mass., 1997), 139.

34 For Krüdener, here and below, see Clarence Ford, *The Life and Letters of Madame de Krüdener* (London, 1893), 238, 263, 265, 280, and passim.

35 *Revue des deux mondes*, July 1, 1837, and September 15, 1849; Charles Eynard, *Vie de Madame de Krüdner* (Paris, 1849): note the contemporary spelling also used by Sainte-Beuve); and Sainte-Beuve, *Oeuvres* (Paris, 1960), 2:764–84, 1327–52. One gets the feeling that Sainte-Beuve dismissed her religiosity as banal: "No different than [that of] numerous sectarians popping up every day in England and the United States." *Oeuvres*, 2:1352.

CHAPTER 8: Apocalypse in Worldly Times

1 *War and Peace*, epilogue, 2:8.

2 Jean-Pierre Séguin, *Canards du siècle passé* (Paris, 1969), 23. In 1832, news that Bréla's comet would cross the earth's orbit on October 23 stirred fears that the end of the world was near. Public anxiety ebbed when it was learned that the earth would not reach that point in its orbit until one month later: November 30.

3 Broadsheet, ibid., 52.

4 Henry James Freeman, *The Story of Prophecy* (London, 1936), 310.

5 E.P. Thompson, *The Making of the English Working Class* (London, 1964), 799.

6 W.H. Oliver, *Prophets and Millennialists* (Auckland, 1978), 112.

7 Thompson, *The Making of the English Working Class*, 801.

8 Paul Gottfried, *Conservative Millenarians* (New York, 1979), 112. Novalis was not the only Romantic fascinated by the seventeenth-

century Rosicrucian promise that a new illumination awaited a world nearing its end. In this view, return to Adam's and Saturn's golden age would bring millennial reformation, an infusion of truth and light, and the turning of earthly dross to spiritual gold. See Frances Yates, *The Rosicrucian Enlightenment* (London, 1972).

9 Ibid., 110.

10 Jacques Anstett, *Pensée religieuse de Friedrich Schlegel* (Paris, 1941), 331–36, 416.

11 M. Rottmanner, ed., *Schlegels Briefe an Frau Christina von Stransky* (Vienna, 1916), 2:89, 145. Gottfried, *Conservative Millenarians*, 95. Schlegel's last published work would be on *The Philosophy of Revelation* (1854).

12 Robert Mackay, *The Rise and Progress of Christianity* (London, 1854), vi.

13 George Eliot, *Letters* (New Haven, 1954), 1:11 (November 1838), refers to "the mighty revolution ere long to take place in our world by God's blessing."

14 See *Le passé et l'avenir expliqués par les événements extraordinaires arrivés à Thomas Martin, laboureur de Beauce*, published anonymously in 1832 by an orthodox legitimist priest, Pierre Perreau; and the informative study of Phillipe Boutry and Jacques Nassif, *Martin l'Archange* (Paris, 1985), especially 145–46.

15 Louis Reybaud, *Jérome Paturot* (Paris, 1842), 40.

16 Jacques Gadille, "Le Jansénisme populaire. Ses prolongements au XIXe siècle: le cas du Forez," *Études foreziennes* (St. Étienne, 1975), 7:160, 162; Laurent, *Les Béguins*, 85; Claude Hau, *Le Méssie de l'an XII et Les Faréinistes* (Paris, 1955).

17 "Car voici le temps des temps, la fin des fins," quoted in Robert Bessède, *La crise de la conscience catholique* (Paris, 1975), 561.

18 Ballanche, in Paul Bénichou, *Le temps des prophètes* (Paris, 1977), 96; Félicité de Lammenais, *Paroles d'un croyant* (Bruxelles, 1834), 34; H. de Lubac, *La postérité spirituelle de Joachim de Fiore* (Paris, 1980), 2:53.

19 Lammenais, *Paroles d'un croyant*, 82.

20 Pierre Pierrard, *L'Église et les ouvriers en France* (Paris, 1984), 199.

21 Ibid., 198–99.

22 Garrett, *Respectable Folly*, 30.

23 In an unpublished paper delivered at the 1998 Conference on Mil-
    lenarianism and Messianism at the University of California at Los
    Angeles, Richard Popkin points out that when Napoleon sailed for
    Egypt in 1798, the official *Moniteur* urged the Jews of Africa and
    Asia to join him in liberating Jerusalem and rebuilding the Temple.
    In 1806, the emperor issued a commemorative medal in honor of
    the Paris Sanhedrin, which in Jewish tradition could not meet from
    AD 70, when Titus destroyed the temple, until the Messiah ap-
    pointed a new one. The medal bore Napoleon's likeness on one
    side and, on the reverse, an image of the emperor handing the
    tablets of the law to a kneeling Moses (or rabbi?).

24 In France, meanwhile, where slavery and the slave trade had been
    abolished in 1793 and 1794, and reestablished eight years later, a
    Committee for the Abolition of the Slave Trade was created in 1815
    by the Société de la morale chrétienne. The trade was abolished in
    1848.

25 Jonathan Frankel, *The Damascus Affair* (Cambridge, 1997), 293,
    for Ashley's delight at "this wonderful event."

26 Ibid., 304–5, 307.

27 Ibid., 391.

28 Boyer, *When Time Shall Be No More*, 100, 186; Timothy Weber,
    Living in the Shadow of the Second Coming (Chicago, 1987), 137–41.

29 In his letter *On the Origin and Life of Antichrist (AD 950)*, Adso,
    Abbot of Montier-en-Der, maintained the tradition that Antichrist
    would be a Jew.

30 Quoted in Emmerson, *Antichrist in the Middle Ages*, 86. See
    C.W.R.D. Moseley's fine modern translation of *The Travels of Sir
    John Mandeville* (London, 1983), 166.

31 Augustine, *The City of God*, Book XX, chapter 29.

32 Cohn, *Cosmos, Chaos*, 27, 30.

33 Marie Caithness, *Les vrais Israélites. L'identification des dix tribus
    perdues avec la nation britannique* (Paris, 1888), vi, 59, 61, 65; the
    United States is identified with Manasse (76).

34 Cohn, *Cosmos, Chaos*, 43, 67, 87–92 and passim. Cohn believes
    that the apocalyptic image of a final struggle against the Jewish

Antichrist and the extermination of the Jews as a prelude to the Germanic millennium were part of the inspiration of Hitler, Himmler, and the SS (189, 254).

35 Arthur Symons, *The Symbolist Movement in Literature* (London, 1899), 16.

36 Beatrice Webb tells us at the beginning of *My Apprenticeship* that her grandmother, Mary Seddon, obsessed with the duty to lead the Jews back to Jerusalem, was confined to an asylum for half a century.

37 J. M. Curicque, *Voix prophétiques* (Paris, 1871).

38 Thomas de Cauzons, *La magie et la sorcellerie en France* (Paris, 1911), 4:610–11, 597ff. Did these women echo what they heard from their priests? See, for example, Jean-Baptiste Bigou, parish priest of Sonnac (Aude) predicting *L'avenir ou le règne de Satan et du monde prochainement remplacé sur toute la terre par une domination indéfinie de Jésus-Christ et de l'Église* (1887) and *Justification du nouveau millénarisme ou glorieux avènement de Jésus-Christ, refoulement de tous les démons dans l'enfer et long règne spirituel de l'Église sur toute la terre* (1889).

39 Nicole Edelman, *Voyantes, guérisseuses et visionnaires en France, 1875–1914* (Paris, 1997).

40 David Blackbourn, *Marpingen* (New York, 1994), 145 and passim.

41 Gerhart Hauptmann, *The Fool in Christ: Emanuel Quint* (New York, 1911), 81, 82. Not all apocalyptists, however, envisaged paradise in the offing. Daniel Paul Schreber, a high Saxon magistrate confined to an asylum through the 1890s, had recurrent visions of the end of the world approaching, "the clocks of the world running out," glaciation, great earthquakes, devastating epidemics, and the appearance of an Antichrist-like figure spreading nervousness, immorality, terror, and fear. See *Memoirs of My Nervous Illness* (London, 1955), especially 93, 97. In their discussion of the *Memoirs*, Ida Macalpine, MD, and Richard Hunter, MD, ignore the eschatological inspiration of Schreber's delusions and attribute them to "procreation fantasies."

42 Geoffrey Ahern, *Sun at Midnight: The Rudolf Steiner Movement* (Wellingborough, 1984), 91.

43 Arden Bucholz, *Moltke, Schlieffen, and Prussian War Planning* (New York, 1995), 315.

44 See Raymond Savage, *Allenby of Armageddon* (Indianapolis, 1926), 21, 289, 302.

45 Edmund Gosse, *Father and Son* (New York, 1909), 310, 347, and passim.

46 Leonard Mosley, *Gideon Goes to War* (New York, 1955), 10, 216.

47 Huzar, *La fin du monde par la science* (Paris, 1859), especially 49, 117, 154.

48 Quoted by Blackbourn, *Marpingen*, 256. Curiously, Haeckel's view was shared by the eschatological Lady Caithness. Her *Serious Letters to Serious Friends* (London, 1888), 37, is unequivocal: "Progress being one of the first laws of God, and therefore infinite and eternal, we *cannot* stop; there is no standing still." As for the great development of science, it confirmed "that we are in the last days of the cycle or dispensation until whose end Daniel had been ordered to seal the book." *Les vrais Israélites*, vii.

49 Bousset, *The Antichrist Legend* (London, 1896), xxv.

50 Bessède, *La Crise*, 524. "Awaiting the final consummation, anything one can write or say on the subject is less than nothing" (522).

51 Flammarion, *La fin du monde*, 360.

CHAPTER 9: Pursuits of the Millennium

1 Frederic Engels, "On the History of Early Christianity," in Lewis Feuer, *Marx and Engels: Basic Writings* (New York, 1959), 168.

2 Cohn, *The Pursuit of the Millennium*, 299.

3 Thompson, *The Making of the English Working Class*, 392 and passim.

4 "Socialism: Utopian and Scientific," in Karl Marx and Frederic Engels, *Selected Works* (Moscow, 1951), 2:101.

5 Lawrence, *Apocalypse*, ed. Kalkins, 65, 67, and passim.

6 Cohn, *The Pursuit*, 14.

7 Oliver, *Prophets*, 94.

8 D.H. Lawrence, in *Adelphi Review*, 1924, 41.

9 In *Joachim of Fiore and the Prophetic Future* (London, 1976), 175, Marjorie Reeves approvingly quotes Roger Garaudy's connection of Joachim with a long Christian revolutionary tradition designed to create the kingdom of God not somewhere else, but in our own world changed by our own efforts.

10 Paine, *Common Sense* (New York, 1946), 57. Abrams, "English Romanticism," 34, mentions Thomas Holcroft, the militant atheist and radical who reads Paine's *Rights of Man* in 1791 and is filled with enthusiasm: "Hey for the New Jerusalem! The Millennium!"

11 Thompson, *The Making of the English Working Class*, 47.

12 Marx and Engels, *Selected Works*, 1:53.

13 *The Life of Frederick Maurice by His Son Frederick Maurice* (London, 1884), 10.

14 Engels, quoted in Pierrard, *L'Église et les ouvriers*, 16–17.

15 Carl Wittke, *The Utopian Communist: A Biography of Wilhelm Weitling* (Baton Rouge, 1950), 26, 71, 87, and passim.

16 Quoted in Michael Barkun, *Crucible of the Millennium*, 70.

17 Owen's *Life*, quoted in Oliver, "Owen in 1817," (Syracuse, 1986), in S. Pollard and J. Salt, *Robert Owen* (London, 1971), 181. See also Owen's own *Book of the New Moral World* (London, 1836), xv: "The time approaches when . . . the evil spirit of the world engendered by ignorance and selfishness will cease to exist, and when another spirit will arise . . . which will create a new character of wisdom and benevolence for the whole human race . . . in which evil . . . will be unknown." John's *Revelation* was right if you read it right. Then you would see that it points to social and economic salvation in a regenerated society.

18 Engels, "Socialism," in Feuer, *Marx and Engels*, 80. G.D.H. Cole and Raymond Postgate, *The Common People* (London 1938), 264–65, class Owenism "among the Messianic religions which arose in the early 19th Century." So does William Dale Morris, *The Christian Origins of Social Revolt* (London, 1949), 170–73.

19 Bénichou, *Prophètes*, 96, 472, 475. In his contribution to Paul Alphandéry, *La Chrétienté et l'idée de croisade* (Paris, 1959) 2, 283ff, Alphonse Dupront suggests that when, in 1833, Prosper Enfantin

and other Saint-Simonians set out for Egypt, they were living a crusade. If one remembers that Enfantin et al. were looking for a female Messiah (and a "Mother" to balance the supreme authority of the *Père* Enfantin), this makes sense. Crusades, after all, were a holy quest designed to precipitate end times.

20 Barkun, *Crucible of the Millennium*, 67.

21 Henri de Lubac, *La postérité spirituelle de Joachim de Fiore* (Paris, 1981), 2:152.

22 Alphonse Esquiros, *L'évangile du peuple* (Paris, 1840), 145.

23 Auguste Viatte, *Victor Hugo et les illuminés de son temps* (Ottawa, 1942), 92.

24 Constant, preface to *Bible de la liberté* (Paris, 1840), quoted in Bénichou, *Prophètes*, 436. "Celui qui fut Caillaux," *Arche de la nouvelle alliance* (Paris, 1840), 117: "God is the People."

25 Another source of influence opened when the abbé Jacques-Paul Migne asked Constant to compile a *Dictionnaire de littérature chrétienne* (Paris, 1851). Léon Cellier, *L'épopée romantique* (Paris, 1954), 212, calls the resulting work an anthology of Constant's own writings. It was to be used by the likes of Baudelaire and Victor Hugo, and, well into the twentieth century, by many clerics preparing their sermons.

26 Judas in Oegger, *Lettre à Mme de Rothschild et à leurs coreligionnaires sur le vrai Messie* (Paris, 1830), quoted in Viatte, *Victor Hugo*, 43.

27 Lubac, *La postérité spirituelle*, 2:33.

28 Edgar Quinet, *Lettre sur la situation religieuse en Europe* (Paris, 1856), quoted in Bénichou, *Prophètes*, 492.

29 Interrupted in 1860, "La fin de Satan" would be published unfinished in 1886.

30 Eugèn Pelletan, *Comment les dogmes se regénèrent* (Paris, 1854), 20: "La fin du progrès est Dieu" (The end of progress is God).

CHAPTER 10: Time's Noblest Offspring

1 McGinn, *Visions of the End*, 284; Pauline Moffitt Watts, "Prophecy and Discovery," *American Historical Review* (February 1985): 73–102.

2 Watts, "Prophecy and Discovery," 74, 96.

3 Kirkpatrick Sale, *The Conquest of Paradise* (New York, 1991), 181, 188ff.

4 See John Leddy Phelan, *The Millennial Kingdom of the Franciscans in the New World* (Berkeley, 1956, 1970).

5 On American Hebrew origins, see, for instance, Elias Boudinot, *A Star in the West: Or a Humble Attempt to Discover the Long Lost Tribes of Israel* (Trenton, NJ, 1816), and Ethan Smith, *View of the Hebrews; Or the Ten Tribes of Israel in America* (Poultney, Vt., 1823).

6 See Perry Miller, "The End of the World," *William and Mary Quarterly*, 3:8 (April 1951):151; *Errand in the Wilderness* (Cambridge, Mass., 1956), 229.

7 Miller, "The End of the World," 235.

8 See Edwards's letter to Thomas Prince, December 12, 1743: "Considering what the state of things now is . . . we cannot reasonably think otherwise than that the beginning of this great work of God must be near. And there are many things that make it probable that this work will begin in America." Quoted in Stephen J. Stein, *Jonathan Edwards' Apocalyptic Writings* (New Haven, 1977), 26.

9 Stephen Stein, *The Shaker Experience in America* (New Haven, 1992), 27.

10 James West Davidson, *The Logic of Millennial Thought* (New Haven, 1977), 15.

11 Jean-Louis Carra, *Esprit de la morale et de la philosophie* (Paris, 1777); Richard Price, *Observations on the Importance of the American Revolution* (London, 1784), 7.

12 Ralph Waldo Emerson, "The Chardon Street Convention," in *The Complete Works* (Boston, 1911), 374.

13 Fawn Brodie, *No Man Knows My History* (New York, 1971), 22;

Oliver, *Prophets*, 177; Robert Reid, *The Seven Last Plagues or the Vials of the Wrath of God* (Pittsburgh, 1828); Barkun, *Crucible*, 67; Ernest Sandeen, *The Roots of Fundamentalism* (Chicago, 1970), 42.

14 J.F.C. Harrison, *The Second Coming* (London, 1979), 112.

15 Stein, *The Shaker Experience*, 210.

16 Gideon Hagstotz, *The Seventh-day Adventists in the British Isles* (Lincoln, Neb., 1935?), 190–91.

17 Edward Wagenknecht, *Harriet Beecher Stowe* (New York, 1965), 202.

18 Walt Whitman, "Years of the Modern," retitled "Years of the Unperformed," in *Drum Taps*, 1865.

19 Robert S. Fogarty, *All Things New* (Chicago, 1990), 9.

20 Charles Grandison Finney, *Lectures on Revivals of Religion*, edited by William McLoughlin (Cambridge, Mass., 1960), ix.

21 C.G. Finney, *Lectures on Revivals* (1835), 306; *The Memoirs of Charles Grandison Finney* (Grand Rapids, 1989), 164, 544.

22 Charles Strozier, *Apocalypse* (Boston, 1994), 184.

23 Savage, *Allenby of Armageddon*, 283. See also Wilson D. Wallis, *Messiahs* (Washington, DC), 74–75.

24 For Riel, see Thomas Flanagan, *Louis "David" Riel, Prophet of the New World* (Toronto, 1979), 125, 140–41, 167, and passim; Gilles Martel, *Le méssianisme de Louis Riel* (Waterloo, 1984), 80–81, 292.

25 M. James Penton, *Apocalypse Delayed* (Toronto, 1985), 57 and passim.

26 Sandeen, *The Roots*, 276.

27 There appears to be some hesitation about the date. While Agnes [Ozman] La Berge, *What God Hath Wrought* (Chicago, nd), speaks of the night of December 31, 1900, to January 1, 1901, H. Caffarel, *Faut-il parler d'un pentecôtisme catholique?* (Paris, 1973), 40, prefers the evening of December 31, 1899, "on the eve of the new century." Both testify to the hold of ends and of beginnings, and to the confusion that Dionysius Exiguus wrought.

28 See William Gentz, *Dictionary of Bible and Religion* (Nashville, 1986), 797.

29 William Pettingill of the Philadelphia School of the Bible, in 1919, quoted by Boyer, *When Time Shall Be No More*, 104.

30 Penton, *Apocalypse Delayed*, 55.

31 Christabel Pankhurst, *Pressing Problems of the Closing Age* (London, 1924), 71: "and nature in convulsion will be one of the terrible features of that time." See also David Mitchell, *Queen Christabel* (London, 1977).

32 For Bryan and Scopes, see Lawrence Levine, *Defender of the Faith* (Oxford, 1965), 287 and passim.

33 H.L. Mencken, *Prejudices* (New York, 1926), 5:73–74.

34 James D. Hunter, *American Evangelism* (Newark, NJ, 1988), 39.

35 Levine, *Defender of the Faith*, 249.

36 Gabelein, in Derek Tidball, *Who Are the Evangelicals?* (London, 1994), 188.

37 Jerry Falwell, *The Fundamentalist Phenomenon* (New York, 1981), 220.

CHAPTER 11: The Twentieth Century

1 William James, *The Varieties of Religious Experience* (New York, 1936), conclusion, 480, 493.

2 Théodule Ribot, *Psychologie des sentiments* (Paris, 1897), 310. Also, Vacherot, *La Religion* (Paris, 1869), 436.

3 Friedrich Nietzsche, "Human, All Too Human," 1878–80. This essay appears in numerous anthologies.

4 Bryan, quoted in Levine, *Defender of the Faith*, 281.

5 Hauptmann, *The Fool in Christ*, 81.

6 See *A Solovyov Anthology* (London, 1950), 26–27, 229–48.

7 Albert Schweitzer, *Out of My Life and Thought* (New York, 1949), 9, 36–37, 214, 53.

8 G. Delanne, *Le phénomène spirite* (Paris, 1897), i. The previous year, 1896, *The Popular Science Monthly*, writing about Marconi, had declared that wireless was the nearest approach to telepathy that has been vouched to our intelligence.

9 Louis-Auguste Blanqui, *L'éternité par les astres* (Paris, 1872), 17.

10 On the comet's passage, see Jerred Metz, *Halley's Comet, 1910: Fire in the Sky* (St. Louis, 1985), 8, 55–56, 83, 84, 90; and Roberta Etter and Stuart Schneider, *Halley's Comet* (New York, 1985), passim.

11 Henri Focillon, *The Year 1000* (New York, 1969), 47.

12 Pankhurst, *Pressing Problems of the Closing Age*, 20; Weber, *Living in the Shadow*, 178ff.

13 Saul Friedlander, *Nazi Germany and the Jews* (New York, 1997), 1:97–98, seems to regard Hitler as a convinced apocalyptist for whom redemptive anti-Semitism makes war against the eschatological anti-Christian Jews who are bent, like Antichrist, on destruction of the world.

14 The third secret of Fatima, revealed to Lucia dos Santos in the summer of 1917 and by her to the pope, was supposed to predict a fiery apocalypse five popes hence.

15 See William A. Christian Jr., *Visionaries* (Berkeley, 1996), 151–52, 351, 100–3; Bernard Billet, *Vraies et fausses apparitions dans L'Église* (Paris, 1973), 24–25.

16 Billet, *Vraies et fausses apparitions dans L'Église*, 28–31; Karl Rahmer, *Visions and Prophecies* (London, 1963), 7, 8, 24–25.

17 Pankhurst, *Pressing Problems of the Coming Age*, 14: "It is entirely conceivable that we may learn to cause destruction on wholesale scale by liberating the energy of atoms."

18 Martha Lee, "Violence and the Environment," in Michael Barkun, *Millennialism and Violence* (London, 1996), 124. *Earth First!* June 21, 1994. See also Martha Lee, *Earth First! Environmental Apocalypse* (Syracuse, 1995).

19 For Reagan, see Stephen O'Leary, *Arguing the Apocalypse* (New York, 1994), 182–83 and passim; for Watt, *Chicago Tribune*, October 25, 1981, B2. Reagan's secretary of defense, Caspar Weinberger, was also fascinated by Revelation: "Yes, I believe the world is going to end—by an act of God, I hope—but every day I think that time is running out." Quoted by O'Leary, *Arguing the Apocalypse*, 273, n21. Curiously, no reference has been made to former President Jimmy Carter, a born-again evangelical Baptist suspect to the religious Right. Returning from the White House to Plains, Georgia in 1981, the Carters joined the Maranatha Baptist Church.

20 Tim La Haye, *Revelation* (Grand Rapids, 1975); Michael Lienesh, *Redeeming America* (Chapel Hill, 1993), 106.

21 See *Samédi–Soir*, July 1, 1950: "Est-ce le début de la 3e guerre mondiale?"; G. Marcel, *Rome n'est plus dans Rome* (Paris, 1951).

22 Cyril Marystone, *The Coming Type of the End of the World* (London, 1963). For Branham, see John Hall, *Gone from the Promised Land* (New Brunswick, NJ, 1987), 292.

23 Boyer, *When Time Shall Be No More*, 55, points out that nothing had changed since the second century, when Ireneus of Lyon taught that Antichrist would reign on earth for forty-two months: precisely the time given by Lindsey and his fellows.

24 Albert Sims, *The Near Approach of Antichrist* (Toronto, nd), 4, 95; Weber, *Living in the Shadow*, 96.

25 *New York Times*, March 25, 1990; David Webber and Noah Hutchings, *Computers and the Beast of Revelation* (New York, 1986), 129; Daniel Wojcick, *The End of the World as We Know It* (New York, 1997), 166.

26 C.S. Lewis, *The World's Last Night* (New York, 1973), 100, 104, 106.

27 Klaus Koch, *The Rediscovery of Apocalyptic* (London, 1972), 13, 14, 131.

28 Reeves, *Joachim of Fiore*, preface, np.

29 *The Times*, July 25, 1990.

30 "Jesus Returns in Judgment," *Washington Evening Star*, June 30, 1973; Jim McKeever, *The Almighty and the $* (Medford, Ore., 1981), 227.

31 Details in T. Bisset, "Religious Broadcasting," *Christianity Today*, December 12, 1980, 28–31.

32 Martin Gardner, *The New Age* (Buffalo, 1988), 236–37, quoting Gerard Straub, *Salvation for Sale* (1988).

33 See *National Catholic Reporter*, June 6, 1975, 13, and Meredith B. McGuire, *Pentecostal Catholics* (Philadelphia, 1982), 40.

34 Strozier, *Apocalypse*, 71.

35 Boyer, *When Time Shall Be No More*, 2; *Time*, special issue, fall 1992, "Beyond the Year 2000"; Lindsey, *Late Great Planet*, 118.

36 James Aho, *The Politics of Righteousness* (Seattle, 1990), 235; Strozier, *Apocalypse,* 117, 158; Pat Robertson, *The End of the Age* (Dallas, 1995), 182–83; For Fundamentalists Anonymous, see Rod Evans and Irwin Berent, *Fundamentalism: Hazards and Heartbreaks* (La Salle, Ill., 1988), 153–55; Strozier, *Apocalypse*, 29, 30.

37 In September 1989, already, Hurricane Hugo, having devastated the islands of Guadeloupe, turned its attention to Charlotte, North Carolina, where televangelist Jim Bakker was being tried for immoral conduct and financial irregularities. Violent winds forced a one-day suspension of the trial, a sign of God's wrath against the persecutors of his prophet. Nevertheless, the trial was resumed and Bakker was sentenced for multiple fraud.

38 See David Spangler, *Rebirth of the Sacred* (London, 1984), 17–18.

39 See Strozier, *Apocalypse*, 231, and Wouter J. Hanegraaf, *New Age Religion and Western Culture* (Leiden, 1996), 521 and passim.

40 The account that follows is mainly based on Martha Lee, *The Nation of Islam* (Lampeter, 1988), and Mattias Gardell, *Countdown to Armageddon* (New York, 1995).

41 Gardell, *Countdown to Armageddon*, 129.

42 Ibid., 136, 131. Compare this scenario with Edward Roux, *Time Longer than Rope* (London, nd), 148–49: In 1921, in the South African Transkei, Wellington Butelezi, posing as an American black, preached that all Americans were black and would soon fly in to free the Bantu people from whites and their taxes. One cargo cult sounds much like another.

43 Hauptmann, *The Fool in Christ*, 81, 82; Mencken, *Prejudices*, 116.

44 G. Klineman and S. Butler, *The Cult That Died* (New York, 1980); David Chidester, *Salvation and Suicide* (Bloomington, 1988).

45 See U.S. Department of Justice, *Report on Events at Waco* (Washington, DC, 1993); James Lewis, ed., *From the Ashes: Making Sense of Waco* (Lanham, MD, 1994); Stuart Wright, ed., *Armageddon in Waco* (Chicago, 1995); Mark Hamm, *Apocalypse in Oklahoma* (Boston, 1997); and a Davidian Seventh-day Adventist movement pamphlet, *The Breaking of the Seven Seals: The Mystery behind the Standoff at Mt. Carmel* (1993).

46 See, above all, *The Cult Observer*, 11 (1994):8, 9, 10, and Ross

Laver, "Apocalypse Now," *Maclean's*, October 17, 1994.

47 See *New York Times*, March 28, 1997.

48 David Kaplan and Andrew Marshall, *The Cult at the End of the World* (London, 1996), passim.

49 Murray Sayle, "Nerve Gas and the Four Noble Truths," *The New Yorker*, April 1, 1996.

50 Kaplan and Marshall, *The Cult*, 17, 31, 101.

51 Ibid., 67, 219–20.

52 See "Aum Terror," *Japan Echo*, autumn 1995, 44–62 and especially 60, 62, and "How Japan Germ Terror Alerted the World," *New York Times*, May 26, 1998.

53 Simon Reeve and Colin McGhee, *The Millennium Bomb* (London, 1997); "The Day the World Crashes," *Newsweek*, June 2, 1997; Edward and Jennifer Yourdon, *Time Bomb, 2000* (Upper Saddle River, NJ, 1998).

CHAPTER 12: Conclusion

1 Quoted in John Headly, *Luther's View of Church History* (New Haven, 1963), 265.

2 John Henry Newman, *Discussions and Arguments* (London, 1891), 44, 102–3. He testifies that Antichrist, his coming and his reign, were present interests in the Britain of the 1830s (107). Maureen Perkins, *Visions of the Future* (Oxford, 1996), 109, confirms the eschatological orientation of the age.

3 The Jewish theme looms at least from Pepys's (February 19, 1666) reference to the Messiah, Sabbatai Zevi, and to the belief, widespread in the Jewish world, that the Messiah would come in 1839–40 (see Frankel, *Damascus Affair*, 294). In his Advent sermon of 1834, Cardinal Newman insists on Antichrist's connection with the Jews (*Discussions and Arguments*, 67). A popular English novelist of the *fin de siècle* goes even further. In *When It Was Dark: The Story of a Great Conspiracy* (New York, 1904), Guy Thorne tells the

story of Antichrist reincarnated as a Jewish agnostic millionaire and member of parliament, who produces world chaos by faking a discovery of Christ's tomb and exploding the Resurrection account. Antichrist is foiled by a humble curate who first confronts him, then frustrates his evil schemes. Under his real name of Cyril Gull (1876–1923), Thorne's writings fill seven columns in the National Union Catalog. *When It Was Dark* was reprinted six times between 1904 and 1906.

4 Tidball, *Who Are the Evangelicals?* 17, 18.

5 Cohn, *The Pursuit of the Millennium*, 212.

6 Josephus, *Wars*, ii, 13–14, quoted in Abba Hillel Silver, *A History of Messianic Speculation in Israel* (New York, 1927), 6.

7 On February 26, 1794.

8 Eliade, *The Myth of the Enternal Return*, chapter 2 and especially 52ff.

9 Ibid., 60.

10 Oliver, *Prophets and Millennialists*, 166.

11 Jean-Marie Lustiger, *Communio*, 15, 2 (1990):13–14.

12 W. Warren Wagar, *Terminal Visions: The Literature of Last Things* (Bloomington, 1982), xiii: "We do indeed live in an end time [surpassing] in scope and destructive potential all others"; Stephen Graubard, *Daedalus*, summer 1997, x: "If, as many believe, we are coming to the end of an era, and not only to the end of a century . . ."

13 C.A.B. Bryan, *Close Encounters of the Fourth Kind* (New York, 1996), 273.

14 Robert Jay Lifton, in Friedlander, *Visions*, 163.

15 Lipset, in Stearns, *Millennium III*, 157.

INDEX

The letter "n" following a page number indicates a note; for example, "242n.2" indicates note 2 on page 242.